# CHASING
# GHOSTS

# CHASING GHOSTS

## A TOUR OF OUR FASCINATION WITH SPIRITS AND THE SUPERNATURAL

### MARC HARTZMAN

QUIRK BOOKS
PHILADELPHIA

Library of Congress Cataloging-in-Publication Data available upon request.

ISBN: 978-1-68369-277-5

Printed in China

Typeset in Adobe Jenson Pro

Designed by Ryan Hayes
Illustrations by Lauren O'Neill
Full photo credits appear on page 254
Production management by John J. McGurk

Quirk Books
215 Church Street
Philadelphia, PA 19106
quirkbooks.com

10 9 8 7 6 5 4 3 2 1

TO MY GRANDPARENTS ON THE OTHER SIDE

# CONTENTS

# A MESSAGE FROM THIS SIDE OF THE VEIL

**M**y first encounter with death happened at the age of ten when my grandmother passed away. In Judaism, bodies are buried within a few days and always in a simple pine box. Wealth, if achieved, does not follow one into the grave. I attended the funeral and listened to the prayers, wept alongside family, and watched the coffin get lowered into the ground. Generally speaking, it was the type of ceremony that's done in all parts of the world—and has been for thousands of years. So it must be the correct way to do things, right? Yet since that day I've wondered, what if it's not? Could humankind have been wrong all this time, leaving countless generations of spirits trapped and suffocating six feet underground?

There's no proven way to know. Not unless, of course, you believe in ghosts. Belief in spirits and in the reasons they appear and disappear vary over time and in different cultures, but those beliefs have always existed. When I started writing this book, I claimed to have never seen a ghost—and firmly believed that was true. But in speaking with parapsychologists, paranormal investigators, ghost tour guides, Spiritualists, a modern-day psychopomp, cultural historians, a professor at the Rhine Edu-

cation Center, and employees of haunted inns and taverns, I'm not so sure
that I've never seen a ghost. Part of it certainly comes down to personal views
but it also depends on one's definition of "seeing a ghost." We have a tendency
to think that ghosts, apparitions, spirits, specters, and wraiths just appear
in front us, like in the movies. A translucent thing that floats through dark,
creepy hallways and cellars. But what if the deceased are projecting themselves
into our minds while we're awake and dreaming? What if we're seeing ghosts a
lot more often than we think and we just can't acknowledge it?

These are just questions swirling in my mind, though other individuals
are clearer on these points. For example, the hamlet of Lily Dale Assembly
in New York, a small community just outside of Buffalo, has been home to
mediums and Spiritualists since the late nineteenth century. Signs reading
MEDIUM hang outside a majority of the homes. Posted inside the church are
the Principles of Spiritualism, which include the tenets "We never die" and
"Spiritualism proves that we can talk with people in the spirit world." The
nature of death and the existence of an afterlife aren't mysteries; they're truths.

Inspiration Stump in Lily Dale Assembly, New York, has been a
pilgrimage destination for mediums across the country for more
than one hundred years.

Quite appealing truths, considering
how this view of death can offer
such peace in life.

Twice a day visitors are invited
to experience these beliefs at
Inspiration Stump—an actual
tree stump standing about three
feet high with a roughly four-foot
diameter that's situated in a quiet
corner of Leolyn Woods (not far
from a pet cemetery). After the
tree was struck by lightning in the
late 1800s, it was leveled off and
filled with concrete. Steps were
added, allowing people to ascend
to its top and feel the vortex of spiritual energy that has built up from the
many mediums who've gathered there over the past century. Rows of wooden
benches facing the stump fill with people ready to receive a reading from one
of the local registered mediums, visiting mediums, or student mediums. For
about an hour, these psychics take turns delivering messages as they come
from Spirit.

The people of Lily Dale aren't the only ones who believe in ghosts. According to a 2019 survey by the data website YouGov, forty-five percent of Americans believe in ghosts. As I was writing this book, I learned some of them

are my friends and coworkers. One of them—let's call her Rebecca—has had many paranormal experiences and always gets a welcome or unwelcome feeling while house-hunting. "The hair stands on the back of my neck," my friend told me. "It's my bar for getting a new home." At her most recent address in New York, she felt nothing and determined the house was "a total blank slate." That is, until Rebecca's three-year-old daughter asked her about "the worker guy that comes here at night" who stands at the foot of her bed and "looks at me." Rebecca gave her daughter some sage advice: "Just tell him to go away. He's not welcome."

Another friend—let's call him Phillip—told me about the time he was in college and wanted to grab some munchies from his fraternity house pantry

Like many locals in the small town of Smithfield, Pennsylvania, ghosts have been known to spend time at the diner.

after a late night. The only problem was the pantry was in a nineteenth-century fieldstone cellar, accessed by a "creepy corridor" and a concrete stairwell. "No one liked going down to the pantry alone at night," Phillip said. "There's nothing more pathetic then a twenty-year-old man in the prime of his life afraid of the dark. Which is why I was incredibly relieved when I entered the cellar corridor to hear a few of the guys shuffling around and laughing. I couldn't make out exactly what was being said, but I was happy as hell to have them there."

He headed toward the voices to say hello, but no one was there. The basement was completely empty. "I immediately bolted up the stairwell back to the first floor, where I hoped to see people directly above where the pantry was located," Phillip explained. "At least that would provide a logical explanation for what happened—but no one was there." A few years later, at an alumni event, Phillip began telling the story and someone else finished it for him, sharing the exact same experience in the same basement.

James, a pharmacist I met in the small town of Smithfield, Pennsylvania, also had stories. Ghosts weren't known to hang around the Advil or antibiotics at his pharmacy, but they did congregate at a diner he previously owned down the street. Knives would fly off the counter, the strings on waitresses' aprons would get pulled from behind, and once a doorbell kept ringing despite the fact that the building didn't have one.

"The most vivid experience I had was on a holiday. We had closed early," James explained. "I went to close the register at, like, one thirty in the afternoon. I was doing the register, and there was a lady in white. I mean, the chills, oh my God! Ghostly looking. I just got so many chills. Middle of the afternoon! She was coming right through the archway into the kitchen. Most of the activity took place in that area. I still get chills thinking about it. It was so real."

These are just ordinary people who've experienced something extraordinary. Given the YouGov survey, I have to think there are millions of stories like these. It's no wonder so many television shows have tapped into the paranormal. It seems there are enough ghosts to feed dozens of programs for multiple seasons. While some are purely escapist entertainment, others strive to balance enjoyment with the presentation of information. When I spoke with the executive producer of *Ghost Adventures*, Michael Yudin, he was quick to stress the importance of that balance.

"We do the history, we do interviews with people, then [the team will] stay [at the haunted site] for forty-eight hours by themselves overnight and film. We cover the whole thing. And we call out what's bullshit if we don't think it's real. We're just trying to represent what we see as the fact. You make your own decisions."

After more than two hundred episodes filmed at allegedly haunted locations across America and witnessing the evidence that the show's host, Zak Bagans, and his crew have produced, Yudin is convinced something is going on. "I have definitely gone from not believing in ghosts to unquestionably believing in the unexplained," he says.

In this book, we'll go on a journey to explore the different relationships the living have had with the dead, from ancient myths to the beliefs of the Victorian Spiritualists to the ghost stories that have shaped our modern conception of the supernatural world. We'll also explore the human effort to capture evidence of the spirit world throughout the ages using period-specific technology. We'll visit famous haunted sites and investigate possible explanations for various paranormal events, from parapsychological to more traditional scientific views. By the end, it will be up to you to decide if the theories presented confirm your beliefs one way or the other—or leave you pondering the possibilities of what might await us all.

# THE GHOSTS OF HUMANS PAST

## THE ANCIENT AND MEDIEVAL BELIEFS THAT SHAPE OUR MODERN CONCEPTIONS OF GHOSTS

"I believe there are few speculative delusions more universally received than this, *that those things we call* spectres, ghosts, *and* apparitions, *are really the departed souls of those persons who they are said to represent.* We see, or pretend to see, our very Friends and Relations actually clothed with their old Bodies, tho' we know those bodies to be embowelled, separated, and rotting in the grave; as certainly as the head and quarters of a man executed for treason are drying in the sun upon the gates of the city: we see them dressed up in the very clothes which we have cut to pieces and given away, some to one body, some to another, or applied to this or that use; so that we can give an account of every rag of them: we hear them speaking with the same voice and sound, tho' the organ which formed their former speech we are sure is perished and gone. These similitudes of things fix it upon our thoughts, that it must be the same; that the souls of our late friends are actually come to revisit us; which is to me, I confess, the most incongruous and unlikeliest thing in the World."

–Daniel Defoe, from *The Secrets of the Invisible World Disclosed*, 1729

O f all the beliefs that have surrounded death throughout the world, it's safe to say that no one has ever perceived it to be a good thing. But if you're a ghost, death has its perks. Play your cards right and you can become immortal right here on earth. It doesn't matter if people believe in you as long as you have a great story for the living to latch onto. Across time and cultures, stories about the dead have endured like no others, laying the foundation for our modern conception of ghosts.

But before we get to the ancient myths and legends that shaped us, let's begin with a classic ghost story from 1693 that perfectly illustrates the impact of the dead upon the living.

## Lady Beresford and the Ghost of Lord Tyrone

Orphaned as a child, John Le Poer, Second Earl of Tyrone, grew up in Ireland with a fellow orphan, Nichola Sophia Hamilton, under the guardianship of a Deist.[1] The two were discussing Deism and Christianity one day and found themselves leaning toward the latter as the correct religion. They agreed that the first to die would come back and report to the other which belief system got the afterlife right.

As they entered adulthood, they went their separate ways. John grew up to be Lord Tyrone and Nichola married Lord Tristram Beresford, becoming Lady Beresford. One morning she joined her husband at breakfast, as usual, but on this occasion she looked pale and wore a black ribbon around her wrist. When Lord Beresford inquired about her strange manner, Lady Beresford said the equivalent of "don't ask" and informed him that he'd never see her again without the band adorning her wrist. "I never in my life denied you a request, but about this I must entreat you to forgive my silence, and never to urge

# THIS GHOST GAVE CONVINCING PROOF

## Said to Have Laid His Hand on Woman's Wrist, After Which Sinews Shrunk.

## CASE OF LADY BERESFORD

## Spirit Came as Result of Fulfillment of a Pact.

New York, Mar. 12.—Have you ever seen a ghost? "For there are ghosts, true ghosts. Science says so," declares an eminent New Yorker, who believes strongly in the spirit world

A childhood pact sealed the fate of Lady Beresford, a seventeenth-century woman who died under circumstances foretold by the ghost of her friend.

---

1   Deists are advocates of science and nature as a governing principle and religion, and though they believe in God, they don't believe in any divine revelation or intervention.

me again on the subject," she told him.

Lady Beresford's behavior grew more bizarre when she repeatedly asked her servant if the mail had arrived. When Lord Tristram inquired about her anxiousness, she explained that she was expecting a letter informing her of the death of her childhood companion, Lord Tyrone.

"He died last Tuesday at four o'clock," she claimed.

At that moment, a letter sealed in black wax did in fact arrive and stated precisely what Lady Beresford had anticipated. Though she mourned her old friend, her sorrow was not without joy. Just as she knew of Lord Tyrone's death in advance of the announcement, she also suddenly knew she was pregnant with a boy. This premonition, too, came to pass, and the Beresfords soon welcomed a son, Marcus, to the family.

The three lived happily for about seven years until Sir Tristram passed away. Nichola vowed never to remarry, but eventually she fell for the charms of a younger man and wed once again. She bore him several more children, but he treated her poorly and left her miserable. Moments of happiness were few and far between, but when her forty-eighth birthday arrived, Nichola believed the event was cause for a grand celebration. As friends and family gathered to join in her merriment, a clergyman cheerfully informed the birthday Lady that he had been going through old church records and discovered she was actually a year younger. A mere forty-seven. The revelation did not

have the pleasing effect intended.

"You have signed my death warrant," Lady Beresford explained, immediately turning the good vibes into unexpected doom and gloom. The party was over. She summoned Marcus and her married daughter, Lady Riverton, to join her in her chambers.

"I have not much longer to live, and must entreat you to leave me at once," Lady Beresford announced to everyone else. "I have something of importance to settle before I die."

Sounding a bit like a drama queen, she told her children about her childhood pact with Lord Tyrone and explained that he had lived up to his end of the bargain. One night, while she was still married to Lord Beresford, Lord Tyrone appeared beside her bed. Startled, she asked what he was doing in her bedroom in the middle of the night while her husband slept next to them. Lord Tyrone said he'd been permitted to return to her and inform her that Christianity "is the true and only religion." Good news, but of course, not so good when delivered by a dead friend. He had other news he'd been allowed to share as well: Lady Beresford would give birth to a boy, her husband would die several years after, she'd end up with a deadbeat and bear him several children, and tragically, she'd die at age forty-seven. Lord Tyrone also predicted that his heiress would marry Marcus, although the ghost had no children before his own death. Still, his predictions had proven correct so far, indicating that her death was imminent.

Before Lord Tyrone vanished from the bedroom and headed back to the afterlife, Lady Beresford made him leave a sign that he'd truly been there. Something that, by morning, would prove to her that the whole thing wasn't some crazy dream. The ghost twisted the curtains of the bed's canopy through an iron loop, claiming "no mortal arm could have done that."

"True, but sleeping we are often possessed of far greater strength than waking," she responded, demanding better proof. Lord Tyrone obliged and this time wrote a note in her pocketbook. His handwriting, he believed, would offer the assurance she needed. Lady Beresford was not impressed.

"When awake, I cannot imitate your handwriting, but asleep it is possible that I might," she countered. Lady Beresford's confidence in her somnambulant abilities may have seemed unreasonable to Lord Tyrone, but who can blame her for expecting a better show from a visiting ghost that demonstrated physical and verbal powers?

Finally, the two decided a hint of violence would be the best way to properly mark the occasion. "He touched my wrist with a hand as cold as marble and, in a moment, the sinews were shrunk up, and every nerve with them," she explained to Marcus and Lady Riverton.

"Let no mortal eye while you live behold that wrist," the ghost told her. "To see it would be sacrilege." With those final words, he was gone.

An hour after telling her story, as Lady Beresford lay resigned in her bed, she joined Lord Tyrone in the afterlife. Her children shared a moment of grief matched only by their curiosity. Carefully they removed the black ribbon from their deceased mother's wrist. The flesh beneath appeared shriveled and withered—exactly as she had described.

Years later, Marcus married Lady Catherine, who happened to be the niece of Lord Tyrone. She'd inherited his entire fortune, just as his ghost predicted.

This story was passed down through the Beresford family and spread in newspapers and books, with details shifting as they tend to do over time. Though stories from centuries ago, like Lady Beresford's, get twisted and distorted through oral retellings and variations in written form, the essence remains. This is especially true of ancient tales. Pliny the Younger of ancient Rome recorded one of the first ghost stories in 100 AD, which has many of the classic elements we still associate with spirits today.

## Pliny the Younger's Tale of Athenodorus

First-century Roman philosopher Pliny the Younger spoke of a large house in Athens reputed to be haunted by the ghost of a gangly old man with a long beard and disheveled hair. His wrists and ankles were shackled and chained together, creating a ruckus every night as he haunted the home. The inhabitants were terrorized, and eventually the house was deserted and put up for sale.

It found a taker in Athenodorus, a Stoic philosopher who read about the property's unpleasantness but was too intrigued with getting a good deal to be bothered by getting a fright. After moving in, he did what Greek philosophers do

ATHENODORUS CONFRONTS THE SPECTRE.

Like a character in a horror movie, the Stoic philosopher Athenodorus couldn't resist a bargain on a haunted house.

and started writing. During his first night in the house, as the evening progressed, a meddlesome clinking and clanking of chains interrupted his flow. Athenodorus looked up from his work and saw the resident specter appear before him. The ghost beckoned him, went outside to the courtyard with the philosopher following, and then disappeared into the earth. Athenodorus marked the spot with leaves and returned the next morning to dig up the ground. He found a skeleton, with bones bound in chains. The remains were given a proper burial, and from that day forward the house was free of all disturbances.

Even back then everyone liked a good ghost story, but for Athenodorus it might have served an additional purpose. "His actions laudably demonstrate the Stoic virtue of mastering the emotions," explains Dr. Leo Ruickbie, a member of the governing council of London's Society for Psychical Research, referencing Athenodorus's cool demeanor in the face of a fright. The ghost had a function, too. "His postmortem mission on earth is to correct the omission of funerary rites, underlining their importance—more important than bringing his murderer to book, for example. Therefore the story serves to glorify Athenodorus and enforce social customs."

## Shamans: The First Ghost Messengers

The notion of using ghosts to enforce social customs is hardly unique to Athenodorus. Shamans across cultures have used spirits for the same purpose. These leaders were the ones who would visit the gods or the worlds of the dead and bring back information to solve problems, like how to stop angering deities to ensure bountiful harvests. Ghosts, in other words, had the answers people needed. For example, aboriginal Canadians in Ontario and Manitoba, along with Native Americans near the northern border, received their messages from spirits from within a cylindrical tent. A shaman would step inside after sundown and conduct a "shaking tent" ceremony, involving singing and drumming to summon the ghosts. When the tent started to shake, it signified the presence of a spirit and the shaman would emerge with cures, hunting tips, or other highly sought knowledge.

In some cultures, if people didn't listen to the messages delivered from the beyond, shamans would use a variety of wondrous tricks to convince followers of their power, such as sleight-of-hand magic and ventriloquism. As some of these shamans grew older, their ghostly or godly advice may have accrued a less-than-stellar track record, forcing them into more nefarious methods of keeping people in line.

A tribe in the Orinoco Basin of South America had shamans that would make life very uncomfortable if, say, you didn't give up your house or chickens when requested.

"You might wake up in the middle of the night and discover that your bed had coral snakes in it," explains historian and performer Harley Newman. "And if that didn't convince you that you needed to give the shaman what he wanted, then you could be walking through the jungle one day and be clubbed from behind." While the victim was unconscious the shaman would stuff packets of herbs in their orifices, then pierce the tongue with a snake's fangs. The victim's tongue would swell up and prevent speech. Over the next few days the organs would start to dissolve from the inside out until death mercifully ended the punishment.

"If you had gone along with what the shaman wanted, you probably would have been in debt to him and become part of the crew who'd stalk people in the jungle and do whatever the shaman wanted," Newman adds.

In many cultures shamans were also busy helping ghosts. Part of their role was to act as a psychopomp—a person who escorts the newly deceased to the land of the dead. Dying is a whole new experience, and the dead often find themselves thrust into it without preparation or acceptance, particularly in the case of a life cut unexpectedly short. Without the guidance of a psychopomp, discarnate souls could get lost and wander aimlessly. And if these ghosts are suffering, they might cause grief for the living, too. Certain shamanic beliefs tell us spirits can cause fear, depression, nausea, bruises, insomnia, nightmares, and self-destructive behavior. Ancient psychopomps helped these souls

escape the earthly plane so they could get on with their next life and let the living live in peace. Ghosts with unfinished business on earth could get information from shamans that might bring comfort and put them at ease. Others might have just needed help getting over guilt, grudges, or confusion.

"Shamans offer nothing less than counseling for the dead," says David Kowalewski, PhD, who has studied with indigenous shamans on multiple continents and authored the book *Death Walkers*. "Psychopomp work, in short, effects the changes needed by the soul to get past its earthbound state and resume its journey of evolving to greater wisdom and power."

As a modern-day psychopomp, Kowalewski is keeping the shamanic service alive. Through clairvoyance, telepathy to the non-earthly realm, aid from "helping spirits," and entering altered states of consciousness in order to take a "soul-flight into a different dimension from the physical, outside of space-time, namely into non-ordinary reality," as he puts it, psychopomps of the past and present have gathered information to help discarnate souls in need.

This general struggle to move on to the Other Side shows up across ancient civilizations in various forms. After all, as long as people have existed, there has been death and ideas about what that means.

## The Ancient Egyptian *Book of the Dead*

Tim Burton's 1988 classic film, *Beetlejuice*, explored the plight of the recently deceased and the strange new world they were suddenly entering. It begins with a young couple dying in a car accident and then heading home, unaware of their predicament until they notice things that seem a bit off, like having no reflection in the mirror and finding a book sitting atop a pile of magazines with the title *Handbook for the Recently Deceased*. Following instructions to draw a door on the wall and knock three times, they create a portal to the Other Side and find their way to the office of a caseworker who helps them understand the whole being-dead thing. Somewhere in the afterlife, ancient Egyptians have been eating eternal bowls of popcorn saying, "Hey, Tim Burton totally ripped us off!"—in their own vernacular, of course.

The Egyptians had no doubt that life continued after death, and like the couple in *Beetlejuice*, the newly deceased had a book to guide them. Mummified in their burial chambers, the wealthy were accompanied by an illustrated papyrus scroll called *The Book of Dead*, containing hieroglyphics of 192 magic spells to guide them through the underworld to the Field of Reeds. There, everlasting paradise awaited with fabulous feasts, friends, and family. It felt just like home on earth so there'd be no pressing need to go back. But the trek through the underworld was no easy feat. En route to meeting Osiris, god of the underworld, one had to face many terrifying trials and tribulations.

"By healing the dead, the psychopomp heals the living from their grief. The shaman helps survivors achieve closure, so that they themselves can move on to their own next adventure. This, in turn, has positive health effects. One might say, then, that the shaman brings the living back to life."

–David Kowalewski, PhD, author of *Death Walkers*, in 2015

That's where *The Book of Dead* came in handy. Spell 33, for example, offered a formula for fighting off serpents. For those who survived them, Spell 40 would help them overcome the horror of the "creature that swallows the ass." Journeying onward, anyone not hungry or thirsty enough to eat excrement or drink urine could depend on Spell 53.

Egyptians encountered twelve gates to pass through, each guarded by an intimidating deity. Naturally, there were spells to get past them. Among the most critical checkpoints was Gate Five, the Judgment Hall. Presiding next to a set of scales stood Anubis, a jackal-headed god waiting to weigh your heart against the feather of truth. If you'd lived a righteous life, your heart would be lighter than the feather and you could go on your merry way toward immortality. If your heart was heavier, all your immortal plans went straight to shit—even if you said Spell 53. Ammit, a demoness that was part lion, part hippopotamus, part crocodile, and all nasty, made sure of that by devouring your heart.

Luckily, your guidebook could help you avoid such a fate with Spell 30B: "O my heart of my mother! O my heart of my different forms! Do not stand up as a witness against me, do not be opposed to me in the tribunal, do not be hostile to me in the presence of the Keeper of the Balance."

As the British Museum's ancient Egypt expert, John H. Taylor, explained to *BBC History* magazine, "Even if you had lived a bad life you could get away with it by using this spell, which prevents your heart from spilling the beans to the gods. This was the first time in history when you see the idea that your fate after death was dependent on your behavior when you were alive. However, it was not carried through to its logical conclusion—because you could cheat your way around that particularly tricky moment."

Whether they cheated their way to eternity or persevered the trials of the underworld, the dead continued to exist. As far as the Egyptians were concerned, that meant communication with them did, too. Friends and family could visit tombs of lost loved ones and leave letters with pleas for help, along with snacks and beverages. Between the paradise of the afterlife and a connection with the living, these ghosts seem to have it made. But, there's always a but. If the ghost didn't respond or, contrarily, if the ghost was seen as a threat, the living could perform execration rituals to essentially erase the essence of the deceased from history. These curses were written on red clay pots or figurines in the person's likeness, along with the ghost's name, and were smashed, spit on, and even urinated on for good measure. Then buried. Goodbye forever, ghost.

## The Underworld of Ancient Greece

The ancient Greeks had their own version of the underworld, ruled by Hades and his queen, Persephone. The dead began their journey by stepping aboard Charon's boat, assuming the soul had a coin for the ride and received a proper burial. If not, no passage would be granted and the spirit would be trapped in the land of living with nothing to do but haunt those who failed to properly prepare him or her. Depicted much like the Grim Reaper, Charon acted as a psychopomp by ferrying his customers across the river Styx to the entrance of the underworld, where they met Cerberus, the three-headed, dragon-tailed dog. Terrifying as the monstrous pooch sounds, he was there to admit all souls—but if you wanted to leave, his heads would have something to say about it.

For a few thousand years the ancient Greek poet Homer has taken readers on a journey to the underworld in the *Odyssey*. The hero of the tale, Odysseus, seeks advice from a dead seer, Tiresias, to find a safe route home after facing a series of dangerous adventures on his voyage back from the Trojan War. To get the seer's attention, Odysseus slaughters a black ram and fills a trench with its blood. The plan works, drawing out the dead like sharks to chum.

"They came, flocking toward me now, the ghosts of the dead and gone," Odysseus says. "Brides and unwed youths and old men who have suffered much and girls with their tender hearts freshly scarred by sorrow and great armies of battle dead, stabbed by bronze spears, men of war still wrapped in bloody armor—thousands swarming around the trench from every side—unearthly cries—blanching terror gripped me!"

Odysseus travels to Hades to learn his fate from the ghost of the blind prophet Tiresias, as depicted by Swiss painter Johann Heinrich Füssli.

He holds his sword, warding off these overeager spirits, but before Tiresias appears, Odysseus encounters the ghost of Elpenor, a fellow warrior who recently died on the island of Circe after drinking one too many and falling off a roof. He's not thrilled about his fatal drunken blunder, or about the fact that his friend left him behind without a funeral. "Do not go on and leave me there unburied, abandoned, without tears or lamentation," Elpenor pleads. Odysseus promises to remedy the situation so the ghost isn't forever trapped at the edge of the underworld.

Elpenor, like Athenodorus's ghost some eight hundred years later and so many others over the millennia, reminds us that the dead just want a little respect. And in many cases, they want a good old-fashioned home-cooked meal, too.

## The "Hungry Ghosts" of Asia

The "hungry ghosts" of Buddhist, Hindu, and Taoist traditions are found across East Asia. These famished souls are typically depicted as ghosts with long skinny necks, tiny mouths, and huge empty stomachs, suffering for having lived a sinful life.

In Japanese lore, hungry ghosts called *gaki* pay for their corrupt, wicked lives by having to eat meals of excrement, whereas another form, the *jikininki*, feast on human corpses.

Regarding the latter, an old tale speaks of a certain village where the bodies of the dead were prayed for and left alone at night as everyone went to the next village to avoid the "strange things" that would happen to the corpses. In the story, a visiting priest who feared no ghosts or demons stayed behind with one such body, and indeed strange things occurred. "He saw that Shape lift the corpse, as with hands, and devour it, more quickly than a cat devours a rat—beginning at the head, and eating everything: the hair and the bones and even the shroud," the legend says. The priest later encountered the creature, which had been living as a hermit on a mountain. "I am a jikininki—an eater

The *gaki zoshi*, twelfth-century illustrated hand scrolls depicting the world of spirits condemned to eternal hunger and thirst, can be seen at the Kyoto National Museum in Japan.

of human flesh. Have pity upon me, and suffer me to confess the secret fault by which I became reduced to this condition," it tells him. The ghost had also been a priest while alive but was selfish and performed his duties only as a matter of business. Since his death, he had "been obliged to feed upon the corpses of the people who die in this district." It begged the priest to perform a special Buddhist service to relieve it of its horrible hunger. The visitor did as he was requested, and the jikininki disappeared.

The *bhoots* of ancient India were hungry ghosts that materialized from those who departed this world unexpectedly early. Dying in an accident, being

killed in battle, and even suicide could turn troubled souls into bhoots. And like ghosts of other cultures, they'd come back especially angry if their body hadn't been buried or given a proper burial ceremony. Recognizing bhoots wasn't terribly difficult. They cast no shadow and spoke with a nasal twang. For anyone still unsure if they were face-to-face with a ghost, bhoots had backward feet to symbolize something gone awry. Hovering around villages, they sought out new bodies—or their old ones—to possess so they could resume their lives. If successful, they'd cause their hosts to tremble, speak nonsensically, and become argumentative with everybody. If a friend or family member suddenly started behaving erratically, it was thought a bhoot had gotten to them.

Aside from craving new bodies, these hungry ghosts would eat almost anything and yearned for water and milk. At times they would chug gallons at a time down their needle necks. Some women feared letting their children leave the house after drinking fresh milk, but if it was necessary they'd put salt or ashes into the children's mouths to ward thirsty bhoots away.

Some scholars speculate the dread of such malevolent spirits led to the practice of cremation in India, so no dead bodies could be reanimated. Prayers and the burning of turmeric were believed to repel the ghosts from inhabiting bodies of the living.

Drifting north of India, the hungry ghosts of China often manifested from the discarnate souls of people who died without descendants to remember them. Every year during the seventh month of the Chinese lunar calendar, hungry ghosts continue to wander freely amongst the living. Festivities offer them public feasts of chicken, pork, rice, fruit and more. And if that's not enough to appease the lonely spirits, they're distracted from causing mischief with puppet shows, pop concerts, and other forms of entertainment. Monetary offerings help, too.

## The Aztec Afterlife and the Origins of Día de los Muertos

Across the globe, the Aztecs, like the ancient Egyptians and Greeks, believed their dead set off on a long journey through the underworld. Their mythology describes a four-year obstacle course through nine treacherous layers of challenges, including a river crossing, heavy snowfalls, obsidian hills, heavy winds powerful enough to blow souls away, piercing arrows thrown by invisible hands, and beasts that open the chests of the dead and eat their hearts. Ultimately, the weary deceased arrive at Michtlān, where the gods of death, Mictlāntēcuhtli and his wife, Mictēcacihuātl, welcome them and bestow upon them the well-deserved reward of eternal rest.

Whereas the Egyptians had a guidebook filled with spells, the Aztecs were cremated or buried with possessions that might be useful on their afterlife adventure. A man, for instance, might be interred with his bow and arrows or other tools; a weaving kit would bid a woman farewell. The funerary tradition also included a Xoloitzcuintle, a hairless Mexican dog, serving as a guide through their underworld adventure.

Meanwhile, the living stayed connected through festivals during the late-summer corn harvest that opened communication with the dead, welcoming them with offerings of feasts and flowers. Following the sixteenth-century Spanish conquest of Mesoamerica, the observance was injected with a dose of Catholicism and moved to early November to sync with All Saints' Day. It became known as Día de los Muertos, or the Day of the Dead.

The annual festival continues to be observed today throughout Mexico and Latin America to celebrate a reunion with the dead. It's believed that during these days the veil between life and death is at its thinnest, and thus permeable. The ceremonies vary, but generally families welcome back dead loved ones by meticulously cleaning their graves, sometimes spending days to make them perfectly presentable. Altars are built and the favorite foods and drinks of the departed, along with *pan de muerto* ("bread of the dead"), are offered both at home and at the cemetery. Candles and marigolds create an aromatic, illuminated runway guiding ghosts back from the Other Side. Joy and solemnity fill the air as the living join with the dead in a brief triumph over the separation of their realms.

# BIBLICAL GHOSTS:
# THE STORY OF KING SAUL
# AND THE WITCH OF ENDOR

In the twenty-eighth chapter of the first book of Samuel, Saul tracks down the witch in hopes of getting military advice against the Philistines from Samuel's ghost. It's a strange quest for the king of Israel since he'd previously banned the practice of necromancy, yet now he seeks help from the dead. In those desperate times, Saul is especially anxious after God failed to answer his pleas through the prophets or his dreams. When the witch is found she fears for her life, given the king's ruling, but he assures her that there will be no punishment "for this thing."

Saul and the Witch of Endor, captured in an 1860 painting by British watercolorist Edward Henry Corbould.

"Whom shall I bring up unto thee?" she asks Saul, implying she has the power to summon anyone. Yet when she complies with the king's request to call for Samuel, she cries out at his arrival as if surprised to see him.

The old prophet, wearing his biblical-style cloak, asks, "Why hast thou disquieted me, to bring me up?" He's in no mood to help because Saul had ignored his advice during the last few years of his life and, even worse, disobeyed God's order to destroy all the Amalekites, the enemies of the Israelites.

The specter admonishes the king for his defiance and informs him that his army will be vanquished the next day. The witch, seeing Saul's visible distress, offers him a morsel of bread to cheer him up, but bread is no substitute for a path to victory. Still, the king's servants persuade him to eat, and they head back to battle with full stomachs. For the last time.

Some interpretations question whether the ghost was truly that of Samuel, or if the phrase "bring me up" implies it was the devil rising from hell and impersonating the prophet. Daniel Defoe, in his 1729 book *The Secrets of the Invisible World*, believed it was neither. Defoe also believed the devil did not have the gift of prophecy, so he would have been unable to fill Saul in on his impending doom. Therefore, the ghost must have been a spirit sent from God and empowered to foretell the unfortunate future.

Defoe's debate is an interesting reflection of eighteenth-century beliefs, but it isn't necessarily the point of the tale. As with most Bible stories, the facts aren't as critical as the lesson to be learned. According to rabbinical scholar Dr. Eric Wasser, "the underlying message in the monotheistic traditions is that if you're going elsewhere to get your answers—sorcery, witchcraft, ghosts, whatever—there's an acknowledgment that you no longer have that connection with God, who is supposed to be the one who is communicating with you." Of course, for those who do read the Bible as fact, the more overt message, based on the presence of Samuel's ghost, is that ghosts clearly exist.

## Making Sense of Ancient History

For all the knowledge we've gained over the centuries, are there things the ancients knew that we've lost? The Egyptians and Aztecs had similar beliefs, despite being separated by nearly eight thousand miles. Cultures all across the planet shared a worldview that saw death as a continuation. The idea of ghosts wasn't a question; it was a fact. It was just how the world worked. Most Western thought today, however, doesn't accept a fact until it's scientifically proven. And though attempts are being made, as we'll see in the last section of this book, the afterlife and the existence of ghosts among us isn't so easily tested through experimentation.

So how do we account for all these commonalities between past civilizations? It's possible that they tapped into a truth beyond this physical world that's since been lost. Or maybe our minds somehow create similar stories for the things we can't answer through our sensory experiences.

"Where might we have thrown the baby out with the bathwater with our overzealous desire to make everything controllable?" asks Joanna Ebenstein, an author and the founder of Morbid Anatomy, an organization that explores the intersections between art, medicine, death, and culture. "This phenomenon still exists. We can doubt the veracity of the reports, but they didn't just go away. We didn't become rationalists and suddenly there's no ghost sightings. It continues on."

Science and rationalism have found many explanations for events once considered miracles. The Bible is full of such wonders, like the burning bush. Colin Humphreys, a physicist at Cambridge University, suggests that Moses may have stumbled upon an acacia bush sitting atop a volcanic vent, an instance not uncommon in the region where the encounter supposedly happened. If hot gases suddenly discharged from below, the bush could have ignited. Similar explanations have been offered for the ten plagues. In 1957, scholar Greta Hort proposed a chain reaction of events beginning with red algae flooding the Nile, which poisoned the frogs' habitats, forcing them onto dry land, and at the same time killed fish, which washed ashore for insects to feast on, who in turn spread the anthrax that infected livestock and caused boils. You get the idea.[2] Things that weren't known or understood were attributed to God or the supernatural—and surely exaggerated a bit for the purposes of storytelling.

We don't hear of the types of miracles described in the Bible anymore, but we do hear of ghosts. All the time. Perhaps discarnate souls do need a *Book of the Dead*, or a Xoloitzcuintle, or more psychopomps to lead them away from

---

2    If you've read a Haggadah at a Passover seder, Hort's theory is like a scientific version of Chad Gadya.

their past lives and into their new ones.

"I often think, looking at the past, and the bulk of historical record, what are the odds that we're the ones who are right and the whole rest of human history was wrong?" Ebenstein says. "I see a lot of arrogance with people thinking that we've proven they don't exist. But we haven't proven they don't exist. We've only proven we can't prove they exist. We don't really know what the world is. We don't know shit, and I love that."

Dr. David Kowalewski is doing his part to keep ancient beliefs alive, but even with a modern shamanic movement growing, it's not enough to handle all the dead. "Just do the math," he says. "Whereas world population tops seven billion with increasing millions dying each year, psychopomp work is rare. Should we then not expect a growing public attention to hosts of ghosts, including hauntings and possessions? Can the global community endure such an assault?"

Might looking to the past and learning from our ancestors teach us more about death and, in turn, create a better way to live? Like any lessons from history, the trick is knowing which parts to take from and which to leave behind. The medieval age is probably a good candidate for the latter.

## Ye Olde Medieval Ghosts: Heaven, Hell, and Everything in Between

Death is always among us, but if it were to look back on human history it might refer to medieval times as the good ol' days. For centuries, the Grim Reaper ran rampant across Europe, reveling in plagues that wiped out whole towns, amassing bodies in hundreds of bloody wars, and possibly wincing at disturbingly creative methods of torture that sent victims into his arms. Life was hell, and it seemed that for many, death wasn't much better. At least, not right away. Early Christians agreed that the trip to heaven or hell wasn't immediate. As French scholar and Lutheran minister Louis Bouyer put it, "Those who end their existence on earth in a state of grace, but without being entirely purified by penance from the traces of their sin, have still to rid themselves of these vestiges through a supreme test before they can attain beatitude." Welcome to purgatory.

Twelfth-century beliefs were far different from ancient Egyptian traditions, but Christians did cling to the concept of an afterlife journey toward the green light to heaven. This temporary rest stop on the way to eternity purified the dead with fire, which was not to be confused with the more punitive flames of hell. Though, according to thirteenth-century theologian Thomas Aquinas, purgatory might have been next-door neighbors with hell, so the same blaze that tormented those who rejected God could also cleanse all the souls en route to heaven. Aside from the efficiency this achieved, perhaps those who'd chosen the righteous path got a glimpse of the other direction to see what they'd avoided. Such knowledge would make heaven that much more satisfying. During this hopefully brief purification period, prayers from the living could help hasten the process and bring relief to the dead.

As all this burning for God's love was going on, ghosts were drifting through forests, cities, and homes all over medieval Europe. Why weren't these dead people in heaven, hell, or waiting in line on a blazing celestial bridge? To account for such an anomaly, a French bishop decided that these wandering souls were on leave from purgatory. But this was no final vacation amongst the living—this was a mission to seek out those much-needed prayers or charitable acts that would shortcut them into heaven. A get-out-of-purgatory-quicker card.

One of these ghosts, however, as a fourteenth-century account tells us, had no such agenda and instead gave an eyewitness account of this purification holding pattern. The story was shared in the year 1343 by Peter of Bramham, who heard it from a Yorkshire chaplain who'd seen his deceased father nine years after his passing. Consider it a game of telephone some five hundred years before telephones were invented, but nevertheless a good one.

The clergyman had been on his way to a church several miles away when two figures approached on horseback. His father's face, unblemished from purgatory torments, was fully recognizable. He held a dead infant in a cradle, presumably belonging to the woman riding alongside him, whose face was hidden. The chaplain was understandably confused by the strange companion and the presence of the child—not to mention the fact that his dead father was talking to him.

The ghost explained that the woman, dead six years, had been the wife of his lord and had a scandalous affair with a knight while her husband was away on business. The chaplain's father was entrusted to watch over her but succumbed to a bribe and allowed the romance to blossom. The resulting love child died before baptism, and now the three of them were cleansing themselves of the mess in purgatory. The wife, it's noted, confessed her sin to God, thereby avoiding a direct ticket to hell. All the chaplain wanted to do was enjoy a peaceful walk to church, and instead he comes face-to-face with his dead dad and a load of drama! The good news in all this, as the ghost finally explained, was that he'd be headed on his merry way to heaven soon. No extra prayers or good deeds done on his behalf were needed.

The father learned this from his personal guardian angel; everyone has one watching over them from the moment of birth to death and right on into purgatory, he claimed. Each busy angel reports back to God with all the good and bad gossip during life and presents their person's soul at death. From there, the amount of purification is determined, and the guardian angel acts as a sort of cosmic cheerleader to keep the tormented spirit's spirits up. This is especially helpful considering that, according to the ghost, they're all trapped in a valley reminiscent of a George R. R. Martin title: a song of ice and fire with darkness, hail, snow, and extreme cold on one side and tar, sulfur, and flames on the other. The souls dance back and forth, accompanied by anyone who's reformed, confessed, and undertaken penance for any and all sins—including, the father adds, bestiality. This last note seems like a curious detail to share, but perhaps he'd had some uncomfortable experiences with such folks in the afterlife, or prior to it.

As if things weren't strange enough for the chaplain, the situation grew more uncomfortable when he changed the subject to ask about his mother, who obviously hadn't been hanging out with his father. Much to his dismay, he learned that she was stuck on a stormy isle near Scotland. "Because, unknown to me, my wife led a wicked life," the apparition explained, "burning in lust, now she suffers great pains on the island of May. Again, because she confessed her sins in extremis she is assigned that place for purgation, thanks to Jesus' goodness, otherwise she would be burning in hell for ever with the Devil." Aside from the revelation that his mother was unfaithful to his father, the chaplain also deduced from this unfortunate piece of information that purgatory isn't one place, but rather many places that might relate to the spot where souls sinned. This might explain why ghosts were observed everywhere. Needy ghosts who were less fortunate than the chaplain's father still sought help to move on to paradise.

The Catholic Church saw this issue as a business opportunity. For a fee, priests could ensure followers that their time in purgatory would be reduced. Somehow, according to this proposition, an all-knowing God would allow savvy souls to pay their way into heaven rather than subject themselves to afterlife prison. To some this may have seemed more like a ticket to hell, but such matters are always subject to opinion. Martin Luther, for one, didn't much care for it. This grievance was among his ninety-five theses that he nailed to the door of the Castle Church in Wittenberg, Germany, in 1517, thus beginning the Protestant Reformation.

If these ghosts played a small part in reforming a religion, more power to them. But it didn't quite fill their purgatory requirements. And sometimes getting the help they needed didn't take anything as drastic as launching a new sect of Christianity. In one recorded case, all a ghost had to do was to carry bags of beans.

Like the tale of the chaplain and his ghost dad, this one, too, took place in the Yorkshire region. But that's where the similarity ends. This helpful spirit appeared as a luminescent bale of hay in front of a man whose horse had fallen and left him walking alone with all his cargo. Upon seeing the other-worldly hay, the man said, "God forbid that you do me any harm." The spirit then shape-shifted into a man, introduced himself, and offered to lug the legumes all the way to the river. To repay the kind deed, the living man had masses sung for the ghost, absolving it and punching its ticket to heaven.

The story, though hardly spooky and completely lacking in ribaldry, was one of twelve tales written by a monk of Byland Abbey sometime around the year 1400. Each was a yarn he'd heard and decided to record in the blank pages of an unfinished twelfth-century manuscript. There they sat, dead to the world, until being brought forth from their own literary purgatory by medieval scholar and masterful ghost storyteller M. R. James, who published them in their original Latin in 1922. In his critique, the stories were "strong in local color, and though occasionally confused, incoherent, and unduly compressed, [they] evidently represent the words of the narrators with some approach to fidelity."

The monk also wrote about a man who suffered a more personal confrontation. The fellow had taken a trip, but made the mistake of leaving his pregnant wife at home. During his travels he witnessed a procession of ghosts along a road, which included a baby rolling along in a sock. The man reached out to the baby and discovered it was his own child, who had been born prematurely, died unbaptized, and been buried disrespectfully by midwives. The father cleansed the baby, who then rejoined the procession walking on his own feet, at peace. Upon his return home, the midwives admitted the child had been buried in a sock. Shaken and angered by the tragedy, the father showed his disgust through divorce papers. The monk, it seemed, didn't think highly of his reaction, claiming it was "very displeasing to God." If the father knew, he may have expressed his own displeasure for his son's death under the Lord's watch. Expressing his grief, however, would have to wait until he made his way through purgatory to heaven, where he could confront God in person. Unless communications could be established without that kind of patience.

By the next century, it seemed such a thing might be possible.

# DANTE'S GHOST
# TO THE RESCUE

In the beginning of Dante's fourteenth-century narrative poem, the *Divine Comedy*, the author (and main character) encounters the ghost of fellow poet Virgil in the forest, and the two head off on a ferry ride with Charon for a tour of hell. Thereafter, Dante paints a vivid picture of the underworld, beginning with the welcome sign reading, "Abandon all hope, ye who enter here," and continuing with a jaunt through nine progressively more terrifying levels. He discovers that whatever sins were committed in life come back to haunt the offenders in the afterlife. Early on they see gluttons standing in decomposing garbage filled with worms, forever trapped in the waste they once disregarded. Later, the visitors encounter fortune-tellers wandering around with backward heads as punishment for infringing on God's job by foretelling the future. Among the

An image from the nineteenth-century illustrator Gustave Doré's series inspired by Dante's *Divine Comedy*.

worst of the worst are the flatterers, eternally buried in excrement as payback for spewing crap all over earth.

Dante and his readers would eventually escape the horrors of hell and find their way through purgatory and on to heaven. The happy ending, however, nearly died with the poet.

Before Dante's passing he'd hidden the final thirteen cantos. Both of his sons, Jacopo and Piero, searched high and low for months in hopes of finding an ending to the unfinished epic. Having had no luck, the two set out to finish the *Divine Comedy* on their own. Both were poets, so surely they'd inherited enough talent to do the job. The world may have soon found out if Dante's ghost hadn't visited Jacopo in his sleep. The startled son asked his father if he were alive and heard him say, "Yes, not in our life, but in the true."

Keeping his wits about him, Jacopo took the opportunity to ask if Dante had finished the poem. "Yes, I finished it," the ghost responded. The spirit then led him by hand to his former bedroom, touched a spot on the wall, and said, "Here is that for which thou hast so long sought."

Jacopo woke up and immediately fetched his brother to renew their search precisely where the dream had indicated. In that very location, a mat covered a small opening. The young poets had never seen or heard about the hidden space. Inside they found some writings, coated with mold from dampness and on the verge of rotting. All thirteen cantos were recovered and salvaged with a careful cleaning, allowing the tale about the afterlife to be completed from . . . the afterlife. Unfortunately, Dante's ghost didn't confirm whether any details of his poem proved accurate.

## Ghosts Creep Out of the Middle Ages

If purgatory wasn't real, how could there be ghosts? This became a pressing question as the Protestant Reformation spread throughout Europe—and beyond—in the sixteenth century. Without this intermediary place for the dead to await their eternity, Swiss Protestant theologian Ludwig Lavater theorized spirits could only return from either heaven or hell. His thoroughly titled 1572 book, *Of ghostes and spirites walking by nyght, and of strange noyses, crackes, and sundry forewarnynges, whiche commonly happen before the death of menne, great slaughters, and alterations of kyngdomes*, recounted ancient ghost stories and tackled this new world of spirits with a mixture of rationalism, demonology, and the occasional acceptance that sometimes souls did return from heaven.[3]

"There happen daily many things by the ordinary course of nature, which diverse men, especially they that are timorous and fearful, suppose to be visions or spirits," Lavater wrote. Rats, cats, weasels, horses, and strange birds were among the natural sources of ghosts mentioned. Echoes, for people who were unfamiliar with the phenomenon, might also cause alarm.

As for any ghost stories that monks and priests had been sharing, "there is no cause at all why we should ascribe much unto them," Lavater said. "Perchance their mind was to bring men to great fear and religion." Like the shamans of long ago, he suggested ghosts had been used as a tool to keep order among the masses.

These explanations were all fine and dandy, but even though "those rumblings of spirits in the night, are now much more seldom heard than they have been in times past," Lavater still had plenty to account for. He acknowledged that God "does use the help and service of good angels, for the preservation of his elect" and that occasionally spirits may return to the living to offer advice or important revelations. That being said, sometimes it seemed that God worked in more mysterious ways when it came to letting a ghost wander free. Like the time a spirit crept into bed with an old companion.

Lavater shared the tale recorded by an Italian lawyer named Alexander ab Alexandro earlier in the century, in which a friend "of good credit" attended the funeral of an acquaintance and encountered the interred soul later that night. The ghost, looking "marvelous pale and lean," quietly undressed, climbed into bed, and embraced the poor fellow. Terrified, the man pushed the ghost away and "by chance touched his foot, which seemed so extremely

---

3   This was Robert Harrison's 1572 English translation of Lavater's original 1569 edition, written in Latin under the title *De Spectris, Lemuribus Et Magnis Atque Insolitis fragoribus, vriisque præsagitionibus quæ plerunque obitum hominum, magnas clades, mutationesque Imperiorum præcedunt*. In the quotes that follow, I've taken the liberty of modernizing the English spellings for your reading convenience.

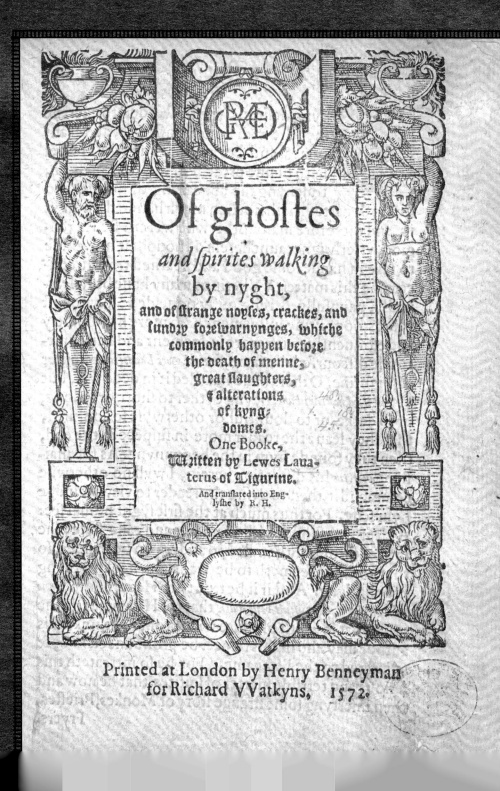

# Of ghostes

*and spirites walking*
by nyght,
and of strange noyses, crackes, and
sundry forewarnynges, whiche
commonly happen befoze
the death of menne,
great slaughters,
& alterations
of kyng-
domes.
One Booke,
Written by Lewes Laua-
terus of Tigurine.
And translated into Eng-
lyshe by R. H.

Printed at London by Henry Benneyman
for Richard VVatkyns,  1572.

cold, as no ice in the world might be compared unto it." The ghost got out of bed, put its clothes back on, and was never seen by the man again. Perhaps it was able to rest in peace in someone else's bed.

Aside from these good souls permitted to return to the land of the living, Lavater's big fear was that the majority of ghosts weren't sent by God. Instead, he claimed, they were most likely demons risen to wreak havoc by luring people into committing crimes, murders, and even suicide. If successful, the demons' recruits would be headed straight for eternal damnation.

William Shakespeare might have agreed—at least from a creativity standpoint. The Bard is believed to be among the many Englishmen who devoured Lavater's post-Reformation diagnosis of ghosts. In *Hamlet*, written in 1599, Horatio is suspicious of the ghost proclaiming to be Hamlet's father. The spirit of the murdered king seeks revenge by urging his son to kill Claudius, Hamlet's uncle and the king's brother. Is this really the soul of Hamlet's father? Or is it a sneaky devil, as Lavater raised concerns about? Before Hamlet runs off to commit murder, he listens to Horatio and ponders the same thing:

The spirit that I have seen

May be the devil: and the devil hath power

To assume a pleasing shape; yea, and perhaps

Out of my weakness and my melancholy,

As he is very potent with such spirits,

Abuses me to damn me.

Like the nature of any ghost, debates about Hamlet's father continue to this day.

## Dr. John Dee and the Philosopher's Stone

Coming out of the Middle Ages, Dr. John Dee didn't want to wait around for ghosts to appear at their convenience or wait till death to chat with angels. Not if he could conjure them at will. Surrounded by a library of some four thousand books, and wearing a long wizard-like beard, Dee was a real-life Albus Dumbledore ready to delve into the supernatural. With the help of a medium, he worked with magical mirrors and wondrous crystals in the 1580s to successfully connect with the dead. Or so he believed.

Dee was born on July 13, 1527, in London. A studious child, he found his way to St. John's College at Cambridge by the age of fifteen, where he grew into a devout Christian while becoming a skilled mathematician, astronomer, and astrologer. As a fellow at Trinity College, his ingenuity began to raise eyebrows and concerns about sorcery when he designed a mechanical flying scarab for a stage performance of Aristophanes's *Pax* that, in Dee's words, caused "great wondring, and many vain reports spread abroad of the means how that was effected."

His prolific knowledge would continue to expand as he traveled through Europe to study the sciences, the occult, and the Kabbalah. Dee hit the lecture circuit as well and made such a great impression that he was offered a professorship in Paris. He declined the position in favor of returning to England, where his reputation earned him employment with the Royal Court under Henry VIII's young successor, Edward VI. All was going well until an illness took the teenage king's life in 1553 and threatened Dee's job security. Fortunately the new queen, Mary Tudor, took an interest in astrology and retained Dee's services. Acting as Her Majesty's chief prophesier, he began casting her horoscopes, as well as those of her half sister Elizabeth. But when word got out that he'd shared a birth map of the queen with the princess, he was accused of plotting her demise and arrested for treason. Dee was eventually acquitted after sitting in prison for two years. Following Mary's death during an influenza epidemic in 1558, Elizabeth welcomed Dee back with open arms and entrusted the learned astrologer with naming an ideal coronation date.

Despite his relationship with the queen and his scholarly wisdom, Dee was far from a wealthy man. Outside his royal duties, he'd been reading up on alchemy and furthering his knowledge of the occult in hopes of remedying his financial situation with an old alchemist get-rich-quick-scheme: finding the Philosopher's Stone in order to turn metals into gold. French alchemist Nicolas Flamel had allegedly done it about two hundred years earlier. Dee believed if he could communicate with spirits, they could help him find the elusive stone.

In May 1581 he claimed to have had his first success in making contact.

A True & Faithful

# RELATION

OF

What paſſed for many Yeers Betw

D.R. JOHN D

(A Mathematician of Great Fame in Q
and King James their Reignes) and

## SOME SPIRI

TENDING (had it Succeeded

To a General Alteration of moſt S T
KINGDOMES in t

His Private Conferences with Rodolphe Emper
K. of Poland, and divers other Prin
The Particulars of his Cauſe, as it was agitated
By the Popes Intervention : His Baniſhment, a

AS ALSO

## The LETTERS of Sundr

and Princes (ſome whereof were p
Conferences and Apparitions of Spirit

OUT OF

The Original Copy, written wit
Hand : Kept in the LIB
Sir THO. COTTO

WITH A

# PREFACE

Confirming the Reality (as to the Point of SPIRITS) of
This RELATION : and ſhewing the ſeveral good Uſes that
a Sober Chriſtian may make of

BY

# MERIC. CASAUBO

LONDON,
Printed by D. Maxwell, for T. Garthwai
North door of S. Pauls, and by other

He knelt in prayer, gazing into his crystal stone, and saw something.

"There suddenly glowed a dazzling light, in the midst of which, in all his glory, stood the great angel, Uriel," Dee recorded in his notes. Known as the angel of light in the Kabbalah, Uriel informed the enthused alchemist that he could continue chatting with spirits through his shiny rock. But Dee had difficulty invoking further visions. He was a man of many talents, but mediumship was not one of them. And book smarts could only take him so far. So he sought a scryer for help.[4]

Dee's search ended months after his initial vision with a psychic collaborator named Barnabas Saul. Though Saul claimed to see the unseen in a globular crystal and was once "strangely troubled by a spiritual creature about midnight," he turned out to be a dud. After just a short stint with Dee, the alchemist noted in his diary that the scryer "confessed that he neither heard no saw any spiritual creature any more." Saul parted ways with Dee and retreated back to obscurity. Fortunately for the ambitious Dee, a new scryer turned up almost immediately afterward.

An experienced twenty-seven-year old, Edward Kelley had previously worked with Oxford scholar Thomas Allen, who also happened to be an occultist and friend of Dee. When Kelley first presented himself at the alchemist's home in Mortlake (now a suburb of London), he asked to see "some thing in spiritual practice." Dee explained that he didn't have that kind of power but sought someone who did—someone to truly aid in his "philosophical studies." Given Kelley's resume, Dee believed he was just the man for the job. The fact that his new sidekick had had his ears removed in the pillory for forging either title deeds or money in 1580 didn't seem to bother Dee in the least. Perhaps Kelley's disfigurement gave the young scryer an aura of mystery that enhanced his appearance as someone who could work wonders. And that he did.

Dee tested Kelley's abilities right off the bat by challenging him to make an angel appear in a crystal. Within minutes Kelley witnessed a spiritual creature: Dee's old friend, Uriel. It would be the first of many séances (which Dee termed "Actions") through crystal gazing to produce Uriel and other spirits, including the archangel Michael and a child called Madini. Kelley received their messages in a celestial language called Enochian, which, according to the angels, was used long ago between God and Adam. One can imagine Dee's delight in bridging his passion for the occult with one of the biggest stars of the Bible. His joy was accompanied by plenty of work as he meticulously and painstakingly transcribed each angelic conversation. These were often of a reli-

---

4   A scryer sees visions in a smooth surface, like a mirror, a crystal, or even a vessel of water.

gious nature, with occasional exceptions, like the time Uriel expressed the need to build a tower with walls made of diamonds, or the time an angel suggested Dee and Kelley share wives. The spirits had bold ideas, but they hadn't exactly unlocked the secrets of the universe.

The alchemist and scryer took their crystallomancy show on the road across Europe, often performing for royalty and nobility. Their demonstrations failed to produce gold, but fortunately their wealthy audience could enjoy the spectacle without relying on the spirits to produce real magic.

Despite their failures, the spirit of Michael encouraged their practice and preached patience. According to Dee, his faith in the angel proved fruitful by December 19, 1586, when he noted in his diary that he and Kelley had produced nearly an ounce of the "best gold." Had the two actually found the formula to the Philosopher's Stone? Or was the manifestation of gold merely a trick by Kelley? Several Dee biographers believe that his scryer was nothing more than a charlatan who, like shamans of antiquity, may have created the illusion of spirit communication through ventriloquism.

On one occasion during the spring of 1587, while staying in Bohemia, in present-day Czech Republic, a spirit carried off Dee's prized crystal while Kelley conducted a séance. A month later the two men were walking in the garden when suddenly the scryer claimed to see two spirits fighting with swords near the banks of a river. One of the ghosts was upset that the other had taken Dee's stone and demanded he return it under his wife's pillow. Dee rushed home, made a beeline for the bedroom, and there, beneath the pillow, lay the pilfered stone. As far as Dee was concerned, the whole ordeal was a supernatural event, though it was more likely explained by trickery from Kelley. It's unknown where the crystal had disappeared to, or what uses may have been attempted with it during its absence.

"This man was Dee's evil genius," wrote British chemist T. E. Thorpe in 1909. "Their connection is one of the most astonishing and perplexing circumstances of his history. How Kelley could have acquired such complete ascendancy over his patron is almost inexplicable. Kelley was a first-class ne'er-do-well, a lover of loose company and of strong waters, and a consummate liar."

Still, the idea of alchemy producing riches was enticing and perhaps the scryer clung to some belief that Dee could make it happen. Greed makes men do strange things, especially when the prospect of magically produced gold is involved.

Though spirits never conveyed the secrets of the Philosopher's Stone to Dee or other alchemists, they eventually offered great detail about the afterlife. At least, if you ask Emanuel Swedenborg.

## Emanuel Swedenborg and Astral Projection

Like Dee, Emanuel Swedenborg was a man who knew more than most but wanted to know more. The Swedish scientist, born on January 29, 1688, learned everything he could about engineering, geometry, chemistry, metallurgy, anatomy, and physiology. Brimming with knowledge, he filled pages with innovative ideas that were well ahead of his time, like "a machine, with whose aid a man could rise into the air and travel aloft" and "a kind of boat in which one could travel underwater wherever one wanted." By 1716, Swedenborg founded his country's first scientific journal, *Daedalus Hyperboreus*, to showcase his inventions and those of others.

A portrait of the Swedish theologian, scientist, philosopher, and mystic Emanuel Swedenborg.

But despite his achievements, at the age of fifty-five he put aside his studies to go where science couldn't take him. Swedenborg, who had unlocked so many secrets of the natural world, set his sights on the spiritual plane. So began a series of out-of-body experiences that led to remarkable places, including all the planets. Mars, he discovered, was full of peaceful, pious people who "acknowledge and adore our Lord," whereas Venus was populated by "savage" folks. Remarkable as interplanetary astral projection was, Swedenborg didn't limit his soul to the boundaries of our universe. He broke through the solar system ceiling and headed straight for heaven to converse with spirits and learn about the afterlife. These experiences were detailed in more than three million words, many of which filled his book *Heaven and Its Wonders and Hell from Things Heard and Seen*. In it, he was able to describe what happens at the moment of death in the only way one could: by dying.

"The actual experience happened to me so that I could have a full knowledge of how it occurs," Swedenborg wrote.

His physical senses vanished, like any dying person, but his capacity for thought remained intact so he could perceive every element of the afterlife and report back on it for the benefit of the living. Once dead, he learned, all is not lost. In fact, the only thing left behind is the physical body. The spirit sees

and touches as before and maintains all its memories and possessions.

"On this account, when man has become a spirit, he does not know, by consciousness, that he is not still in the body in which he was when in the world; consequently, he does not know by consciousness, that he has died."

So when you die, you won't even know it. But at this point you've entered what Swedenborg termed the "world of spirits"—a place situated between heaven and hell. From there, people are sorted into those who go to either the good place or the bad place. The process is reminiscent of the Egyptian journey through the underworld, but without the hideous monsters or an eternal judge weighing your earthly deeds. God oversees both realms and leaves it up to the dead to decide how they wish to spend eternity. Spirits reunite with their deceased friends and family and find their way to heaven if they choose a path of love and wisdom—or, if they're more comfortable among evil spirits, they congregate with them and enjoy their rotten company in hell. To each their own.

Those who choose heaven and reach its highest level grow "exceedingly beautiful." Swedenborg claimed to have "seen faces of angels of the third heaven, which were so beautiful that no painter, with all the resources of his art, could impart such brightness to his colors, as should equal a thousandth part of the light and life which appeared in those countenances."

All these beautiful angels live busy afterlives, not unlike their time on earth. They have their houses, communities, parks, and cities and stay occupied helping one another or attending to the newly dead. And if angels were married on earth, their union may continue in heaven, though things would be a bit different without a physical body. Marriage, Swedenborg described, "is the conjunction of two into one mind" and since those minds are joined together, "two married partners are not called two, but one angel."

On the other end of things, those who choose to go to hell also stay active in their own communities. There are no fiery pits, no boiling brains, and no head honcho devil poking people with a sharpened trident. None of that is necessary since spirits in hell torture themselves perfectly well through fear, manipulation, and the types of persistent power struggles that spread misery on earth. The worst of these hells, Swedenborg said, are inhabited by those who "had been full of self-love, and, consequently, full of contempt of others, and of enmity against those who did not side with them, and, at the same time, full of hatred and revenge against those who did not treat them with respect and make their court to them."

Considering these spirits' penchant for such unpleasantness, Swedenborg's hell is their version of heaven. Whichever way the dead go, there's no turning back to earth. Spirits, he believed, could not appear in the physical world. People who thought otherwise had their senses deceived in some manner. If he's right, Swedenborg never had a chance to revisit earth and see all the sub-marines, airplanes, and other inventions that came to life long after he passed.

The theologian's unique ideas about the afterlife developed into a religion called Swedenborgianism, which grew in popularity following his death in 1772 and into the nineteenth century. But by the 1840s, ideas about the dead were rapidly changing. And any notions of spirits being unable to return to earth were undone by a burgeoning movement of mediums conjuring the dead to knock on wood, levitate furniture, scribble messages, and excite millions among the living.

"From all my experience, and which I have now enjoyed for many years, I can declare and affirm, that angels, as to form, are in every respect men; that they have faces, eyes, ears, a body, arms, hands, feet, and that they see, hear, and converse with each other; in short, that they are deficient in nothing that belongs to a man, except that they are not super-invested with a material body."

—Emanuel Swedenborg in the 1885 edition of
*Heaven and Its Wonders, the World of Spirits,*
*and Hell: From Things Heard and Seen*

# THE SALEM WIZARD TRIAL

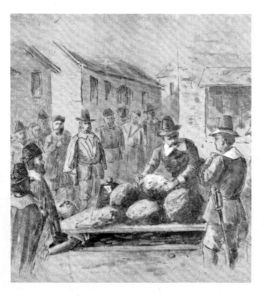

The Salem witch trials left many innocent women dead in the late seventeenth century. But one victim stands out among them: eighty-one-year-old farmer Giles Corey, who was accused of being a wizard in 1692 and refused to stand trial. Had he entered a plea, he would have forfeited his property and his family would have lost their inheritance. Corey was already going to lose his churchgoing wife, Martha, who'd been convicted of witchcraft and was sentenced to be hanged. So he opted for death.

The accusation against Corey had been exacerbated by the words of a ghost who'd appeared to Ann Putnam, a meddling teen known for accusing more than sixty people of witchcraft. The supposed spirit was that of a farmhand Corey had allegedly kicked to death in 1675 for stealing apples. (The murderous farmer apparently weaseled his way out of jail time and paid a fine, despite standing trial.) Young Ann shared her spectral vision with her father, who took the liberty of writing a letter to one of the witchcraft trial judges detailing the notes provided by the apparition. "Whereupon there appeared unto her (she said) a man in a winding sheet, who told

her that Giles Corey had murdered him by pressing him unto death with his feet; but that the Devil there appeared unto him and covenanted with him, and promised him, he should not be hanged," began the missive.

Ann's indictment may have simply been based on local stories she'd heard, forcing Corey to finally pay the price for the crime he committed (without the use of wizardry) seventeen years earlier. The judges accepted the ghost's testimony, possibly to make amends for having let the old man get away with murder, or possibly because, in a world believed to be full of witches, why not believe a ghost? These delusional lawmen also decided to allow the devil to keep his word. Instead of hanging on the so-called Gallows Hill, it was determined that Corey's death would mirror his victim's. The chosen method was called pressing—a torturous punishment that involved piling heavy stones atop a board laid across a person's chest. "More weight, more weight!" Corey cried defiantly as his accusers watched. The sheriff shushed him with his cane, shoving the supposed wizard's protruding tongue back into his mouth as he died.

Local legend has it that Corey became a ghost as well. Some believe he haunts Salem and emerges whenever disaster is about to strike the town. One account in particular claims Corey was seen floating through the cemetery the night before the Great Salem Fire of 1914. With its dark history, Salem is certainly rich with lore, but according to the Salem Witch Museum's assistant director of education, Jill Christiansen, the ghost of Giles Corey is nothing more than an invention from the 1970s. The tale has been traced back to Robert Ellis Cahill, an ex-sheriff of Essex County, Massachusetts, and the author of numerous books on New England history and folklore.

"None of it is true," Christiansen says. If only those words had been heard and believed in 1692.

# CONVERSATIONS
## WITH THE DEAD

MODERN SPIRITUALISM THROUGH
THE ROARING TWENTIES

"It is no proof of wisdom to examine certain phenomena because we think it certain that they are impossible, as if our knowledge of the universe were already completed."

—Professor Oliver Lodge, circa 1890s

I n 1927, an entrepreneurial medium named Nellie C. Moore decided to earn a little extra cash by playing matchmaker between the living and the dead. For the past seven decades, communicating with lost loved ones had been a thriving business, but why stop at old flames when there are so many new spirits to meet?

Moore had been working with a seventy-one-year-old Kansas farmer named John Seybold. She roped him in by first summoning the spirit of his deceased son, and then after earning his trust, she introduced him to "Sarah" during a séance. Sarah was a spirit apparently looking for a relationship back on good ol' earth and probably wasn't too picky given her discarnate situation. Seybold and Sarah flirted through the séances and soon enough, he proposed. Always the opportunist, Moore offered her services to conduct the marriage ceremony. Like any wedding, there were attendees from both sides. Seybold's were alive; Sarah's were not.

Not surprisingly, this unusual form of marital bliss did not last. In fact, Seybold may have started to sour on his spirit bride before they ever made it to the honeymoon.

"An empty chair was provided for 'Sarah', who failed to materialize despite assurances she was there," an article reported.

So Seybold sued.

The wedding had cost him one hundred dollars, plus he bought roses for Sarah, purchased a wedding gown and a ring, and handed over deeds to 480 acres of land to Moore. It was a pricey affair for a bride who wouldn't—and couldn't—show up.

As if that weren't bad enough, he'd forked over thousands more based on suggestions given by other ghosts that Moore conjured. This included payments for her rent, new furniture, and her children's education. At times, Seybold claimed, this money was "whisked away in the darkened séance room by an illuminated hand."

For these damages, the farmer's lawsuit sought a $7,500 judgment against Moore. The medium defended herself, claiming that all transactions were business dealings. Seybold, she testified, came to her in poor health and "he wanted to promote spiritualism and leave something good behind him to perpetuate his memory."

He had the money, and she was more than happy to provide the spiritual-istic work he allegedly desired.

Despite the absurdities of a spirit wedding, the judge ruled that Seybold couldn't reclaim his money unless he could produce a contract with the medium that was illegal. Sadly, Seybold and his attorneys could not.

Mediums like Moore had been swindling money under the guise of Spir-

# Husband of 'Spirit Bride' Sues Woman Medium for $7,500 as 'Gold Digger'

**Vacant Chair Left at Table During Wedding Supper for Wife That Never Came, So Seybold Goes to Court to Recover $7,500 He Spent to Win Heart and Hand of His 'Unseen Sweetheart'**

*Special dispatch to S. F. "Examiner."*

WICHITA (Kan.), Nov. 26.—A. Conan Doyle, eminent interpreter of spirits, has lately maintained that shades carry on their earthly professions, and John Seybold, retired farmer of Wichita, is in entire agreement with him.

For, John says, he has but lately been mixed up with a gold digger of no mean sort who for the past year has wasted her spiritual sweetness on the arid Kansas air—wanted it to the extent of $7,500 of John's money, when she might have been lifting far larger amounts from unrefined butter, egg and oxidized iron men.

At that she had to marry John to get her hands on his money, or to get his check pen flowing freely.

### Cost Him $7,500

The unusual story of how this meek and lovely young woman of the spirit world, Sarah, was married to elderly John Seybold, whom two wives had already divorced, and how she cajoled him into giving her money and spending more on the medium than married them, has just been told in a Wichita court—one of the queerest cases ever heard in Kansas, where natural and supernatural phenomena vary from tornadoes and floods to Carrie Nation and anti-cigarette laws.

John Seybold, 71, and a somewhat disillusioned inquirer into the mysteries of the other world, brought the suit against Mrs. Nellie C. Moore, Wichita medium, who arranged his courting, marriage and —Seybold now claims—the expenditure of his $7,500.

Mrs. Moore, 36 and comely, denied all the ex-farmer's allegations and it is now being decided by a District Court judge whether Mrs. Moore did fraudulently secure money through suggestions of his "spirit bride" or whether the bride was bona fide, in so far as a spirit bride conveniently can be, and in addition a gold digger of the first Kansas water.

Seybold said his eyes were opened and he lost faith in the reality of his cold and calculating bride, whom he had often seen as a dim figure in the darkened room, but whom he had touched only to place on her finger a diamond ring that had cost him $200, when Mrs. Moore suggested that he sell two valuable farms, one in Kansas and one in Oklahoma.

When, in the course of the trial, Seybold took the stand he told the court how he had given up farming, how he had come to town and how his interest of thirty years in spiritualism had been fostered when he went to live at the home of Mrs. Moore, who also "developed" him in seances at $2 a development.

He told how Mrs. Moore had in-

**SPOOKY!**—This is said to be the only photograph ever taken of Mrs. Nellie C. Moore, Wichita medium, who is alleged to have arranged the marriage of John Seybold to his "spirit bride." John is suing her for $7,500 he spent during the "courtship."

troduced him to his spook bride-to-be, Sarah; to Indians, doctors, a jeweler and his own dead son, who acted as financial advisor to him. He told how he had come to believe that Sarah was his soulmate who had been wailing down the winds of eternity waiting to be put into concert with him; of his joy at finding her; of how he bought flowers for her and finally was married to her by Mrs. Moore and spent "close to $50" on a wedding supper and party that lasted from early evening to early morning.

The delicate question of reopening the homosexual attic between these two, so incongruously lovers—he of the earth earthy and comparatively flush, and she of the ether clear and ecstatically poor—the cash—he did not tell of specifically. It may be that there are no conventions in this land of the spirits, and it is altogether likely that Sarah did the question popping, considering later events, for she let her phantasied farmer buy the goods for her wedding dress, which Mrs. Moore turned over to a dressmaker.

her, after which she would return to him warranty deeds to the land, that he become suspicious.

She had asked, he swore, that she they go to a bank and put up the deeds as security, and borrow all the money he could. But this was too much. It appeared to him, he declared, that the medium wanted to get all his money from him and turn him out in the cold, and though the world likely fancied his entrance into the same stuff as his beloved Sarah, he was not in favor of it. It opened his eyes, Seybold said.

I told her she was a fake, I broke away, I took the doll made out in her favor and marked it "null and void."

He then voiced how the medium had cautioned him not to touch anything in the darkened room. To touch a spirit meant death. He was to do nothing until advice had been passed on to him by the "managing guide."

Pondering over the scenario, his eyes continued to open. He came to believe that the spirits were no more than Mrs. Moore, who dressed in a raiment of floating robes touched with phosphorescent material that made them glow with a weird and unearthly light.

He recalled how at one time Sarah had expressed a desire to own a small diamond as Mrs. Moore's. Mrs. Moore told him that she had several times received $50 on the ring to take her ever so slight "hoist" periods. To ensure him that the ring was worth the price set out in the shade of a raiment jewelry expert was brought forward and he placed a value of $150 on the ring. Seybold recalled how he had been allowed to slip the ring on the little finger of his hazy fiancee, or so he thought at that time.

### Sausalito N. D. G. W. Will Fete Leader

Sea Point Parlor No. 196, Native Daughters of the Golden West, of Sausalito, tomorrow evening will entertain Grand President Miss Mae Hines-Noonan of San Francisco. There will be a reception, degree work and a collation, with a program of addresses. A presentation will also be in the honor chief officer of the Parlors, other visits in the itinerary of Grand President Noonan are:

Wednesday, November 30, Buena Vista Parlor No. 167, Oakland; Thursday, December 1, Bonaldon Parlor No. 183, Manlius; December 5, Darina Parlor No. 114, both of San Francisco; Tuesday, December 6, Tamalpa Parlor No. 231, Mill Valley; Wednesday, December 7, James Lick Parlor No. 237, Fresno; December 8, Twin Peaks Parlor No. 185, both of San Francisco; Monday, December 12, Wichita Parlor No. 198, San Rafael; Wednesday, December 14, Linda Vista Parlor No. 116; Thursday, December 15, Oro Fino Parlor No. 9, both of San Francisco; Tuesday, December 13, Richmond Parlor No. 147, Richmond.

### Burning Tobacco Big Cause of Fires

EXAMINER BUREAU, SACRAMENTO, Nov. 26.—Indicating a surprising ignorance of fire laws, are caused by the carelessness of man, and responsible for open the menace, Fred C. Stevens, State director of natural resources, revealed today that 864 out of the 1,564 fires in California this year, notably natural forests, w...

itualism for nearly eighty years, all thanks to two young girls and the help of their older sister, known as the Fox sisters.

## The Fox Sisters and the Beginning of a Movement

With a series of raps and knockings, Maggie and Kate Fox, age eleven and nine respectively, kicked off the modern Spiritualism movement in the spring of 1848 from their small wooden farmhouse in Hydesville, New York, near Rochester.[5] The Fox family had just moved in the previous December, and within months they began to hear noises. *Ghostly* noises. Knockings startled the girls and sent them running scared to their parents' bedroom. Try as they might, Mr. and Mrs. Fox couldn't find the source of the unusual sounds. The haunting was just warming up, though. On March 31, things went to a whole new level when their younger daughter, Kate, interacted with the spirit—and addressed it by name.

"Here, Mr. Splitfoot, do as I do," she challenged. With every snap of her fingers came a knock. The spirit, in fact, repeated every pattern Kate offered, like an otherworldly game of Simon. The dead, it appeared, had been resurrected. This glorious day was like a new Easter celebrating this strange new kind of Messiah called Mr. Splitfoot. It was an odd moniker to have been

---

5   Depending on the source, the sisters' ages range from as young as eight to as old as fifteen at the time of the initial rappings. I've gone with eleven and nine, which are the ages engraved on the monument to their home in Lily Dale Assembly, New York. The home of Spiritualists should know best.

used by a child, given its association with the devil, who is often portrayed in popular culture with cloven hooves. But who had time to worry about things like that when the dead were trying talk?

Amazed and dumbfounded, Mrs. Fox began asking questions, and the apparent spirit rapped out its responses. She asked, for example, how many children she had. Seven knocks sounded. *Wrong!* thought Mrs. Fox, until she remembered her six children had a sibling who had died early. The spirit followed up by rapping out their correct ages. Kate, the youngest of Mrs. Fox's daughters, suggested someone might be playing an April Fool's joke. She might have been on to something, but her suggestion was disregarded. They believed the effect was too real, too accurate, and too downright spooky to have been faked by someone nearby.

So who was this spirit? What did he want and why was he suddenly communicating through two young girls? Mrs. Fox described her chat with Mr. Splitfoot in hopes of finding some answers:

---

I then asked: "Is this a human being that answers my questions so correctly?" There was no rap. I asked: "Is it a spirit? If it is, make two raps." Two sounds were given as soon as the request was made. I then said: "If it was an injured spirit, make two raps," which were instantly made, causing the house to tremble. I asked: "Were you injured in this house?" The answer was given as before. "Is the person living that injured you?" Answered by raps in the same manner. I ascertained by the same method that it was a man, aged thirty-one years, that he had been murdered in this house, and his remains were buried in the cellar; that his family consisted of a wife and five children, two sons and three daughters, all living at the time of his death, but that his wife had since died.

---

Now that they knew a bit more about their invisible guest, they wanted to share the phenomenon with their neighbors. Word spread quickly and people rushed to the tiny shack to witness the girls' powers and speak to the mysterious ghost. A crowd of three hundred reportedly packed in and around the small house and awaited more news from beyond.

The curious Foxes tried a new method of gathering information by reciting the alphabet and waiting for raps to stop at the correct letter. Though tedious, they eventually learned Mr. Splitfoot, a peddler, was actually named Charles B. Rosna and was killed on a Tuesday night at twelve o'clock. Through another series of raps they discovered the motive had been money: a theft of five hundred dollars.

MISS MARGARETTA FOX.    MISS CATHARINE FOX.    MRS FISH.

Maggie, Kate, and Leah Fox of Hydesville, New York, known to history as the Fox sisters, are credited with the birth of the Spiritualism movement.

The next morning, April 1, Mr. Fox and a few eager neighbors started digging in the cellar for remains. They found water but nothing more. The men, however, were not dismayed and vowed to continue the search as soon as the water settled. Meanwhile, in the weeks that followed, Kate and Maggie continued chatting with their dead companion. Returning to their Simon-like game, Kate experimented by simply touching her thumbs to her forefingers rather than snapping. Sure enough, Mr. Splitfoot rapped in return. He could *see* as well as hear.

As summer approached, Mr. Fox and friends finally resumed their digging. This time they hit pay dirt by finding human hair and bones. Not a full skeleton, but human bones nonetheless (though a 1904 report claimed a skeleton was, indeed, found within the walls of the Fox home). The findings were enough to convince people that the girls' powers were genuine. With the help of their much older sister, Leah—some twenty years Margaret's senior—the Fox sisters were about to embark on a journey to fame and fortune.

At the time of the first knockings Leah lived in Rochester and taught music to support her daughter after her husband had left her. All the family excitement brought her to Hydesville, where she shrewdly realized there was money to be made with her sisters. She knew from experience that it wasn't easy to earn a living as a woman and second-class citizen.

"A woman could be a mother or housewife, maybe a nurse, maybe a teacher. If you were religious you could become a nun maybe, maybe a secretary or some clerical work, and all of a sudden a new job opening came up—which was goddess," explains historian and performer Todd Robbins. "I think Leah glimpsed this and said, let's run with this."

If Kate and Maggie had any ideas of ending the charade, Leah put the kibosh on it. She started monetizing her sisters' abilities in Rochester and Buffalo, where the Fox sisters were raking in $100 to $150 a night.

"John Fox and his wife appear to have been of the 'good, honest,' but not mentally keen type of farmer folk. Of the two, the wife was the more 'simple minded,' and when the 'nervous, superstitious woman' began to hear unusual noises, which she could not account for, and which seemed in some peculiar manner connected with her children, she concluded at once that the sounds were 'unnatural' and began to brood over the matter. Her fears increased with the persistent recurrence of the mysterious sounds, and before long she took some of the neighbors into her confidence. They were as puzzled as the mother, the Fox home became an object of suspicion and the neighborhood set itself the task of solving the mystery. . . . The possibility of duplicity in such children never occurred to anyone in Hydesville."

—Harry Houdini, in
*A Magician among the Spirits*, 1924

Despite the success, not everyone was enamored with the young girls. In February 1850 three physicians set out to discover the true source of the rapping sounds. They had the opportunity to observe Maggie and Leah (Kate was staying with an aunt at the time) and determined that Maggie willfully created the noises. "She evidently attempted to conceal any indication of voluntary effort, but in this she did not succeed," they reported. "A voluntary effort was manifest, and it was plain that it could not be continued long without fatigue."

The doctors went on to explain that the joints could create the mysterious sounds "under certain circumstances"—in particular, the knee joint. Leah didn't take too kindly to the accusation, so she sent a letter issuing a challenge:

As we do not feel willing to rest under the imputation of being impostors, we are very willing to undergo a proper and decent examination, provided we can select three male and three female friends who shall be present on the occasion. We can assure the public that there is no one more anxious than ourselves to discover the origin of these mysterious manifestations. If they can be explained on "anatomical" or "physiological" principles, it is due to the world that the investigation be made, and that the "humbug" be exposed.

The challenge was accepted and the examination began the next evening with Maggie and Leah seated on a sofa, ready to go. The doctors asked the "spirits" if they would answer a few questions, and the responsive raps were interpreted as a yes. Knowing that, the real test could commence. The doctors repositioned the girls so they were seated on chairs with their legs extended and elevated, resting on cushions of chairs opposite them. With their feet not resting on each other or any resisting surface, the doctors felt certain the sounds could not be effected. Sure enough, after a half hour of waiting, "the 'spirits,' generally so noisy, were now dumb."

The doctors then allowed Leah to sit normally, suspecting Maggie of being the real noisemaker.

"The 'spirits' did not choose to signify their presence under these circumstances, although repeatedly requested so to do," they reported. Thus, they concluded the ghosts were nothing more than Maggie's joints.

Yet, the physicians' report of "The Rochester Impostors" mostly served to bring out supporters of the Fox sisters and build even greater public interest in their abilities. But regardless of what locals thought, it was time to move on to the bigger and brighter gaslights of New York City. The Fox sisters were moving up in the world.

Upon their arrival they booked a suite in Barnum's Hotel on the corner of Broadway and Maiden Lane and attracted a host of curiosity seekers, including poet William Cullen Bryant, newspaper editor Horace Greeley, and author James Fenimore Cooper.[6] As many as thirty people gathered around their table to hear ghosts rap out messages. Tours of the rest of the United States and parts of Europe followed. Along the way the sisters continued attracting anyone who was anyone, most notably one of the few women who still had greater name recognition: Queen Victoria.

Aside from spirits and dollars, the sisters also managed to find love. Maggie married an Arctic explorer, Dr. Elisha Kane, and Kate fell for a London barrister named H. D. Jenckin. Over the years, however, Maggie and Kate each struggled with a drinking problem. Both were eventually widowed and suffered from depression and poverty. Even in the 1800s, it seemed, child stars grew up to lead troubled lives. Meanwhile, big sister Leah moved on to her third marriage, to a wealthy banker and Spiritualist named Daniel Underhill, and was doing just fine.

It may seem odd that these women's childhoods could've sparked a global wave of commotion, excitement, and opportunity. But not to those inclined to believe. As ardent Spiritualist Sir Arthur Conan Doyle wrote:

Remember that a falling apple taught us gravity, a boiling kettle brought us the steam engine, and the twitching leg of a frog opened up the train of thought and experiment which gave us electricity.

6    Barnum's Hotel wasn't owned by P. T. Barnum, though one wonders how things may have been amplified if it was. This Barnum was a cousin of the famed showman.

So the lowly manifestations of Hydesville have ripened into results which have engaged the finest group of intellectuals in this country during the last twenty years, and which are destined, in my opinion, to bring about the far greatest development of human experience which the world has ever seen.

---

Maggie Fox wouldn't have agreed. By 1888 she decided to come clean. Lo and behold, she and her sister were not the bridge between the living and dead. As suspected decades earlier, they were nothing more than masterful pranksters and manipulators of their toe and knee joints. Maggie made her confession before a large crowd attending a Spiritualist conference at the New York Academy of Music. All these years later she now appeared as a short woman with dark eyes and dark hair, dressed in black and wearing black-rimmed glasses with a black cord. Kate watched silently and attentively from a stage box as her sister began to explain that they were "very mischievous children" who wanted to "terrify our dear mother, who was a very good woman and very easily frightened."

The initial bumps in the night, she explained, were made after they went to bed. They would tie an apple to a string and pull it, causing the apple to bang on the floor. Their mother "could not understand it, and did not suspect us of being capable of a trick, because we were so young." The girls then discovered, of course, that they could make noises without a piece of fruit.

"The rappings are simply the result of a perfect control of the muscles of the knee, which govern the tendons of the foot and allow action of the toe and ankle bones that are not commonly known," Maggie explained. "Such perfect control is only possible when a child is taken at an early age and carefully and continually taught to practice the muscles which grow stiff in later years."

To prove her abilities, she slipped off a shoe, sat on a chair and put her feet on a sounding board. As a murmur swept over the audience, a series of "rat-tat-tat-tat-tat" knockings emanated from her toes, loud and clear.

What started as a childish prank grew into a global business under Leah's leadership and vision. "Katie and I were led around like lambs," Maggie said, referencing their extensive touring. "All during this dreadful life of deception I had been protesting. I have always rebelled against it. I have been going to expose it time and time again."

Her husband had urged her to forget about her past and move on. After his death, she was ready to share her story, but Leah's spell over her held strong. "She wanted to establish a new religion," Maggie announced, "and she told me that she received messages from spirits." These spirits, Leah said, had spoken to her before her sisters were born and claimed the girls were "destined for great things."

By the time of Maggie's admission there were more than eight million practicing Spiritualists and thousands of mediums in America, with dozens of Spiritualist newspapers helping to keep them connected.

"I trust that this statement, coming solemnly from me, the first and most successful in this deception, will break the farce of the rapid growth of Spiritualism, and prove that it is all a fraud, a hypocrisy and a delusion," she said.

It would seem that her demonstration and confession would've been damning to the movement, but it wasn't. Some claimed the fact that she was paid $1,500 for the appearance was proof that she only said such things for a desperately needed paycheck. Maybe the public just couldn't accept Maggie's admission because it would be bad for business.

One medium claimed the Fox sisters' ill health was the cause of such ramblings. "Mediums are generally very erratic creatures," she told a reporter. "Their mode of living makes them so, and as their years increase many of them will say and do things which almost justify others in regarding them as utterly irresponsible. Either this is the explanation of it or else the women are controlled by a band of evil-disposed spirits."

If it was a band of spirits, Maggie soon freed herself of them. Shortly after her confession she retracted it. Perhaps the money was simply better in being a proponent of Spiritualism versus lecturing against it.

# THE FOX SISTERS' HOME
# GETS A NEW HOME

After the Fox family left their haunted cottage, ownership traded hands from one family to another, and the home became more and more rundown along the way. When talk of razing it began in 1915, a resident of Lily Dale Assembly in western New York refused to let it happen. He purchased the home and transported it to his small community, where it could stand as a shrine to Spiritualism. This, of course, was no easy task. The home had to be disassembled, carried across country roads, floated along the Erie Canal, then trucked to Lily Dale, where it was reassembled. If Mr. Splitfoot was still there, he had quite an adventure.

For decades the shrine served as a Mecca for Spiritualists all over the world. Then, on September 21, 1955, the Fox cottage went up in flames, and in minutes the landmark to Spiritualism became a spirit itself. Today, the empty lot is still marked by an original monument noting that the cottage was where the Fox sisters "received the first proof of the continuity of life."

Though the small farmhouse left Hydesville, the town hasn't lost sight of its significance. A memorial was erected in 1927, reading: "Birthplace of Modern Spiritualism. Upon this site stood the Hydesville Cottage, the home of the Fox Sisters through whose mediumship communication with the spirit world was established March 31, 1848. There is no death. There are no dead."

Whatever you believe, there's no question that the movement and the story live on.

## The Rise of Spiritualism

Forty years before Maggie's admission, when the Fox sisters' business kicked off with those first Hydesville rappings from Mr. Splitfoot, an entire spiritual awakening was already brewing in the region. Joseph Smith, for example, had moved to the area as a teenager in 1817, and by 1820 he had visions that led to his publication of the Book of Mormon in 1830. The Shaker movement, which enjoyed its heyday from 1820 to 1860, saw many women taking on spiritual leadership roles. And a preacher named William Miller had his followers, the Millerites, believing Christ was about to make his return and that the world would end on October 22, 1844.

Ron Nagy, a historian at western New York's Spiritualist community, Lily Dale Assembly, suggests that the area might have been especially ripe for new ideas, given the area's geographical location. "New York was said to be the gateway to the West, and the fertile land attracted settlers," he wrote. "The majority of settlers were of the younger generation, an age group of people in their twenties who were all open to new ideas and were undisturbed by orthodox tradition."

Among these young folks was Andrew Jackson Davis. Born in 1826 near Poughkeepsie, New York, as the son of a shoemaker, he was raised with limited education. Despite having, by one account, "not an hour's schooling," he did have a curious mind and read books—particularly controversial religious ones—to sharpen and form his thinking. As a teenager he began developing psychic powers that allowed him to hear voices offering advice. This clairaudience was followed by clairvoyance after his mother passed, giving him a vision of a wondrous land of brightness where she was spending eternity. Davis would eventually call this place Summerland. This home of the dead was, by his estimate, sixty-five billion miles from earth.

"It is a spiritual planet, revolving on its own axis, around its own spiritual sun, and in its own spiritual solar system," Davis explained. He also noted that it was far more beautiful than the most beautiful landscape to grace earth and was filled with cities that boasted marvelous architecture and streets paved with enamel that shines like gold. This version of heaven sounded as good as one could hope.

"Angels come to us, and
we go after death to dwell
with them, in accordance
with the laws of design."
—Andrew Jackson Davis, in his 1885
autobiography, *Beyond the Valley*

But before Davis would ever make his own journey to Summerland, he had more powers to develop. A traveling mesmerist known only as Mr. J. S. Grimes indirectly helped bring them to light during a stop in town. Mesmerism was an early form of modern hypnosis. Its practitioners believed an invisible force existed within all living beings on earth and could be used to bring about physical effects and healing. Grimes pulled the seventeen-year-old Davis from his audience to participate in the performance, but the budding psychic turned out to be a dud on stage. The village tailor, William Levingston, was called up next and had much better luck. Davis must have been disappointed in his lack of respon-

Before the Fox sisters shot to fame, Andrew Jackson Davis, known as the "Poughkeepsie Seer," demonstrated psychic powers in well-attended public performances.

siveness with Grimes, because in the days that followed he paid Levingston a visit so the two could give it another try. Levingston, energized by his newly discovered talents, found success in their experiment. Suddenly Davis exhibited remarkable powers of clairvoyance by describing places he'd never seen—like he had with Summerland—and reading from books with his eyes covered in bandages. Locals were abuzz, and for the next three months Davis and Levingston put on amusing performances in which the boy read from sealed letters and astounded all those who came to witness his strange abilities.

The teen sensation found excitement in these performances, but he wasn't looking for a life of showmanship. Seeking something deeper, Davis disappeared one night to do a little soul searching. To find a greater purpose. The next day he returned, claiming to have spent the night forty miles from home in the Catskill Mountains. There, he reported an encounter with two spirits, one of which upheld the ideals of medicine, and the other, morals. He identified them as Galen and Emanuel Swedenborg. His lack of schooling suggests he wouldn't have ever heard of either, but it's possible he discovered them in books and absorbed much more than anyone suspected.

Davis was empowered by the experience, and his gifts were growing. He became known as the "Poughkeepsie Seer" and captivated attention by going into trances and locating lost objects or diagnosing diseases and suggesting medications. Galen, the ancient Greek physician, had apparently imbued Davis with the ability to look into the human body, as if it were transparent, and spot disease where an organ's brightness was dimmed. Davis provided these services free of charge to those in need, which perhaps enhanced the view that his powers were authentic and altruistic.

Swedenborg's spirit, meanwhile, seemed to have filled Davis's head with religious, philosophical, and scientific thoughts. In a March 1846 lecture the seer spoke of eight planets—six months before Urbain Le Verrier confirmed the existence of Neptune. Davis also suggested a ninth planet was orbiting the sun with the rest of us, though Pluto wasn't found until 1930. Impressive, but don't get too excited. His discussions of planets also included a description of a Saturnian orangutan: "Its mental organization nearly represents that of the human being, with the exception that its knowledge and power of *exterior* understanding, surpass that of man existing on the earth!" The people of Jupiter were also, allegedly, superior to us earthlings.

But it was a prediction in his 1847 book *Principles of Nature* that is key to this story: the rise of Spiritualism. Davis wrote:

It is a truth that spirits commune with one another while one is in the body and the other in the higher spheres—and this, too, when the person in the body is unconscious of the influx, and hence cannot be convinced of the fact; and this truth will ere long present itself in the form of a living demonstration. And the world will hail with delight the ushering-in of that era.

A year later, of course, Mr. Splitfoot knocked, the Fox sisters answered, and modern Spiritualism was let in. And enough talented mediums followed their lead to build the case for Davis's prophecy and to strengthen people's beliefs—whether those rappings were made by joints or not. Let's start with two of the earliest to capitalize off the Foxes' phenomenon: two brothers, Ira and William Davenport. The boys' séances would soon develop into an extraordinary exhibition unlike anything anyone had seen before.

## The Davenport Brothers: Spiritualist Predecessors to Harry Houdini

Ira and William were born in Buffalo, about one hundred miles west of Hydesville, in 1839 and 1841, respectively. The Rochester knockings were well known and offered inspiration to any ambitious and inventive medium wannabes such as the young Davenports. As children they learned the art of rope-tie escapes from their father, a detective who had witnessed others perform such feats—clearly with a keener eye than most. This skill allowed them to develop a séance performance in which the boys could be tied to their chairs before connecting with spirits, then loosen themselves enough to create manifestations in the darkened room and slip back into their ropes after. As the "ghosts" came to life, they typically played guitars, banjos, tambourines, bells, trumpets, and violins left in the center of the room.

After performing for local séance circles in early 1855, the Davenports gained notoriety and within months earned an invitation to follow the Foxes' lead and bring their show to New York City. Their first performance in a hall at 195 Bowery had room for thirty spectators, which was hardly enough to appease Manhattan's anxious crowds that lined up outside and offered obscene amounts of money for a ticket, ranging from ten dollars to a ridiculous two hundred. Those lucky enough to get in were seated against the wall, leaving the open space for the spirits to play their postmortem concert while the boys remained tied up at a table in the center of the room.

As P. T. Barnum wrote in his 1865 book *Humbugs of the World*, "the noise made by 'the spirits' was about equal to the united honking of a large flock of wild geese." Sometimes, he noted, a guest would "get a 'striking demonstration' over his head!"

The boys, whose perfect innocence was assumed, were getting along just fine until a policeman attending one of their shows decided to spoil the fun by lighting a lantern in the middle of the séance. Ira and William were seen running around with the instruments in their hands. That soured the show, and the duped audience left in anger. The Davenports tried to salvage their New York run with private séances, but further flubs didn't help. Neither did their claims that spirits were responsible for any deceptive acts that may have been witnessed.

The boys and their father retreated to their home near Buffalo, where, as Barnum put it, "they continued to hold 'circles,' hoping to retrieve their lost reputation as good mediums—by being, not more honest, but more cautious."

Being more cautious led to the development of the spirit cabinet, allowing for a controlled environment where skeptical audience members couldn't so easily disrupt the experience. This Davenport cabinet was about six feet wide, six feet high, and two and a half feet deep. It was split into three sections with three doors: the left and right segments had a bench for each brother to sit on, facing each other; the middle section held an array of instruments, and its door had a small window at the top with a black curtain. The entire cabinet was elevated from the floor by three sawhorses.

Shows began with volunteers being called onstage to tie the Davenports at the wrists and feet, and to their benches. Then one boy's feet were bound to the other's. As far as anyone could tell, the young men were securely trapped inside. The doors closed and, after a brief period, were opened to reveal that the brothers had been freed of the ropes. The doors were shut once more and after a couple of minutes opened again. This time, Ira and William were fully bound once more. The spirits, it seemed, were quite adept at rope ties and escapes.

But the real show began once the doors closed again. This time, as Henry Ridgely Evans described it in his 1897 book *The Spirit World*

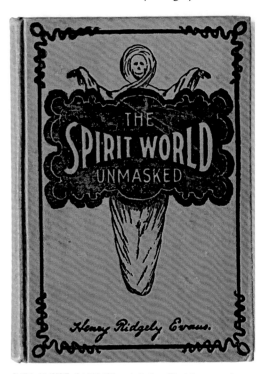

Published in 1897, *The Spirit World Unmasked* by Henry Ridgely Evans exposed methods used by the Davenport brothers and other Spiritualists.

*Unmasked,* "Pandemonium reigned. Bells were rung, horns blown, tambourines thumped, violins played, and guitars vigorously twanged. Heavy rappings also were heard on the ceiling, sides, and floor of the cabinet, then after a brief but absolute silence, a bare hand and arm emerged from the lozenge window, and rung the big dinner bell."

Adding to the spectacle, the Davenports would invite an audience member into the cabinet. After the ruckus inside, the volunteer would emerge with his hat pulled over his eyes and his coat turned inside out. At times, the brothers would even hold a fistful of flour in their hands. After the "spirits" finished their concert, Ira and William would be seen still holding the flour, secure in their ropes.

Audiences were mystified and the press loved it. Adding to Evans's description, the *New York Daily Tribune* reported that "twice a bare arm was thrust forth, almost as mysterious as that which rose out of the lake (in the legend) and took King Arthur's sword. This arm and these hands may have belonged to the Davenport Brothers; but if they did, the Davenport Brothers are the cleverest jugglers of this age, or of any age in

The Davenport brothers' most famous illusion involved binding themselves in a "spirit cabinet" with musical instruments, which would play while the brothers appeared to still be bound.

which juggling has been known."

After the cabinet portion of the show, the Davenports held a dark séance in which they were once again tied up, and the instruments ran amok for another gig. This second act wasn't far from their original New York City performance, but they were now more skilled and even added phosphorescent oil to the instruments, creating a glowing effect as they appeared to float around the stage.

Throughout the shows, Ira and William remained quiet, dressed in all black and sporting matching mustaches and goatees. They simply performed their feats and let people think what they wished. Were they magicians or mediums? Lecturers introducing them often spoke of Spiritualism, but it was up to the audience to decide. Many believed, but the brothers had their share of naysayers who claimed they were frauds. It didn't hurt business, though. Fortunately for them, there was no social media or TV so they were a fresh act from town to town.

By the mid-1860s the Davenports looked to expand their market and brought their talents abroad to Europe. There, the media and audiences began challenging their authenticity. One such example came after playwright Dion Boucicault (who had plenty of experience with theater trickery) hosted the brothers for a group of friends and, after a two-hour performance, detected no deception. The press thought he'd been fooled, but Boucicault defended himself in the *Spiritual Magazine* by stating, "Some persons think that the requirement of darkness seems to infer trickery. Is not a dark chamber essential in the process of photography? And what would we reply to him who should say, 'I believe photography to be humbug; do it all in the light, and I will believe; otherwise, not till then?'"

The Davenports survived the media skepticism, but then they ran into bigger troubles. Some audience members decided to tie knots with a bit more skill than the average volunteer had. Knots tight enough to draw blood frustrated the brothers, who complained and had the ropes cut. End of show. But they took their biggest hit in 1865 when a budding young magician named John Nevil Maskelyne happened to catch a peek through the window at a moment when the drapery fell. Ira could be seen loosened from his ropes and manipulating the instruments.

"There sat Ira with one hand behind him and the other in the act of throwing," Maskelyne later recounted. "In an instant both hands were behind him. He gave a smart wriggle of his shoulders, and when his hands were examined he was found to be thoroughly secured—the ropes, in fact, were cutting into his wrists."

Maskelyne, along with a partner and cabinet builder, George Cooke, soon replicated the apparatus, learned the Davenports' technique, and began doing their own show. Other imitators would soon follow.

The Davenports' mastery of escape was helped by the knowledge that volunteers wouldn't be experts at tying knots, especially if they selected high-profile businessmen or celebrities in attendance—the kind of people who aren't typically skilled in the art of rope tying. If they felt too much pressure, a simple grunt or tensing of the muscles would signal to the volunteer, who'd naturally ease up.

Audience members who joined them in the cabinet were simply shills. And as for the flour in the hand, well, they deposited it in their pockets, then grabbed another handful before revealing themselves at the end.

Still, despite being exposed and imitated, business continued even after William's death in 1877. Ira carried on the act with longtime promoter William Fay into the 1890s.

The Davenports' secrets were revealed to Harry Houdini just before Ira's death in 1911. The magician had paid him a visit out of respect and curiosity. Ira shared his secrets and explained the methods of their rope escapes. Afterward, he smiled and said, "Houdini, we started it, you finish it."

# NOW PLAYING OHIO: KING SPIRIT AND HIS BAND OF GHOSTS

The Davenport brothers may have been innovators in the world of musical ghosts, but around the same time a farmer and his eight children were helping spirits host full concerts in a remote dilapidated log cabin in the middle of Nowheresville, Ohio.

Jonathan Koons's interest in Spiritualism began in 1852 after he attended a séance and was informed that he and his entire brood had the gift

of mediumship. The spirits told the family to build a one-room cabin, sixteen by twelve feet, to be used exclusively for spirit manifestations. To maximize those manifestations, the room was furnished with a table and racks to hold a suite of instruments, including drums, tambourines, violins, and triangles. This was all done as directed, right next to their house.

A New Yorker named Charles Partridge paid Koons a visit and described his bizarre experience in a letter to the *New York Tribune*. It began by intermingling with a crowd of thirty to fifty people who "looked respectable" outside the cabin, each awaiting their turn to go inside the spirit room to talk to their spirit friends and witness manifestations.

The chitchat was, of course, complemented by the concert. One by one, groups squeezed into the small cabin and sat around the table as the doors and windows were shut to block out the light. The festivities began with the beating of drums that could be heard a mile away. After about five minutes, the "King Spirit" graced Koons and company with his presence and the toots of his trumpet, and then invited requests from the audience. "Really this was obliging," Partridge noted, though he didn't mention what, if any, requests were made. Regardless, the spirits soon began to sing. This band of spirits was said to be composed of more than 160 ancient ghosts.

"I think I never heard such perfect harmony; each part was performed with strict attention to its relative degree of sound or force," Partridge wrote. "There was none of that flopping, floundering, and ranting which constitutes the staple of what is latterly called music; harmony rather than noise seem to constitute the spirits' song."

Within the darkened spirit room luminous hands could be seen swiftly moving the instruments in front of people's faces. Partridge was especially impressed with the tambourine player, mentioning that he'd seen the "best performers in the country" but "they cannot perform equal to these spirits." Sometimes, however, instruments accidentally smacked sitters on the head. But hey, even in the afterlife no one's perfect.

Others, too, had reported the wonders of Koons's spirit room and rejoiced in their abilities to shake hands and converse with spirits. One group of visitors wrote to their local paper raving about the marvels they witnessed, including spirit writing, "which is performed about three times as fast as human penmanship is exhibited—crossing the t's and dotting the i's, and punctuating at the same time." The impeccable writing compelled "mankind to seek after truth" about its mortal and immortal existence.

"People think nothing more of having a chat with a ghost than with one of their friends in the body," said another reporter. "Some of the goblins are at times quite jocular," he added, urging readers to visit and experience it for themselves. Being dead never sounded so joyous.

## D. D. Home: The Great Levitator

Music and table rappings were impressive, but while the Fox sisters and the Davenport brothers were doing their thing, Daniel Dunglas (D. D.) Home was taking the art of séances to another level by elongating and shrinking his body, levitating, and performing other astonishing acts.

Home was born in Scotland in 1833 to a family that allegedly had a history of "second sight" abilities. Daniel, for unknown reasons, was adopted by his aunt and uncle, who immigrated to Connecticut when he was nine. One day young Daniel and a friend, Edwin, were playing in the woods and began telling stories. Edwin shared the tale of Lady Beresford (which you can read about in the first section of this book). This idea of being able to return from the dead stuck with him, and the boys decided to make the same pact that Nichola and John had. Not long after this event Home had his first vision. He had stayed at a friend's house late one evening and feared getting in trouble when he got back to his aunt's place. Luckily for

him, she was already asleep. He said his prayer and was about to pull his sheet over him when a sudden darkness interrupted the moonlight. The darkness grew more and more dense until a gleam of light illuminated a spiritual presence. "This light increased," Home later wrote of the event, "and my attention was drawn to the foot of my bed, where stood my friend Edwin."

When he told his family of the vision, he claimed Edwin had died three days earlier. A day or two later a letter arrived announcing the boy's death after an illness, just as Home had said.

These visions continued, including one of his mother's death, as Daniel's powers developed. By 1850 rappings filled the house with strange noises and his aunt with fear. She'd heard about the Fox sisters and blamed their phenomena on the devil. As far as she could tell, her nephew was possessed and she wasn't going to stand for demons in her house. It was time to call in the local priests for help.

"Don't be frightened," one of the pastors told Daniel, "if this is the work of Satan, it is your misfortune and not your fault." The holy men started praying in hopes that God would enter the fray and silence Satan, but instead their words only elicited more rappings. Home said they sounded as if they were "joining in our heartfelt prayers." The priests were disappointed by the continued sounds, but Home took them as a sign from God and claimed the moment was a turning point in his life, resolving to "place myself entirely at God's disposal."

The sounds continued and were soon joined by moving furniture. One instance recorded in a biography of Home recounts a table moving across a room with no one near it. His aunt ran for the family Bible and slammed it on the table. "There! That will drive the devils away!" she cried. But it didn't. The vivacious table only grew more animated.

As far as his aunt was concerned, if Satan wasn't going to leave Daniel, Daniel would have to leave and take the devil with him. Kicked out of the house, Home set off on his own to share his emerging gifts with the world. Curious clients frequently took him in as a guest as he moved from town to town, performing séances and stirring wonder and amazement.

By this time, he had grown into a tall, thin man with long blond hair draped over his broad shoulders. Large, sharp teeth, pale gray eyes, thin bloodless lips, and long, bony hands adorned with rings added to his mystique. "You knew, without touching them, that they were icy cold," one nineteenth-century writer remarked.

D. D. Home was able to levitate to great heights during séances, capturing the attention of Spiritualists and befuddling scientists.

Despite increasing fame and demand, he rarely accepted money for his work, as he was convinced that such a mysterious gift was not something to profit from. Room and board and the occasional diamond (who could resist?) were payment enough.

As Home's legend grew, so apparently did his abilities, enabling him to travel the world and schmooze with European royalty and the wealthiest curiosity seekers. Séances produced a variety of wondrous phenomena—all without the need for total darkness. In addition to chats with the dearly departed, attendees would witness floating tables and sofas that slid across floors in fully lit rooms, and sitters occasionally had flowers, books and other objects delivered to them by mysterious hands. Oh, and accordion music would play. Yes, Home's séances frequently featured the sounds of the accordion allegedly played by spirits. Those attending would bring their own instrument for Home to use. There, in front of all gathered and with no fingers touching it, the accordion, according to one witness, "executed a charming air, which voices were distinctly heard accompanying."

If he wasn't busy moving furniture or producing music without a musician, he was creating physical effects with his own body. In 1868, a journalist witnessed Home contort himself: "We sat in a room well lighted with gas. . . . Mr. Home was seen by all of us to increase in height to the extent of some eight or ten inches, and then sank to some six or eight inches below his normal stature."

He reached even greater heights not by growing, but by lifting himself right off the ground. More than a hundred accounts of such feats have been recorded. One claimed Home floated around a room and moved pictures on a wall, each beyond the reach of anyone standing on the ground. On another occasion a witness said, "I once saw Home in full light standing in the air seventeen inches from the ground."

But Home's masterpiece, his Spiritualist magnum opus if you will, was the levitation most frequently mentioned by those sharing his story. During a séance, Home had been in a trance for some time and then walked uneasily into an adjoining room. In the words of one of the three witnesses who all swore the event was genuine: "We heard the window in the next room lifted up, and almost immediately afterwards we saw Home floating in the air outside our window. The moon was shining full into the room. My back was to the light; and I saw the shadow on the wall of the windowsill, and Home's feet about six inches above it. He remained in this position for a few seconds, then raised the window and glided into the room feet foremost, and sat down."

The windows were seventy feet off the ground and about seven and a half feet apart.

Home's showmanship was undoubtedly extraordinary, but was it truly powered by spirits? Sir William Crookes devised a series of experiments to find out. Crookes was a British chemist and physicist and, as evidenced by his title, a well-respected one. The study would pit the power of scientific apparatuses against the power of psychic abilities. Happy to play along, Home submitted himself to any and all of Crookes's elaborate contraptions and still managed to mystify him. The medium had passed the tests to Crookes's satisfaction; however, he determined it wasn't due to contact with spirits, but rather to a new type of force "in some unknown manner connected with the human organization." He called it the "psychic force."

Others were less impressed. Home's accordion feat, for example, was typically done under a table—a place where spirits seemed to find comfort, and perhaps mediums tended to find secrecy.

In 1922, a student of magic, Rev. Carlos María de Heredia, explained a simple way of replicating Home's "spirit" music:

"I offer the same demonstration in my lectures. After a few minutes of expectation I give a signal to a friend behind the partition who plays a tune on another accordion. As he is invisible and as the source of the sound is not discoverable, especially when attention is riveted on the visible instrument, the effect is as convincing as the humbug is simple."

Granted, Heredia wasn't there in person, but in 1865 investigators from *Fraser's Monthly* were. Their report cast doubt on Home's legitimacy, noting "the manifestations at these exhibitions were invariably of the same character, and became strong or weak in exact proportion to the abundance or lack of faith in the company. The greater wonders were never attempted, at all events they never succeeded, with an unbeliever in the room."

The magazine went on to compare him to Joseph Smith, the founder of Mormonism, who asked his followers if they believed he could walk across water. When they responded "yes," he said that was as good as him actually doing it. His supporters gladly agreed.

"Mr. Home beats Joe Smith hollow," *Fraser's* remarked, "for he persuades people that they hear what they do not hear, that they see what they do not see, that an accordion, which makes an irregular noise, is playing a popular tune, and that he is floating near the ceiling when he is simply standing on his chair with one foot touching a disciple's shoulder."

During a séance, the *Fraser's* investigators said they were most struck by the "mental condition" of the other five people seated with them. They were there, ready to believe, yet Home "did nothing but what might obviously and easily be done by hand and foot, for the whole of the so-called manifestations took place under a table of limited dimensions, with a green cloth lapped over the edge, which we were warned on no account to lift. After two hours spent in shaking and slightly raising the table, ringing the bell, sounding the accordion, twitching ladies' petticoats, pinching their knees, &c., &c., there was a pause of twenty minutes to rest Mr. Home or the spirits."

An attempt to levitate failed since the "spiritual ladder was broken." *Fraser's*, however, shared an account from 1860 in which Home was seated against a window before rising off the ground. "Through the semi-darkness his head was dimly visible against the curtains, and his hands might be seen in a faint white heap before him. Presently he said, in a quiet voice, 'My chair is moving; I am off the ground: don't notice me; talk of something else,' or words to that effect."

Not noticing Home certainly helped create the illusion. This strange retelling continued:

---

In a moment or two more he spoke again. This time his voice was in the air, above our heads. He had risen from his chair to a height of four or five feet from the ground. As he ascended higher he described his position, which at first was perpendicular, and afterwards became horizontal. He said he felt as if he had been turned in the gentlest manner, as a child is turned in the arms of a nurse. In a moment or two more, he told us he was going to pass across the window, against the gray silvery light of which he would be visible. We watched in profound stillness, and saw his figure pass from one side of the window to the other, feet foremost, lying horizontally in the air. He spoke to us as he passed, and told us he would turn the reverse way and recross the window, which he did. . . . He hovered round the circle for several minutes, and passed this time perpendicularly over our heads. I heard his voice behind me in the air, and felt something lightly brush my chair. It was his foot, which he gave me leave to touch. Turning to the spot where it was, on the top of the chair, I placed my hand gently upon it, when he uttered a cry of pain, and the foot was withdrawn quickly, with a palpable shudder. It was evidently not resting on the chair, but floating; and it sprang from the touch as a bird would. He now passed over to the farthest extremity of the room, and we could judge by his voice of the attitude and distance he had attained. He had reached the ceiling, upon which he made a slight move, and soon afterwards descended, and resumed his place at the table.

---

This witness, it appeared, had not actually witnessed anything. The entire illusion worked through the power of suggestion, aided by effects to enhance the experience. But a few doubters hardly slowed Home or other mediums. Business was in fact booming through the Civil War and the years immediately following. The frighteningly high number of wartime casualties left many clinging to hope that they could still communicate with their lost loved ones. With opportunity knocking, more and more mediums happily obliged grieving families.

## Mary Todd Lincoln Reaches across the Veil

By the mid-nineteenth century, séances were being held in houses all across the country—even the White House. Mary Todd Lincoln worked with mediums to reach her son Willie, who died of typhoid fever in 1862 when he was just eleven. She believed her bond with him was so strong that his presence could be felt without the aid of a medium.

"Willie lives," she told her half sister. "He comes to me every night and stands at the foot of the bed with the same sweet, adorable smile he always had. He does not always come alone. Little Eddie is sometimes with him."

One of Mrs. Lincoln's mediums, Mrs. Nettie Colburn Maynard, claimed President Abraham Lincoln joined one of the séances, during which a spirit warned him not to delay his Emancipation Proclamation. She claimed the event left a powerful impression and noted that the proclamation was issued shortly after. Maybe she was right and took a pivotal role in the abolition of slavery, although it's more likely that the president was supporting his wife's interest and may have simply been awed by the theatrics Maynard conjured up. Regardless, if ghosts had any influence whatsoever on the proclamation's timing, it's nice to know they were being put to good use.

Another medium known to have regularly graced the Lincoln White House was Charles Colchester. Bell ringing, table rapping, reading sealed letters, and producing messages in blood-red writing on his forearm were among his specialties. But of all the messages he may have delivered to the Lincolns, the one of most interest likely came from a human source rather than a dead one. It just so happened that Colchester had also been spending time in Washington, DC, with John Wilkes Booth. The actor and would-be assassin took up Spiritualism in 1863 after the passing of his sister-in-law. He and his widowed brother began attending séances, hoping to find comfort from communication with her. Booth didn't stop at grieving, though; he continued attending séances, including those performed by the Davenport brothers. And Colchester.

John Wilkes Booth's biographer, Terry Alford, contends that the two were more than just medium and client. They spent a lot of time getting drunk together and talking about who knows what. Could Colchester have been privy to Booth's planning?

"In the weeks before the assassination, Booth roomed at the National Hotel on Pennsylvania Avenue, just six blocks from the Capitol and even closer to Ford's Theatre," Alford wrote. "Colchester visited him there often. Besides his ability to contact the dead, Colchester could also tell the future—a useful ability to Booth, who was beginning to think the unthinkable."

The president acknowledged Colchester's warnings, but others had cautioned him of danger as well. There were no definite threats, but given the national climate he knew his well-being was at risk. If Colchester was aware of Booth's plot, did he treat the information as coming from the spirits, or did he offer the president specific details? And if the latter, was his information disregarded because the president didn't share his wife's faith in his honesty?

After the assassination, Mrs. Lincoln continued practicing Spiritualism in hopes of finding her husband, just as she'd seen her children. In 1872, she even had her picture taken with his spirit standing behind her, resting his hands lovingly on her shoulders. Neither Eddie nor Willie made an appearance, though it's believed her youngest son, Thomas, who passed away in 1871 at age eighteen, can be seen behind her as well.

The First Lady wasn't the only one who wanted to hear from the assassinated president. Mediums knew a president beloved by so many would be a good draw at séances. Lincoln's spirit could talk about the wonders of Summerland or offer political advice in times of turmoil and have an audience ready to trust his message.

Those who wanted to know what happened after Lincoln's fateful night at Ford's Theater found out through a process called psychography, or automatic writing. Mediums achieved this by supposedly falling into a trance with a pen in hand and paper before them, allowing a spirit to take control and write a message. Lincoln's description of passing into the spirit world came through the mediumship of Mrs. S. G. Horn and included the following passage:

---

On that fatal night which ended with my life's tragedy, when I fell mortally wounded in the theatre, and after a few moments of anguish—a brief time of mental despair followed by unconsciousness—I awakened to find myself a spirit among spirits, and to realise that I was being actually crowned with a wreath of laurels by the hand of Washington, and that I was surrounded by an innumerable company of spirits "which no man could number,"—when I heard the grand vibrations of heavenly music surging through the air, filling my soul with an ecstatic bliss beyond mortal comprehension; then a weight was removed from my heart, and I experienced a happiness that I had not felt for ten long years!

---

Lincoln and other former presidents remained popular figures to channel well into the next century. In 1917, for example, Lincoln's ghost delivered a message that was part politician, part cheerleader for America as the Great War waged: "The struggle looks like an extended one as to time, but victory comes at the price of vigilance. We can win."

"If we grant a continued existence after death, a survival of memory and affection, and that there is a possibility of intercommunion between the two worlds, it seems but natural that such men as Lincoln, Washington, and Jefferson should seek to impress and guide those who are directing our public affairs or molding public opinion. Unless these patriotic men have lost their interest in our republic's welfare or their power to manifest it, we cannot conceive of their being mere idle spectators when this nation is passing through political or moral crisis."

—Dr. B. F. Austin in an address at
Plymouth Spiritual Church in
Rochester, New York, on October 22, 1906

# NECESSITY IS THE MOTHER OF SPIRITUALIST INVENTION: THE CREATION OF THE OUIJA BOARD

Receiving messages from the dead by calling out the alphabet and waiting for table raps to stop at certain letters proved tedious and laborious. By 1853, inventive mediums were hastening the process by attaching a pencil to a small basket and resting their fingers on its edge. As Allan Kardec, a French Spiritualist, described it, the basket would be placed on a piece of paper and "set in motion by the same occult power that moved the tables," in order to "trace letters that formed words, sentences, and entire discourses, filling many pages, treating of the deepest questions of philosophy, morality, metaphysics, psychology, &c., and as rapidly as though written by the hand."

The world had its first planchette. The basket soon evolved into a teardrop-shaped board with two small wheels at the back and a pencil at the tip. Though it was an improvement, the spirits proved to have poor penmanship since the boards blocked the messages as they were being written.

"The words are usually created in a difficult cursive in an unbroken line, often under the influence of two practitioners at the boards whose subconscious minds might have different ideas of what the writing should produce," says Brandon Hodge, occult historian and founder of the website MysteriousPlanchette.com.

Some mediums substituted their hand for the planchette and let the spirits guide the pencil as they held it. This allowed for neater handwriting, but as Hodge notes, "in doing so robbed participants of the cooperative and collaborative nature of the planchette that made their writing so mysterious to begin with."

When the Ouija board arrived in stores in 1890, it supported collaboration with clear results and swift responses to yes/no questions. Plus, after forty years of planchettes, it had the advantage of being the shiny new object. As Hodge describes it, "Talking boards certainly represented a 'next step' or the latest and greatest do-it-yourself spirit communicator in the public eye."

As for the curious name of Ouija, the Kennard Novelty Company, which made the parlor game, claimed it came from an ancient Egyptian word for "good luck." Today's manufacturer, Hasbro, might agree that's what every Ouija user needs to make it work.

## Dead Celebrities Sell

The idea of channeling spirits like Lincoln's was part of an entire brand of mediumship: celebrity ghosts. Working with cultural icons allowed mediums to go beyond personal messages from lost loved ones and provide dispatches from the Other Side that everyone would want to hear. This either generated greater profits or created new ways to preach religious beliefs—or sometimes both. Either way, psychics knew celebrity sells.

Anyone who was anyone before death had a lot to say. Among the chattier spirits was Edgar Allan Poe, who died on October 7, 1849—just a year and a half after the Fox sisters opened the floodgates. In one message, Poe condemned his darkness on earth and reveled in the light of the afterlife. "I now am a spirit given, through God's kind grace, to good works," he wrote through a medium's hand. His added notes indicated a little irritation about the way he lived: "No kind spirit offered to *write* through *my* hand. But, I think, many a dark spirit had my brain in his power—yea, the power of the demons of HELL."

Poe's prolific nature remained unchanged. Mediums cranked out stacks of new poems from the discarnate master of the macabre, including a revised version of *The Raven*. One in particular, named Lizzie Doten, published an entire collection of poetry she claimed to have channeled through Poe's spirit in 1863.

Other famous dead writers couldn't put their pens (or quills) down either. Mark Twain wrote two short stories and a novel, one letter at a time, on a Ouija board through a St. Louis medium and novelist named Emily Grant Hutchings and her medium cowriter Lola V. Hays. These posthumous new works were penned between 1915 and 1917 and titled *Up the Furrow to Fortune*, *A Daughter of Mars*, and *Jap Herron*.

"That the story of Jap Herron and the two short stories which preceded it are the actual post-mortem work of Samuel L. Clemens, known to the world as Mark Twain, we do not for one moment doubt," Hutchings wrote in her introduction to the novel. "His individuality has been revealed to us in ways which could leave no question in our minds."

Twain's ghost allegedly emphasized that his individuality not be messed with, except

# TWAIN BOOK CAME OVER OUIJA BOARD, WOMAN DECLARES

Mrs. Emily Hutchings to Print 50,000 Words She Says She and Mrs. Hays Received.

Emily Hutchings claimed the ghost of Mark Twain was writing novels through her between 1915 and 1917. Unfortunately, they didn't receive the accolades of Twain's credited works.

in trivial instances. "There will be minor errors that you will be able to take care of. I don't object," he told the two mediums. "Only—don't try to correct my grammar. I know what I want to say. And, dear ladies, when I say d-a-m-n, please don't write d-a-r-n. Don't try to smooth it out. This is not a smooth story."

In life, Twain frequented séances for their entertainment value. If his ghost really was out there making two women painstakingly write stories one letter at a time through a planchette, he was surely enjoying the same brand of amusement from the beyond.

One entity that was not amused was Twain's publisher, Harper and Bros. The company held the rights to all of the writer's works and contended that it maintained those rights despite Twain's passing seven years earlier. Hutchings had given Harper first crack at acquiring the *Jap Herron* manuscript, but they rejected it for two reasons: first, they didn't believe it was dictated by Twain's ghost through a Ouija board, and second, they felt it "lacked literary merit." The case went to the US Supreme Court and though Hutchings never retracted her claims, Harper dropped the lawsuit after the psychic agreed to destroy whatever copies had been produced. Fortunately, at least one copy of the novel remained. It's since been digitized and granted *Jap Herron* immortality.

# MARK TWAIN'S GHOST WRITES A STINKER
## (AND SO DO OTHER OUIJA BOARD WRITERS)

Tom Sawyer and Huckleberry Finn are classic characters ingrained in American literature and culture. Jap Herron, not so much.

Twain's ghost told the story of a young boy in a small Missouri town who begins life in poverty but gets work at the local newspaper, grows into a productive man, and helps reinvigorate the village. Emily Grant Hutchings said Jap's character was "reminiscent of young Sam Clemens." Critics didn't find *Jap Herron* reminiscent of Clemens or Twain at any age, as indicated in the book's less-than-stellar reviews:

> "If this is the best that 'Mark Twain' can do by reaching across the barrier, the army of admirers that his works have won for him will all hope that he will hereafter respect that boundary."—*New York Times*, September 9, 1917

> "The Ouija board has had a demoralizing effect upon the alleged author's style and humor."—*Detroit Free Press*, August 26, 1917

> "It is a feeble piece of work, and, if one were to accept the assertion of its authorship, it would be with profound regret that the conditions of the spirit life had effected so great deterioration in a style once so charming."—*Living Age*, October 20, 1917

> "If anything disturbs his spirit, it would be the linking of his name to 'Jap Herron.'"—Agnes Repplier, essayist, October 1917

Hutchings and Hays were backed by Twain's celebrity, but another St. Louis medium and friend of Hutchings, Pearl Curran, had been successfully writing poems, prose, plays, and novels through the ghost of a complete unknown. Her name was Patience Worth, and she was believed to have lived a few hundred years earlier during the colonial period. Like Twain's work, Worth's was dictated through a Ouija board. Each revealed letter formed words in a distinct archaic English dialect. Psychic investigator James Hyslop believed it was influenced by local speech in the nearby Ozarks, where Curran had spent time in her youth, and the works of one of her husband's favorite writers, Geoffrey Chaucer.

One of Worth's books, a telling of the story of Jesus Christ called *The Sorry Tale*, weighed in at over six hundred pages. Published just before *Jap*

*Herron*, it fared slightly better and earned mixed reviews. A local and perhaps sympathetic writer for the *St. Louis Globe-Democrat* wasn't concerned with the source of the tale, because "simply as a story it is truly remarkable" and it painted a "moving picture, a vivid panorama of the time."

Agnes Repplier, whose review above showed she wasn't a fan of Twain's ghost, wasn't a fan of Worth or any other ghost writer either. "We are told that once, when Patience Worth was spelling out the endless pages of *The Sorry Tale*, she came to a sudden stop, then wrote, 'This be nuff,' and knocked off for the night. A blessed phrase, and, of a certainty, her finest inspiration. Would that all dead authors would adopt it as their motto; and with Ouija-boards, and table-legs, and automatic pencils, write as their farewell message to the world those three short, comely words, 'This be nuff.'"

Twain's ghost listened. Worth, however, directed a few million more words until a month before Curran's death in 1937.

## Shakespeare: Not Even Death Could Stop Him

Prolific as Twain's ghost was, he was outdone by the spirit of history's most prolific writer: the Bard himself, William Shakespeare. Of note was 1916's *Hamlet in Heaven*, written through the mediumship of Charles Lincoln Phifer. The psychic said he'd been receiving messages "purportedly" from the Bard for twenty years, but this Hamlet sequel was channeled just in time for the tricentennial milestone of Shakespeare's passing. Phifer claimed the timing of the event "did not enter my head" and the play's theme of death "seemed to be Shakespeare's contribution to the forthcoming world celebration of the event."

The five-act play reunited Hamlet with his father, who had appeared as a ghost in the original *Hamlet*. But before Hamlet can find his dad, he has to find out that he, too, is dead. Thus, the play begins with that revelation through a conversation with a physician spirit guide:

> PHYS. But art thou brave enough to learn the truth,
> That thou art dead?
>
> HAM. —Dead? I am not dead.
>
> PHYS. Yet thy disgusted soul hath exit made
> From gates of flesh.
>
> HAM. —Give me my sword.
> If I can swing it as I one time did,
> I am not dead; if I can push its point

Into thy thigh, I live; if I can sheathe—.
But give me not the venomed instrument.

PHYS.     It is not needful that thou take a sword.
Strike at me—so.
                    [*He squares his breast. Hamlet*
                    *strikes at him, and his arm*
                    *goes through physician's body.*

HAM.                         —Merciful Heavens!
Am I indeed among the shades of souls?
I flout the thought. Did I not see my father,
A spirit, when my belly bulged with woodcock?
Because I sense another, then, proves nothing.

PHYS.     Hamlet is dead indeed.

Indisputable proof comes when Hamlet discovers his body in the cemetery. "'Tis a lump of flesh to which the worms hold title," the physician tells him. And on it goes, but we'll leave the rest for the Afterlife CliffsNotes.

Shakespeare's ghost also gave interviews and penned sonnets, including a collection of twelve delivered through Gregory Thornton and published in 1920 as *Sonnets of Shakespeare's Ghost*. This followed a much larger volume of poems, notes, and essays from the year prior, *Shakespeare's Revelations by Shakespeare's Spirit*, which was dictated through a medium named Sarah Shatford.

According to the foreword to *Revelations*, also written by Shakespeare's ghost, Shatford was the only medium he worked through, meaning he either disavowed his earlier posthumous work or those other mediums were channeling an impostor. Then again, something was wrong in the spirit state of Denmark because Shakespeare's ghost seemed awfully cranky in his introductory notes: "To pettifoggers who declaim and spume at length a mess of balderdash to befuddle the seeker of truth, proclaiming no advance where worlds divide, I say, who spell through her these lines, Avaunt dissembler: you who know the truth and lie to shield your muggy braincells under a cloak of Science, you fool not any but yourself."

Or maybe Shatford was just being defensive.

## The Art of Spirit Slate Writing

Automatic writing became big business for mediums, even without the aid of dead superstars. With Dr. Henry Slade leading the charge, slates became the latest and greatest canvas for spirits in the mid-nineteenth century. Mediums placed them under tables with a piece of chalk or pencil, and ghosts scribbled messages from the beyond onto the board. The effect, with its personalized handwritten notes, appeared miraculous.

Slade, like many before him, started young. If an 1876 biography from a Spiritualist newspaper called the *Medium and Daybreak* is to be believed, rappings were heard "in the vicinity of the child from his cradle." However, this would've been in 1835, before the Fox sisters, and thus before modern Spiritualism was a thing to pay attention to. That meant Slade's crib rappings went ignored. As he entered adolescence, a series of visions ensured that his developing medium powers wouldn't go unnoticed any longer. At breakfast one morning, for example, he told the family that an older sibling who'd been absent for several years would be making a grand return and was already in the village. That morning, young Henry's brother, James, showed up as predicted.

Slade's history echoed that of Andrew Jackson Davis after he crossed paths with a traveling mesmerist passing through his hometown of Johnson Creek, New York. The entertainer detected Slade's mediumship and encouraged his pursuit of it. That day, seated around a table with his family, all the classic physical phenomena began. The table tipped, lifted into the air, and had strange forces rapping on it. Now, as if drawing straight from D. D. Home's youth, the story alleged that Slade's mother concluded such manifestations could only be the work of Satan. That put an end to the home séances. But eventually Slade moved out and took his evolving show on the road.

Tall, muscular, with dark curly hair and dark eyes, Slade had an appearance that commanded the room as well as the alleged spirits. His invisible performers, it seemed, were as enthralled as his paying customers, for they wasted no time in manifesting and ensured people got in and out of séances in twenty to thirty minutes. Efficiency was good for business—but so was innovation.

The introduction of slate writing made a good show far better. The *Medium and Daybreak* reported it all started during a séance in New Albany, Indiana, at the home of a fellow named Mr. Gardiner Knapp:

"Dr. Slade's attention was attracted by a noise of scratching on, in, or under the table, as if writing were being done with some instrument. He was impressed to give the spirits an opportunity that he might discover whether they intended to write. Accordingly, he placed a piece of chalk on a slate and held it under the table, thinking that the chalk would make a mark with the slightest effort."

The experiment worked. The first letter scratched onto the slate was a *W*. A few scribbles later it had spelled out *William Maynard*. Slade's audience recognized the name as a friend who had passed into spirit life. From here, the wonders increased and the performances grew in complexity. A Mrs. Louisa Andrews described a Slade séance that produced a message inside a folding slate that she had provided. Beforehand, she wrote a few lines to a deceased friend, put a fragment of pencil in between the slates, and screwed it together. At the séance table she claimed to have almost immediately heard the scratching of the pencil. When she later unfastened the slate, a reply to her message appeared inside, signed by her friend.

"Whether written by this spirit or not I cannot say, and any opinion I might form on that point would be worthless except to myself," she wrote in her description of the event. "What I *know* is that some power caused writing to be done on the inner side of a folding slate, which did not leave my possession, and which remained firmly screwed together till I myself unfastened it."

Henry Slade's gift for spirit slate writing was covered in a biographical feature by the *Medium and Daybreak* in 1876. His act would later be debunked on multiple occasions.

Perhaps, without even realizing it or remembering it, that slate did leave her possession—even if just for a few moments at the table. Slick and skilled as he was, Slade's slate writing was eventually exposed. Several times.

The first came in 1872 after Spiritualism investigator John W. Truesdell sat with Slade in New York City for a second time. His initial visit ended in disappointment. Truesdell told Slade that the physical phenomena during the séance were "bunglingly executed" and that the written messages on the slate came from unknown spirits and were "vague and meaningless."

The criticism took Slade by surprise. He defended the theatrics of the séance but admitted the slate writing was less than impressive. However, it may have been Truesdell's fault, not his own. Recalling the experience, Truesdell said he was told that "I was too much alarmed to allow the safe appearance of my immediate spirit-friends, and that strangers had, therefore, been substituted to prepare the way."

Months later Truesdell gave Slade another shot. This time he decided not to divulge his name to the assistant in the medium's lobby. He explained that he would be much more impressed if the spirits could determine his name on their own. He also laid a trap. Before entering, Truesdell removed his name from the lining of his hat and left an unsealed letter in his coat pocket where the snooping assistant could find the name Samuel Johnson of Rome, New York.

While waiting for Slade to appear in the séance room, Truesdell did some snooping of his own and noticed a slate tucked beneath a sideboard. A message was already written on it. Slade would just swap out a blank slate during the séance for this one. The generic note read:

---

We are happy to meet you in this atmosphere of Spirit research. You are now surrounded by many anxious friends in the Spirit life, who desire to communicate with you, but who cannot until they learn more of the laws which govern their actions. If you will come here often, your spirit friends will soon be able to identify themselves and to communicate with you as on earth life.—Allie.

---

To believers the message would appear miraculous, while also serving as an ad to spend more money at Slade's spirit room. Truesdell took advantage of his find and added his own message to it: "Henry, look out for this fellow. He is up to snuff.—Alcinda." He knew Alcinda was the name of Slade's recently deceased wife. Truesdell replaced the slate and took his seat just in time for Slade's grand entrance and the start of the show. Luckily, the medium didn't recognize his repeat customer, so Truesdell's name remained unknown. As empty chairs began to move, Truesdell detected Slade's long legs in action. After the physical phenomena act concluded a slate was brought out—an exact replica of the one he'd found. The name Mary Johnson soon appeared, and Slade told Truesdell it was his sister. So Truesdell informed him that she was not. Slade attempted to receive another message on the slate, but this time he dropped it, a convenient move that allowed him to make the exchange with the slate beneath the sideboard.

Slade was stunned when he saw the new message that had been added.

"Had a thunderbolt from heaven fallen at his feet, he could not have been more astounded," Truesdell wrote. "For several minutes he continued to gaze

"When you see them they're oddly photographic and so beautiful. But for Spiritualists, all of their art is two-fold, so it's not just enough to be art; it has to be evidence as well."

—Shannon Taggart, who spent nineteen years visiting and photographing Lily Dale Assembly for *Séance*, in 2020 upon the slate in blank amazement—then, suddenly turning upon me, his countenance livid with rage and excitement, he exclaimed, 'What does this mean? Who has been meddling with the slate?' 'Spirits,' I coolly replied."

As they discussed the matter afterward, Slade attempted to explain how Spiritualism works and proclaimed Truesdell to be a medium. Despite all the evidence staring him in the face, Truesdell accepted the idea that wicked spirits were responsible for the mishaps he'd experienced and went home to experiment with his own private circles. Mean-spirited spirits made excellent scapegoats, and they proved that Slade's sleight-of-tongue may have been even better than his sleight-of-hand.

Following the Truesdell snafu Slade continued astonishing sitters with spirit messages on slates in America and Europe. In 1876, he ran into trouble again when two London professors caught him swapping out a slate for one with marked with a prewritten message. Once the local papers caught wind of the story, Slade was tried and sentenced to three months of hard labor. Luckily for him, an appeal was sustained due to a technical flaw in the indictment. Still, he was done in England. Paris heard the news and didn't want any part of him. So Slade moved on to Germany, Russia, and Australia.

While in Leipzig toward the end of 1877, Slade found himself performing a new kind of show for a rather different audience. Professor Johann Karl Friedrich Zöllner, an astrophysicist who dabbled in Spiritualism, wanted to prove the existence of a fourth dimension. This, he believed, would explain the marvels performed by mediums. Slade wowed the professor with his usual bag of tricks, including, of course, slate writing. Zöllner's astonishment led him to write a book, *Transcendental Physics*, in 1878. Henry Ridgely Evans would later call the professor Slade's most famous victim, saying that he "lacked entirely the necessary critical faculty, and became an easy prey of fraud."

Slade may not have summoned real ghosts to produce slate writing, but his popularity proved he was quite adept at his act. It just required a skill of a different sort. One of the ways in which Slade created the messaging was to slip a thimble on his finger with a tiny piece of lead attached. With the slate held under the table, he'd scratch the message from beneath the table without having his eyes on it. No easy feat. The less-than-perfect penmanship gave the messages a ghostlike feel. On the other hand, slates that had been prewritten featured more elegant script.

## Art Lives Forever—and So Do Some Artists

As Spiritualism blossomed toward the end of the nineteenth century and mediums around the world preached the good word of the dead, western New York continued to be a hotbed of activity. William Alden, a Spiritualist in the community of Laona, owned farmland along Cassadaga Lake and welcomed other believers at his property for an annual camp that featured speakers like Andrew Jackson Davis. By 1879, a year after Alden's passing, a committee of Spiritualists purchased his land, along with the property just north of it, and started building. Situated right next to the lily-covered lake, the twenty-plus acres of land became known as Lily Dale. Today, Spiritualism remains the only religion in the small community. As historian Ron Nagy puts it, "Lily Dale is to Spiritualism as Rome is to Catholicism."

Of the many mediums who spent time there, four of the most unique and most creative were the Bangs sisters and the Campbell brothers. Around the turn of the century, the two pairs, who worked independently of each other, both offered spirit messages through slate writing and even spirit typewriters. Both were also the only mediums known to produce precipitated paintings, portraits that would appear on a canvas during a séance without the aid of a human hand. In just minutes, spirits created paintings that would take living artists hours. Examples of their artwork can still be seen today in Lily Dale at the Maplewood Hotel. They're strik-

A precipitated spirit painting of Leolyn Pettingill by the Bangs sisters at the Maplewood Hotel in Lily Dale Assembly.

ing, particularly in the lack of visible brushstrokes. Whatever medium the alleged spirit artists used isn't known for certain, but the paintings on display in Lily Dale have a pastel-like quality. At the time of their creation pastels were fashionable in America, popularized in particular by French impressionists like Edgar Degas and Édouard Manet.

If you paid Lizzie and May Bangs for a painting, you would join the sisters in a room with a blank canvas placed in front of a window on an easel. A black cloth framing the canvas would block out light, and in front you'd find a small table with a pot of paint atop it. Various colors would fill the container, offering a suitable palette for whatever the spirits might need. You'd sit at the table facing the canvas with Lizzie and May next to you on opposite sides, each holding one of your hands. With their free hands grasping the frame, the sisters would call out to the spirits and request your desired painting. Then, with everything in place, an artist from the after-life would get to work. Details would soon start to appear on the canvas, like a darkroom photograph being developed in a tray of chemicals. If a change was requested, a portion of the painting might fade away, then reemerge as if the spirit had made the adjustment.

"We were so carried away with the marvel of the performance, that reason gave place to sentiment," wrote one witness.

According to another account, by the time it was done the pot of paint looked untouched, as if only the color had left. Like a soul leaving its flesh behind.

Looking at the Bangs sisters' painting of Leolyn Pettingill at the Maplewood Hotel, it almost feels as if that soul escaped into the painting. The softness of the blended colors and her upward gaze combine to create a sense of ghostly disembodiment.

The Campbell brothers, like the Bangs sisters, produced their paintings with the type of speed no human artist could replicate. They typically used watercolors and oils and, more important, a cabinet in which the spirits could paint in privacy. Or was the privacy for someone whose job was to substitute blank canvases for paintings?

Allen Campbell and Charles Shourds (they weren't actually brothers; they were instead rumored to be a gay couple) worked with the spirits to produce portraits of some of history's most famous men, like Abraham Lincoln and Napoleon.

A precipitated spirit painting of Azur the Helper, the spirit guide of the Campbell brothers, at the Maplewood Hotel in Lily Dale Assembly. Six witnesses signed an affidavit swearing that the image of Azur appeared on the canvas while one of the brothers was in a trance.

During their time in Lily Dale and throughout their world travels, they were also known to deliver portraits of sitters' spirit guides who, unlike a friend or relative, would be unrecognizable.

Lizzie and May didn't shy away from known subjects. Clients raved about receiving paintings of family members the spirit artists had never seen before. This was long before everyone had a camera in their hand, so photographs were rare and oftentimes the subjects of the paintings had never been photo-graphed. This made the likeness all the more strange and remarkable.

Harriet Duhl, from Elmira, New York, shared such a story in a 1905 issue of the *Sunflower*, a Spiritualist publication. The Bangs sisters had just invoked spirits to paint her son and daughter. "I never had a photograph taken of either, so no one could say they were copied," Duhl wrote. "My son's portrait was finished in just seven minutes by my watch, and my daughter's in eighteen, no earthly hand touching the canvas. I sat in front of the table on which the canvas rested, and my eyes were on guard every moment."

Lizzie and May's clientele also included judges, senators, and even Dr. Isaac C. Funk. That's Funk as in Funk & Wagnalls. If you were born anytime before 1980, one of his encyclopedias was—and maybe still is—on your bookshelf. Funk reportedly paid $1,500 for at least one of their paintings. Look up *inflation* in one of his books and you'll see that's equivalent to more than $40,000 today.

How were the Bangs sisters doing this? Were their medium abilities real? Nagy says art experts have examined the paintings "and cannot explain the medium used; it is not paint, ink, pastel, nor any known substance."

In his book, he offers a Spiritualistic explanation: "The pot of multicolored paint that contains all the colors of the spectrum reacts to the combined magnetism of the mediums, along with everything else in the room or space that is being used for the precipitation séance. The walls, rugs, curtains, and even flowers (which were often used) react to the magnetism and transforms into the fine dust-like substance that creates the painting."

Others have claimed Lizzie and May had hidden help, employing slits in the floor through which one would pass a substitution. However, after a charge of fraud in 1905, a Chicago detective visited their home and found no signs of trickery.

"There is nothing here," the detective told a reporter joining him on the inspection. "I used to be a carpenter before I went on the force and I know when a floor or ceiling has been disturbed. There not only is nothing here now, but neither floors, walls nor ceilings of these rooms have been disturbed or replaced for years."

The irritated sisters touted their many happy customers and emphasized in particular how pleased Dr. Funk had been with their work, even sharing his complimentary letters. May also expressed her frustration with claims that images were hidden beneath the paint to help create the effect.

"If a print was there, there would be some trace of it," she reasoned, offering the detective a sample portrait. "Now you erase this one and see if there is a print underneath it."

The detective and journalist took erasers to the image of a young girl's face and found nothing but white canvas beneath.

"Neither my sister nor I is an artist," Lizzie announced defiantly to the press. "We have never taken a lesson in our lives. We are ignorant of art's first principles." All they knew was that the spirits who worked through them "were masters of the brush in life and have forgotten nothing in death."

These dead masters and the Bangs sisters impressed many people, but magician and paranormal investigator David P. Abbott wasn't one of them. In his 1909 book *Behind the Scenes with the Mediums*, he theorized that mediums like the Bangs sisters could be using a variety of chemicals that remain invisible until activated. Sulphate of iron for blue, nitrate of bismuth for yellow, and on and on, enough to impress the most creative chemists. The colors would develop after being sprayed with a solution from a hidden mechanism. The level of detail the mediums would've achieved through invisible ink would've been truly extraordinary—almost as magical as channeling spirits. But Abbott later changed his mind after receiving more information on what the spirit painting experience with the Bangs sisters was like.

In a letter to Abbott, a witness described the selection of two blank canvases prior to beginning the séance. When Abbott learned of that important detail, he decided there must be a simpler means by which the mediums were creating the effect. He began to experiment and finally cracked it. The two canvases were facing each other, with the light from the window shining in from behind. Since Abbott did not for a second believe that spirits were painting the portraits, he realized the second blank canvas must be the key to the illusion.

"It surely was merely to have the front one conceal from the sitter what happened to the one behind it," he wrote in 1913. "When both were in position in the window, and the side and upper curtains drawn and pinned to the front frame, anything could happen to the rear canvas and the sitter would know nothing of it."

Abbott believed the canvases were thin and had a degree of transparency. The rear canvas, in a move any good magician could achieve, would quickly be substituted with a finished painting. As the mediums held the frame with their free hands, they could control movements of the rear, painted canvas, slowly shifting it closer to the front canvas. With the light shining from behind, and the painting gradually getting closer or moving backward, the front canvas would show details emerging or fading. Abbott surprised himself with how well it worked during his home tests—and how convincing the effect could be. As for the unusual paint used that no one seemed able to define, he suggested a formula of pastels mixed in vegetable fat.

The mediums could even advise agreeable changes along the way, shifting the rear painting accordingly to make it appear as if the spirits were fine tuning their art per the sitter's requests.

Once finished, the two canvases were covered by a third, according to Abbott's witness, who added that those in attendance placed their hands on it in order to "set the colors." This new cover and the front canvas were presumably removed to reveal the final painting on the rear canvas.

Other tricks helped, too. If a sitter requested a painting of their nine-year-old daughter who'd passed away, the mediums would have a series of paintings prepared of young girls. A network of mediums sharing information could also supply useful details to be integrated into the prepared portraits. The painting might even show a girl who looked older than she should be, but this was excused by explaining that spirits age differently. If a photograph was brought to the session, the mediums might find ways to see it, either in plain view or surreptitiously, then claim the spirits weren't able to paint at that time and request a second sitting, when a painting could be prepared in advance.

Mediums also knew who a good customer would be. If they detected a threat of being caught or a suspicious sitter, the session would simply not produce a painting.

"The ability to choose whom to work for is part of the art of the psychic," Abbott said. "This is why some of them are so successful for so many years. They are so cunning at judging the dispositions and mental characteristics of persons that they make no mistake, and only get results for persons whom they are sure they can 'handle.'"

Abbott shared his secret with a few magician friends, including Howard Thurston, who replicated the illusion for the stage.

Some Spiritualists argued that Abbott himself never personally witnessed the Bangs sisters, and that his ability to replicate the effect proved nothing. Many continued to believe that mediums produced the paintings through spirits, whereas magicians worked through illusions. One thing everyone could agree on, however, is that the portraits were beautiful. Somewhere out there, true talent was shining—whether the artist was alive or dead.

If ghosts were making art, not all of them wanted to paint portraits on demand, take directions from the living, and help mediums earn a fast buck. Some spirits, it seemed, were more interested in doing their own thing. One British artist, Georgiana Houghton, claimed to have such free-spirited spirits working through her, beginning in 1861. Her pencil drawings evolved into ethereal watercolors and ink rich in colors with swirling, whirling, fluid lines and layered patterns. It was unlike anything other contemporary artists—Spiritualist or not—were doing. Perhaps the best term to describe her art was one that was not yet used in the art world: *abstract*. That would eventually change. In 1988, the premiere issue of *Modern Painters* called Houghton

the first true abstractionist. By accepting that proclamation, one can say
that the abstract art movement didn't begin with Wassily Kandinsky or Piet
Mondrian, but with a few ghosts operating through the hand of a Victorian
woman who attended a séance in 1859 and soon after developed mediumistic
powers.

Houghton claimed several spirit guides worked with her, beginning with
Henry Lenny, who she described as "a deaf and dumb artist."

"He immediately controlled my hand, which was resting on the planchette, to form various curved lines," Houghton said. They started with a simple
flower. But Lenny's spirit soon gave way to more household names, such as
the Italian Renaissance painters Titian and Correggio. Leaving the planchette
behind, Houghton's style evolved as she began taking direction from a group
of ghosts she referred to as the "high spirits."

By 1871, Houghton's work received an audience at the fashionable New
British Gallery in London, featuring 155 of her spirit drawings. Despite
the abstract nature of her work on display, she believed it involved a certain
degree of specificity from the spirit world: "When the water-colour drawings
were commenced, I gradually gained faint glimmerings of their meaning, but
nothing detailed except the positive fact that they were representations of real
objects growing in spirit regions, and not simply allegorical, as I had thought
probable."

In her spirit flowers, for example, she explained that "each tint, whether
strong or delicate," would be "clearly understood by spirit beholders," but to all
of us "dwellers upon earth the pictured representations require interpreting."

Houghton included these meanings and interpretations on the backs of
many of her spirit drawings, giving the "high spirits" a chance to explain their
work rather than leaving it to Victorian art critics or those that would follow.

Shortly after, around the same time the Bangs sisters and Campbell
brothers were selling spirit portraits, Swedish artist Hilma af Klint followed
in Georgiana Houghton's Spiritualist footsteps. A trained portrait, landscape,
and botanical artist, af Klint took up an interest in Spiritualism in the late
1870s and began attending séances. The untimely death of her ten-year-old
sister in 1880 may have deepened her intrigue; Spiritualism offered hope of
communication with her lost sibling.

By the mid-1890s, af Klint had formed a Spiritualism group with four
other women artists. Meeting once a week, they were determined to explore
the spirit world and make contact with the Other Side through automatic
drawing and writing. They called themselves the Five. It's not known how
often they believed they found success, but a séance in 1904 clearly offered a
breakthrough. Af Klint claimed a "spirit world leader" had commissioned her

to "execute paintings on the astral plane" to represent the "immortal aspects of man." This grew into a monumental work comprising 193 paintings over the course of a decade collectively titled "The Paintings for the Temple."

Af Klint worked with vivid color combinations and free-flowing organic shapes that, like Houghton's pieces, were unusual and innovative for the time. Some of her paintings stood nearly ten feet high—almost twice the height of the five-foot, two-inch artist. "Af Klint worked on many of them on her studio floor like a cosmic Jackson Pollock," noted art critic Jennifer Higgie in 2016.

But the medium was simply working as the spirits guided her. "The pictures were painted directly through me, without any preliminary drawings, and with great force," af Klint later explained. "I had no idea what the paintings were supposed to depict; nevertheless I worked swiftly and surely, without changing a single brush stroke."

After completing the series of paintings, she spent years attempting to figure out what her work meant. She wrote more than 1,200 pages in the process, culminating in a text entitled *Studier over Själslivet* (Studies on Spiritual Life).

The spirits were hardly done with her after the Paintings for the Temple. Af Klint continued working at a prolific pace, ultimately creating more than 1,200 paintings, a hundred texts, and 26,000 pages of notes and sketches by the time of her death in 1944. Yet, much like her guiding ghosts, her work was unseen till long after she'd crossed over to the spirit world. Af Klint had stipulated that her art was not to be shown until twenty years had passed after her death. She may have been shy about exhibiting her art after being criticized in 1908 by fellow Spiritualist and eventual founder of anthroposophy Rudolph Steiner. He suggested that no one would understand her work for fifty years. Or maybe her hesitancy had more to do with the raging evil of World War II. Af Klint simply may have wanted her work to wait for the world to be in a better place.

Twenty years passed, as she requested, followed by another twenty-two. Her work was finally featured in a 1986 exhibition of abstract artists, including Kandinsky, Mondrian, František Kupka, and Kazimir Malevich.

Both af Klint's and Houghton's work has received renewed appreciation in the past decade, with the former being exhibited at the Guggenheim in New York City and the latter at London's Courtauld Gallery and Serpentine Gallery, as well as the Monash University Museum of Art in Melbourne, Australia.

While their creative expression of Spiritualism has found a home in the art world, the work of other mediums was met less with praise and analysis by art critics and more with scrutiny by scientists, most of whom found their art of spirit manifestations anything but artful. On the other hand, some thought Spiritualism's proof was piling up. Particularly in the case of Leonora Piper.

## The Curious Case of Leonora Piper

Leonora Piper didn't need paints or slates or table raps or darkened rooms to deliver messages from beyond. All she needed was a nap. While in a trance state, Piper astounded the scientific community, and all those around her, by delivering information she seemingly had no access to.

Her first experience began in Boston shortly after she gave birth to her first child in 1884. After she suffered the effects of an illness, her father-in-law sought the help of a local blind medium, J. R. Cocke, who had built a reputation for providing successful medical diagnoses and cures, and who apparently outperformed sighted physicians. During the consultation, as Piper watched and listened, she found that Cocke's "face seemed to become smaller and smaller, receding as it were into the distance, until gradually I lost all consciousness of my surroundings."

A week after this strange sensation she and her father-in-law joined the blind clairvoyant at his regular Sunday evening circle. The medium walked along the circumference, pressing his hand on each sitter's forehead. When arriving at Piper, he seemed to have activated the mediumship bubbling inside the young woman. At that moment, she claimed to have felt chills and saw before her "a flood of light in which many strange faces appeared." She stood, walked to a table in the center of the room, wrote a message on a sheet of paper, then handed it to another member of the circle and returned to her seat. Afterward that member, an elderly gentleman called Judge Frost, approached Piper and said, "Young woman, I have been a spiritualist for over thirty years but the message you have just given me is the most remarkable I have ever received. It has given me fresh courage to go on, for I know now that my boy lives."

Frost's son had been fatally injured in an accident thirty years earlier and had spent the last months of his life in a coma. Piper's message gave the boy's name and assured his mourning father that he "lived" and that his comatose head had been cleared.

And with that, a new Spiritualist star was born.

The new trance medium began offering similarly spooky utterances for family and friends, including relatives of Professor William James of Harvard University. James had taken a keen interest in Spiritualism and became a founding member of the American Society of Psychical Research in 1884. Naturally, he was intrigued by Piper's abilities, and after multiple sittings he was not disappointed. The information James received offered news about family members that at times he hadn't been aware of but discovered to be true shortly after. In one case, she told him his Aunt Kate, who was living in New York, had passed away early that morning. James later remarked, "On

reaching home an hour later I found a telegram as follows—Aunt Kate passed away a few minutes after midnight."

Piper's trances began at a table with seemingly normal conversation until she would suddenly lean her head forward onto an awaiting pillow and fall into a trance. Consciousness disappeared and her body fell inanimate—except for her right arm and hand, which lifted a pencil and began writing facts and information believed to have been directed by an intelligent discarnate spirit control. Over the years she had several controls with varying degrees of knowledge, including a French physician who died in 1860 and was known only as "Phinuit."

Based on James's experience, he saw no means of producing the wealth of information she offered through fraud.

"If you wish to upset the law that all crows are black, you must not seek to show that no crows are; it is enough if you prove one single crow to be white. My own white crow is Mrs. Piper," he said. "In the trances of this medium I cannot resist the conviction that knowledge appears which she has never gained by the ordinary waking use of her eyes and ears and wits."

His enthusiasm was joined by an entire crew of curious scientists who spent decades studying her. Among them were many of the top minds in psychical research: Columbia University professor of ethics and psychology James Hyslop, renowned physicist Sir Oliver Lodge, psychical researcher Dr. Richard Hodgson, and our spirit-painting enthusiast Dr. Isaac Funk.

Hodgson's studies began in 1887, and like James, he found Piper's accuracy with personal details about deceased friends, relatives, and his childhood to be unexplainable by known means. Tests included sittings with at least fifty people he knew to be strangers to Piper. Careful to take precautions against deception, Hodgson hired detectives to ensure no information about the sitters was gathered in advance by Piper, her husband, or anyone connected to her. Still, Piper prevailed. She gave details during her trance state that went beyond "chance coincidence and remarkable guessing" and "could not be accounted for except on the hypothesis that she had some supernormal power."

Piper's talents earned her a trip to Cambridge, England, in 1889 for further studies with Lodge and his team, where she continued to do her thing across eighty-three sittings with staggering results. Years later, Hyslop wrote a 785-page analysis about his seventeen sittings for the American Society for Psychical Research.

Both he and Lodge were so stymied by Piper's trances and strongly believed the only source of her information could be spirits. As Lodge put it: "On the question of the life hereafter the excavators are engaged in boring a tunnel from the opposite ends. We are beginning to hear the strokes of the pickaxes of our comrades on the other side."

Funk wasn't as convinced, responding to Lodge's claim, "But, we must hear more than the pickaxes. We must meet beyond any possibility of doubt the comrades themselves."

Funk suggested that she might be receiving messages telepathically from the living, not the dead. Piper didn't disagree. She didn't consider herself a Spiritualist and didn't know the source of her mysterious knowledge. In 1908, she noted:

---

I have never heard of anything being said by myself while in a trance state which might not have been latent in (1) my own mind, (2) in the mind of the person in charge of the sitting, (3) in the mind of the person who was trying to get communication with someone in another state of existence of some companion present with such person, or (4) in the mind of some absent person alive somewhere else in this world.

If thought could be unconsciously transferred to me from a person in the room I do not see any reason why that person could not have received a thought message from somebody at a long distance and then telephoned it, so to speak, in thought, direct to me. If telepathy is possible between two people, why not among three?

---

So did Piper actually possess some form of superpower, be it telepathic or spiritual? Some people were skeptical, including Granville Stanley Hall, president of Clark University, and his assistant, Dr. Amy Tanner, who studied Piper in 1909. During several of their sittings, Piper allegedly channeled the spirit of Dr. Hodgson, who'd died in 1905. When asked about a fictitious niece, Bessie Beals, Hodgson's spirit acknowledged her as if she was real. When questioned about it, the spirit got defensive and eventually claimed he was mistaken about the person he was thinking about. "Her name was not Bessie, but Jessie Beals," he said. Had Piper been caught in a trap like the one John W. Truesdell laid for Henry Slade decades earlier, or does occasional confusion follow us into the spirit world?

Other skepticism comes from some of the strange, nonsensical utterances Piper had given, like the time in 1895 when she muttered about evil monkeys living inside the sun. Further doubt was cast in 1898 when magician Joseph Rinn attended a Piper séance and reported that she held the hands of Hyslop and Hodgson. This, he believed, allowed her to sense feedback and perform what mentalist performers call muscle reading.

Still Piper's case gave researchers great cause for excitement. And she wasn't the only one. Around the same time that Piper began her trances in Boston, another medium some four thousand miles away in Italy was making a splash with a host of physical phenomena.

## The Physical Powers of Eusapia Palladino

Sitting at a séance with Eusapia Palladino, one might experience table levitation, the appearance of spectral hands and faces, flashes of light, foreign
tongues rambling on, a dead rat appearing out of nowhere, and solid objects
moving on their own. These objects, as one report described, were of the big
and heavy variety: "bookcases and bedsteads get up and dance barn dances,
and do other incomprehensible things." Palladino even emitted a cool breeze
from a one-inch scar on the left side of her forehead—the mark being a result
of a bad fall when she was one year old. The scar wasn't in the shape of a lightning bolt, but its effect was as mysterious as that of Harry Potter's. All this
happened while the short, stout, uneducated
psychic was supposedly in a trance, bound in
a chair with her hands and feet held by those
in attendance.

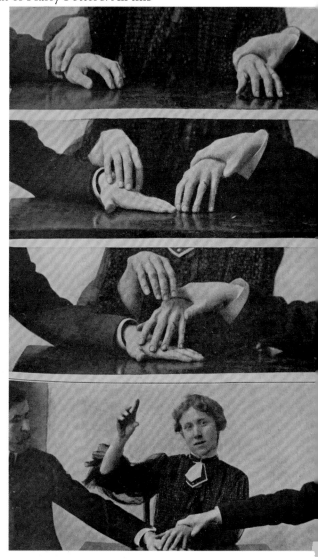

"At the beginning of a trance Mme.
Palladino is hoarse and tears and perspiration flow," a reporter for the *Baltimore Sun*
described in 1909. "Then come tremors and
twitchings. She becomes rigid. Finally her face
turns a deathly pallor and her eyes roll in so
that the eyeballs are barely visible." Once fully
in this trance, the writer added, "she exhibits many of the signs peculiar to epilepsy or
nervous hysteria. She laughs spasmodically
and wildly and chews frequently. She utters
strange words occasionally in foreign tongues,
which she could by no possibility have knowledge of in the flesh. When more important
phenomena occur she moans as if in agony or
else drops into a semi-comatose state."

Palladino began attracting the attention of
scientists from around the world shortly after
her first mediumistic experience as a teenager.
She'd attended a séance and caused a ruckus
by psychically tilting the table and then
lifting it completely off the ground. Astonished as anyone, Palladino began holding her
own sittings in her small Italian village and
building notoriety over the next few years. At

This series of photos depicts a method the medium Eusapia Palladino used to secretly free one of
her hands during a séance.

some point during this early period of her mediumship (the timing is unclear) she married a conjurer. She later denied he was a magician and claimed only that he had been "connected with theatricals" and knew his way around stage mechanisms and trick devices. The young medium had married a mentor, yet this did not seem to concern the many scientists who would soon descend upon her.

Among her first of these befuddled observers were astronomer Giovanni Schapiarelli, who first spotted the lines on Mars that were believed to be canals; celebrated Italian physician Cesare Lombroso; and French physiologist Charles Richet. Their detailed studies of Palladino left them in utter disbelief and of the opinion that her phenomena were "unfathomable." With brilliant minds like these giving her the stamp of approval, her fame skyrocketed. Soon the peasant woman was pulling in as much as five hundred dollars per séance—a fee wealthy families were more than happy to pay.

In the early 1890s, after being sold on Leonora Piper, Oliver Lodge examined Palladino in England and concluded that much of her phenomena was genuine. But by 1897, fellow Piper fan Dr. Richard Hodgson cast a cloud of doubt over Palladino's uncanny spirit world. He just wasn't as gung-ho as everyone else.

"I have found in my experience that learned scientific men are the most easily duped of any in the world," Hodgson wrote, regarding the earlier investigators' beliefs. Richet stood by his group's analysis and agreed to bring Palladino to Cambridge, England, for further tests. She ran through her typical repertoire of spirit manifestations, but Hodgson was unimpressed. While holding her hand during a séance, he noticed that she would cleverly substitute one hand for both, so that the sitters on both sides of her believed they were each holding one hand. He believed she did the same with a foot.

"Given a free hand and a free foot, nearly all the phenomena can be explained," he wrote. "She has very strong, supple hands, with deft fingers and great coolness and intelligence."

Hodgson added that strings may have been attached to objects to help move them, and faint outlines of ghostly visages and limbs may have just been "clever representations of the medium's own free hand in various shapes." Perhaps the uneducated peasant wasn't so uneducated after all. Or maybe this was all part of an act to enhance the effect of her remarkable abilities.

Despite these findings, Palladino remained popular and continued to amaze audiences with her performances. These included her biggest fan, Hereward Carrington, a prominent member of both American and English societies for psychical research.

"I have been asked many times for my own explanation, but I have none. I know only that I can feel the force; that it seems to flow out of me; and that I obtain it in part from others. . . . Perhaps some day we will know all about this force. Only God and his people know now, and perhaps—the devil."

—Eusapia Palladino,
in *Cosmopolitan* magazine in 1910

Eusapia Palladino levitates a table at the home of Professor Camille Flammarion in 1906.

Carrington, who looked like Harrison Ford and acted like an occult version of Indiana Jones seeking artifacts of the spirit world, traveled to Italy to inspect this newest mediumistic sensation. He'd written extensively on the subject and frequently exposed the tricks of psychics. If Carrington had doubts about her authenticity, Palladino would soon erase them.

Throughout the course of his examinations, he filled several books with his observations. These included notes on Palladino's famed table levitations, which "completely levitated" and rose forcibly against his own hand to six inches off the ground, and her unusual breezy forehead that let out a "distinctly perceptible" coolness, even when he held her mouth and nose to prevent her from breathing.

Carrington, however, was a seasoned researcher and not so easily fooled. As his studies continued, he, like Hodgson, detected moments of trickery. But he could not attribute everything to deception. Fraud, he determined, became an option when spirits weren't cooperating and Palladino wanted to please her sitters. In other words, when people wanted a show, she gave them one. This tendency caused problems for Carrington's star medium when he brought her to New York in 1909 for her American debut. Séances and studies continued through 1910, and further exposures resulted. A Harvard psychologist, Dr. Hugo Munsterberg, smuggled an assistant into one of the séances to crawl on the floor and observe Palladino's feet. Similar to Hodgson's discovery, the assistant spotted her slipping her foot out of her shoe while the shoe remained in position to make others think the foot was still restrained.

"That released foot does all the tricks of the performances," Munsterberg reported, noting its ability to play instruments, tug at sleeves, and levitate tables. "It is a strong foot and an agile one. It really should have all the credit."

Though he couldn't explain everything, Munsterberg had learned enough to determine Palladino was nothing more than another clever fraud. Still, Carrington defended her as genuine and believed she cheated on occasion "simply and solely because of her love of mischief" and her delight "in seeing onlookers mystified at the phenomena produced through mediumship."

"There was a very strong belief among the male population that women were not smart enough to deceive them. When you have scientists approaching this and they're not looking for deception because they don't think that women are smart enough to deceive them because they're *important, intelligent* men, it was a lot easier to just do that."

—Todd Robbins, performer and historian, on the ability of female mediums to stymie investigators, in 2020

# THE MAN WHO DIED TO PROVE THERE'S NO DEATH

Whether they used slate writing, Ouija boards, voices, or other manifestations, mediums offered many ways to talk to the dead. But in 1921, a student of Spiritualism named Thomas Lynn Bradford wanted something more conclusive. And he was willing to die for the cause.

Bradford lived by himself in a small, dingy rented room above a store in Detroit and spent his time writing about and lecturing on Spiritualism and the occult. He decided that if he had a partner—two minds perfectly attuned—they could stay connected after one left its body. So the ambitious forty-eight-year-old placed the kind of curious newspaper ad one might find on Craigslist today, searching for a special someone who was interested in communications with the dead. Ruth Doran, a forty-year-old local woman, answered.

Given that he was a Spiritualist, Bradford's belief in being able to make contact from the beyond doesn't seem outrageous. Yet, he only met Doran for one conversation at her home. This hardly seemed like enough time for two minds to connect, let alone form a pact over his death. Shortly after, on a Friday night, he turned on the gas in his room, lay down in bed, and began his experiment.

The next day his landlord found him dead. Near his body on the floor were several typewritten pages with the title, "Can the Dead Communicate with the Living?"

Bradford had mentioned his visit with Doran to the landlord, which sent investigators on a search for his apparent partner. When they found her two days later, she was shocked and denied being involved with his morbid scheme. Doran

also noted she wasn't a Spiritualist and thought the ad sought psychological conversation, not a psychical one. Besides, she added, if she had entered into such a pact, she wouldn't have let him die in such a depressing manner. "I would have had flowers and music."

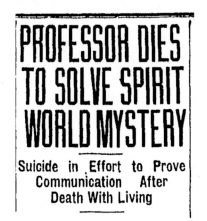

## PROFESSOR DIES TO SOLVE SPIRIT WORLD MYSTERY

### Suicide in Effort to Prove Communication After Death With Living

Still, she felt a connection with Bradford and wanted to honor his experiment by awaiting any possible message. During a vigil a week later, almost to the hour of his death, Doran sat in the parlor of her home with three non-Spiritualist friends when suddenly she claimed to have gone into a trance. It was 9:15 p.m. Others around town had joined in on the vigil, and as one reporter said, "spiritualists and psychics throughout Detroit, through prearrangement, 'concentrated' to hasten or help the return of Bradford's spirit."

Doran placed her hands on her temples, asked a friend to turn off the lights, and told another to write down the next words she would utter. In a low, slow voice she delivered a series of short sentences:

I am the professor who speaks to you from the beyond. I have broken through the veil. The help of the living has greatly assisted me.

I simply went to sleep. I woke up and at first did not realize that I had passed on. I find no great change apparent. I expected things to be much different. They are not. Human forms are retained in outline but not in the physical.

I have not traveled far. I am still much in the darkness. I see many people. They appear natural.

There is a lightness of responsibility here unlike in life. One feels full of rapture and happiness. Persons of like natures associate. I am associated with other investigators. I do not repent my act.

My present plane is but the first series. I am still investigating the future planes regarding which we in this plane are as ignorant as are earthly beings of the life just beyond human life.

By ten o'clock she'd snapped out of it and turned the lights on. Doran said the message unquestionably came from Bradford. She was convinced the experiment had worked, regardless of what others might think. "I know the dead can talk," she said.

It would seem other forces may have been at work beyond sheer curiosity and dedication to Spiritualism. However, Dr. I. L. Polozker, a Detroit psychologist, said the whole thing was perfectly sane. "His action, while bordering on the line of insanity, did not cross it," he told the press of Bradford. "Whether right or wrong, he was logical. He believed the dead can talk—his scientific mind demanded proof. The way to prove a premise is to prove it. Prof. Bradford adopted an entirely logical manner of trying to do so."

Bradford's experiment didn't seem to win over new converts, but fortunately it didn't inspire any copycat Spiritualists either.

## Eva Carrière Gives Birth to Ectoplasmic Ghosts

For an uneducated peasant, Eusapia Palladino displayed remarkable brilliance and ingenuity. But as the twentieth century progressed, so did the manifestations of other physical mediums. The latest and greatest shock came in the form of a gooey substance called ectoplasm. That's right, the stuff from *Ghostbusters*.

The spirit world was oozing into the living through the orifices of numerous mediumistic marvels. Perhaps the most notable psychic of this particular genre was Eva Carrière, better known as Eva C. and originally known as Marthe Béraud. The French phenom first discovered her mediumship in the early 1900s after her fiancé, the son of a general, died in Algiers. His distraught parents began holding séances led by their once future daughter-in-law. Béraud discovered during this time she had a talent for materializing spirits, and after a few publications of her wonders she drew the attention of Charles Richet. During the physiologist's visit to this latest Spiritualist marvel, Béraud held séances and brought forth the spirit of a three-hundred-year-old Brahmin Hindu called Bien Boa. Richet sensed the spirit's breath and felt its touch, convincing him of Béraud's powers.

"The personage in question is neither an image reflected on a mirror, nor a doll, nor a lay-figure," Richet reported. "In fact, it possesses all the attributes of life."

It did indeed have lifelike qualities because the old ghost was alive. Bien

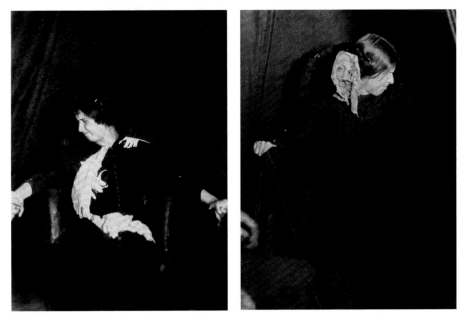

Medium Eva Carrière and her "materialisations" of ectoplasm, captured in *Phenomena of Materialisation* by Dr. Albert von Schrenck-Notzing.

Boa would eventually be revealed by less credulous investigators as a not-so-old man wearing a cloak and beard over his flesh and blood. Exposed, it was time to move on.

Béraud moved to Paris in 1909 for a fresh start under the name Eva Carrière. There, she found a benefactor and lover in a wealthy older woman, Madame Juliette Bisson, and attracted the interest of a German physician and psychical researcher named Dr. Albert von Schrenck-Notzing. And then things really got weird.

A series of séances over the next decade, into the early 1920s, resulted in

hundreds of photographs of Eva's "materialisations" emanating and stretching from her nose, eyes, ears, and vagina as her face strained and winced amidst groans and gasps. Von Schrenck-Notzing said it was reminiscent of a woman in labor, as if the spirits put her through a mighty struggle to give birth to them in the realm of the living. Oftentimes these ectoplasmic births appeared with images of expressive faces. Maybe the ghosts were just as surprised by these bizarre happenings as everyone else.

Such manifestations took place in a darkened cabinet behind a curtain after Eva was allegedly hypnotized. But before the show began, the cabinet would be inspected to ensure against fraud, and Eva would undress in an effort to prove she wasn't hiding bits of muslin or chiffon or anything else that could create the ectoplasm instead

Elizabeth Ann Tomson producing ectoplasm during a séance, captured by the *San Francisco Examiner* on July 15, 1923.

of a ghost. Madame Bisson added to the thorough examination by inserting her finger into Eva's vagina. She found nothing there, but the examination may have been as much for pleasure as it was for science. Von Schrenck-Notzing, of course, watched the whole thing and reported on it, along with every other detail of the séance on a nearly minute-by-minute basis. He felt pretty sure Eva's body was in the clear.

"Assuming that a female medium wished to use the vagina as a hiding-place for closely rolled packets, e.g., chiffon gauze, she would have to attach some kind of cord or ribbon to the packet beforehand, in order to be able to withdraw it," he wrote in his voluminous book *Phenomena of Materialisation*. "This cord would be detected during the exploration at the mouth of the vagina, and any finger introduced into the vagina would feel the foreign body. In the case of persons with a very wide vaginal entrance, it might be possible to withdraw the packet by means of the fingers, deeply inserted."

He went on to exonerate her other orifice as well, stating "the hiding of objects in the anal aperture, and their withdrawal from it, is even less possible, on account of its closure by a firm ring muscle, which hinders the introduction of a finger" and that sneaking materials inside would be "almost unthinkable without the use of Vaseline."

So he was convinced the ectoplasm and the faces appearing on its surface were legit. He met opposition from other investigators, like Richet in Algiers, who weren't so sure about Eva's act. The faces looked like images cut out from a magazine because they were. So were lines of text from newspapers and words from *Le Miroir*. Regarding this last peculiarity, a puzzled von Schrenck-Notzing wrote, "I cannot form any opinion on this curious result." Another psychical researcher, Eric Dingwall, had less difficulty, saying Eva's ectoplasm was nothing more than chewed-up paper. Regurgitation, it seemed, was her true power.

Teams of investigators and years of photographic studies were hardly the only way to expose ectoplasm-producing mediums. In 1923, for example, Mrs. Elizabeth Allen Tomson produced the spirit goo at a séance in New York City with a particularly curious attendee named Richard Gallagher. It was his first experience with such a manifestation, so he decided to find out more about the viscous substance. Tomson typically undressed herself in a cabinet with an inspector giving an Eva C.–like search and then emerged cloaked in yards of white ectoplasm like a cliché Halloween ghost. When she did so on this particular night, Gallagher decided to test the substance in a way other sitters hadn't.

"Just as [the ectoplasm] was about to embrace him he bit it vigorously," a reporter wrote. The gauzelike material ripped and came apart.

"When that spook put her arms around me, I just began eating ectoplasm as fast as I could. I filled my mouth with it and when she yanked away, the ectoplasm just poured out of my mouth," Gallagher said. "All that I could hold on to was a tatter that caught on one of my teeth."

Gallagher said he wasn't afraid of the stuff and had only one regret about the experience: "I might have got enough of that ectoplasm to screen the porch next summer."

Mrs. Tomson, who'd been caught years earlier with flowers hidden under her breasts and a snake tucked away in her armpit, was not pleased and scolded Gallagher for not paying her the courtesy due to a lady. The ectoplasm eater didn't seem too concerned with hurting the medium's feelings, though, as the reporter claimed that he boasted being "the only man who ever bit a spook and got away with it—or some of it!"

## Arthur Conan Doyle, Harry Houdini, and the Great Debate

As the First World War waged in the early 1900s, mediums popped up in even greater numbers to work their supposed miracles around the world. Much like in the Civil War era, wherever there was grief there was a medium nearby to console the griever. Mighty as their powers seemed to be, there were two even greater forces at work pushing for and against Spiritualism: Sir Arthur Conan Doyle and Harry Houdini.

Doyle is immortalized as the creator of Sherlock Holmes, though he firmly believed such status would be attainable without the help of a fictional character. His first inkling of the afterlife came after he joined a séance in 1880, which compelled him to proclaim, "After weighing the evidence, I could no more doubt the existence of the phenomena than I could doubt the existence of lions in Africa." But his steadfast belief in spirits didn't come till decades later, when he believed he heard a personal message from his son, Kingsley, who had died in a World War I battle.

Doyle put Sherlock Holmes to rest so he could focus on multiple books touting the new breakthrough that Spiritualism offered humankind and lecturing on it across Europe and America. Though he excelled at writing detective stories, his detective skills in reality seemed to be lacking. Doyle acknowledged some mediums were phonies, but he was quick to believe in the powers of many. One of his books, *The Coming of Fairies*, even announced the existence of tiny fairy-tale-like creatures and included photos. Years later the teenage girls who'd taken the fairy images admitted the obvious hoax.

Still, Doyle had a lot of clout and a lot of passion for advancing Spiritualism. So wherever he went, people listened. In 1925 at the International Spiritualist Congress in Paris, they even rioted for the chance to hear him speak. A mob of 1,500 people battled to get inside a crowded hall already packed with 4,000 attendees from all walks of life.

"This is the most important message that has come to man in two thousand years and he has laughed at and insulted it," Doyle told the throngs of believers in response to the many non-Spiritualists who were hellbent on exposing mediums and ruining all the fun. "The raps of the medium are a knocking at the door of life. . . . The last fifty years have been given to the study of protoplasm. I prophesy that the next fifty years will be given to the study of ectoplasm."

In the meantime, he and Houdini had struck up a friendship in 1920. But the famed magician was hardly as exuberant about mediums. He was open

# Do the Dead Really Die?

### Is it possible to talk with the spirits of the departed?

See

# "Is Conan Doyle Right?"

*Two parts*

Louder and louder grows the discussion as to whether there is anything in Spiritualism.

It is talked of in the home, the pulpit, the street and the office.

Here is the real and vital topic of the day in a sensationally interesting picture.

Who is there in your community who doesn't want to know about it and see the picture?

*A real attraction*

*Written by*
Cullom Holmes Ferrell
*Directed by*
J. J. Harvey

Pathé
Distributors

to the possibility of legitimate mediumship, but fraud disgusted him. He had worked as a medium himself in the 1890s, conducting séances and producing the types of effects common amongst psychics. Doyle, in fact, believed Houdini had genuine powers, despite the magician's assurance he did not. A frequent exchange of letters saw Doyle exalting the merits of Spiritualism and Houdini countering with the merits of a genuine display of ability, which he'd yet to witness.

Houdini, in fact, had been busy exposing every medium as was humanly possible given his busy schedule. Sometimes this involved inviting mediums to shows and calling them out right from the stage—exposing their tricks in front of the full audience. Other times he visited mediums in disguise under the name F. Raud, as in *fraud*. And when he couldn't expose a charlatan, he had a team of others doing it, including his niece, Julia Sawyer; a magazine writer named Clifford Eddy Jr.; and an investigator named Ruth Mackenberg, who would pose as a widow, a jealous wife, a schoolteacher, or other seemingly innocent characters. Fellow magicians Joseph Dunninger and Joseph Rinn worked heavily alongside Houdini as well. Rinn even offered Doyle $5,000 to speak with one of the ghosts the writer had communicated with. Doyle declined.

Harry Houdini offered a $10,000 reward to any medium who could physically prove the existence of spirits.

Houdini's crusade took the fight all the way to the United States Congress in February and May 1926, where he served as a star witness at a hearing before the House District of Columbia Committee on a bill to prohibit fortune-telling for fees. Spiritualists, mediums, fortune-tellers, and astrologers filled the committee room, ready to defend their right to profit from ghosts. Houdini explained that he wasn't opposed to any legitimate practice or religion, but that he absolutely opposed individuals who deceived others. The idea that mediums might be influencing policy surely wasn't appealing either.

Rose Mackenberg joined the magician at the hearing and testified that Dr. Jane B. Coates, head of the Spiritualist Church of America in Washington, DC, held table-tipping séances at the White House with President Coolidge and his family. Coates denied the accusation, explaining that all séances were held "under the shadow of the White House."

Houdini, being the master showman he was, demonstrated slate writing and other mediumistic techniques right in front the committee. He even offered a $10,000 reward to any medium in the audience who could produce a physical manifestation that he couldn't prove to be fraudulent. One medium, Madame Marcia, accepted the challenge by announcing that she had predicted the election of President Harding and his death to Mrs. Harding. Houdini was unimpressed. No money changed hands. Undeterred, Marcia proudly informed everyone that senators and congressmen "consult me constantly."

Politics aside, Coates insisted that Spiritualists have every right to advise congregants or anyone else.

"I have saved many young girls from marrying the wrong man and have kept others from going wrong," she announced. "My religion goes back to Jesus Christ. Houdini does not know I am a Christian."

"Jesus was a Jew," Houdini shot back, "and he did not charge two dollars a visit."

Such exchanges elicited amusement and hissing throughout the bizarre hearing. But the mediums had the last laugh when the bill failed to pass.

Before it was all said and done at the hearing, Houdini called his old friend Doyle one of the biggest dupes in the world. Their opposing views, as one might imagine, had put a damper on the men's friendship over the years. One episode that perhaps caused the most damage was the one that got the most personal, involving Doyle's wife, Jean, and Houdini's beloved deceased mother. Lady Doyle, by what Doyle must have believed to be some wondrous coincidence, claimed to have developed her own psychic powers and began channeling ghosts. In 1922, the Spiritualist couple invited the master of escape to a sitting in an Atlantic City hotel room. There, Jean planned to channel Houdini's mother and produce a message through automatic writing. By the end of the séance, she'd scribbled fifteen pages of notes from the magician's mother. Houdini, not surprisingly, wasn't buying it. After all, his mother's English was terrible—she couldn't have possibly said any of what was written. Houdini didn't appreciate Lady Doyle's attempt, and Doyle didn't care for the magician's dismissal of his wife's mediumship.

Lady Doyle would later channel an ancient Arabian from a Mesopotamian city called Ur. This wondrous spirit's name was Pheneas, and he claimed to have lived before the time of Abraham. Perhaps eager to have someone to finally talk to again, he spoke quite often with the Doyles throughout the mid-1920s. "Say just 'Pheneas' and I will come quicker than if you said a number on the telephone," he told them, as if he was their own personal genie. Pheneas gave them business advice, suggested travel dates for the couple, and even helped them find a new home in a region of southern England called the New Forest. "It is a wonderful place," he said in May 1924. "The atmosphere is perfect."

He also liked predicting doom and gloom for the world. More specifically, the old man from Ur predicted doom for Doyle's friend the nonbeliever, Houdini. On April 12, 1925, Pheneas told Jean, "Houdini is doomed, doomed, doomed. He will not be allowed to stand in the way of God's progress." The great magician died just over a year later, on October 31, 1926, after suffering a ruptured appendix.

## The Housewife Who Challenged Houdini: Margery, the Witch of Lime Street

But let's not leave Houdini for dead just yet. Not before we discuss his greatest psychic foe: a housewife from Boston named Mina Crandon, better known as Margery, the Witch of Lime Street.

Their story began in 1924 when *Scientific American* held a contest in search of a medium who could produce a genuine psychic manifestation. Any such medium deemed authentic by the magazine would receive $2,500. The publication's investigative committee included an all-star cast of brainpower: J. Malcolm Bird, the magazine's managing editor; Dr. William McDougall of Harvard University; Dr. Daniel F. Comstock, formerly of the Massachusetts Institute of Technology; Dr. Walter Franklin Prince of the Society for Psychical Research; Hereward Carrington, champion of Eusapia Palladino; and of course, Houdini.

Mediums jumped at the chance to snag the prize money. Elizabeth Allen Tomson, whom we met earlier when her ectoplasm got eaten, was first to bat but never made it to the plate. After making the trek from Chicago to New York, Tomson's husband asked Bird about the location for his wife's test and was not pleased with the law library that had been designated. He preferred a stage or a friend's apartment, suggesting these would be more appropriate for the sitting. Bird disagreed; Tomson cancelled.

A young Italian medium named Nino Pecoraro made some noise by playing a toy piano and spinning a tambourine in the air while tied up, à la the Davenport brothers. Manifesting the voice of the late Eusapia Palladino, in her native Italian no less, added a nice touch and enhanced his mystique. It was a good try, but Houdini quickly dispatched the contender after personally spending nearly two hours expertly tying him up and stifling the spirits. Things were looking bleak until a new challenger from Boston entered the fray: a beautiful young blonde who never expected to one day butt heads with the great Houdini.

Mina Crandon's life had already been through twists and turns since she moved from Canada to Boston as a teenager in the early 1900s, but the biggest change came one night in 1923 after she attended a séance and heard a spirit suggest that she had the gift of mediumship. She found her gift to be quite powerful as she began hosting her own sittings for friends and family at her home on Lime Street. Her deceased brother, Walter, who was tragically crushed between two train cars on a railroad in 1911, regularly attended and addressed the guests from the great beyond.

Mina stood out from other mediums because she didn't address spirits for profit. She had no history of being associated with magicians or other psychics, and her mediumship was strictly private. As her great-granddaughter, Anna Thurlow, notes, Mina's mother was her most loyal sitter, which suggests that the channeling of Walter may have been for her benefit. It also suggests that Mina's manifestation of him was so convincing that his own mother believed it was really him.

The other sitter always at Mina's side was her husband, Dr. Le Roi Crandon, a well-respected physician who'd been married twice before and took an interest in Spiritualism after hearing a lecture by Sir Oliver Lodge in 1920. Mina, too, had been previously married, to a grocer named Earl Rand, and worked as a secretary at a church. The couple had a son together, but Mina later met Crandon during a minor surgery and divorced Earl shortly after. Her status, along with Le Roi's penchant for taking new wives, may have also contributed to Mina's desire to suddenly spice things up with her newfound mediumship.

"He was really a lot to keep up with," Thurlow says. "So I could see someone pulling out whatever it took to keep things happy—you can't get divorced twice at that age as a woman and survive, especially with a child. She'd have no reputation left if she got divorced again."

So as the séances went on, Mina found herself busily keeping her husband interested and her mother happy, all while raising her son with the help of their butler, a Japanese man named Noguchi. At the same time, she may have found her unexpected profession a creative escape. As evidenced by so many of the women mentioned earlier in this section, mediumship had a strong appeal for women. Women did not have a public voice, but spirits gave them one. And suddenly Mina was empowered to say just about anything.

Thurlow suggests mediumship may have also been a way for women to explore new ideas in the privacy of their own living rooms and still maintain a reputable social status. "Women just didn't go out and become astronauts or doctors or scientists at that time," she notes. "But you could be in your living room and very respectfully explore 'new worlds'. I can imagine that had a lot of appeal."

Mina was exploring new worlds like few others had, and things were going along just fine. But it was only a matter of time until gossip spread around town, and when it did it caught the ear of William McDougall at nearby Harvard. From there things took off. Soon she was paraded around numerous investigators and Spiritualists, and not surprisingly, Sir Arthur Conan Doyle arranged a meeting. He was an immediate believer in her powers and urged her to enter the *Scientific American* contest. Her cherished privacy was about to go very public. Despite attempts to protect her identity by entering her simply as "Margery" (a variation of her middle name, Marguerite), the media soon learned her identity as the wife of a prominent physician. But the pseudonym stuck.

The investigative committee was enthralled with its visits—all except Houdini, who, being the busy showman he was, missed the first forty-seven séances and the host of wonders wrought in Margery's darkened chambers. The judges witnessed ectoplasmic limbs extruding from her body and felt their touch—and possibly got hit by a tossed thing or two—before they were reabsorbed into her person. Sometimes they even left fingerprints in wax. A bell enclosed in a box rang on command. Objects appeared out of nowhere. The table tilted and levitated. And as mentioned, the spirit of Walter spoke freely.

Walter Prince of the Society for Psychical Research marveled at the possibilities if these phenomena proved real and believed much more was on the line than $2,500. Voices produced by a nonliving being requiring the presence of a "peculiarly-constituted person" would have "deep significance for physics, psychology, and physiology." He also expressed excitement about the appearance of live pigeons and flowers during a séance, "either by special creation or by passage through matter" that, if legitimate, "would considerably enlarge the domain of either biology of physics."

"Mediumship circumvented the structural barriers that excluded women from religious leadership. By communicating directly with spirits, mediums bypassed the need for education, ordination, or organizational recognition. . . . Spirit communication carries its own authority. If one accepted the message, one had little choice but to accept the medium."

—Ann Braude, Harvard Divinity School teacher, in her 1989 book *Radical Spirits*

Prince and his team thought they'd found a winner. Carrington found even more, having fallen in love and started an affair during the investigation. When Bird and the publisher, Orson Munn, finally filled Houdini in on the committee's consensus, the magician was shocked and angered that he hadn't been brought in earlier.

"Do you believe that this medium is genuine?" he asked Bird at Munn's office.

"Why, yes, she is genuine," Munn responded, standing next to his boss for support. "She does resort to trickery at times, but I believe she is fifty or sixty per cent genuine."

Houdini knew he could bring that percentage down to zero. He also knew the consequences of prematurely awarding the prize would be severe. Turning to Munn, he said, "If you give this award to a medium without the strictest examination, every fraudulent medium in the world will take advantage of it. I will forfeit a thousand dollars if I do not detect her if she resorts to trickery. Of course if she is genuine there is nothing to expose, but if the *Scientific American* by any accident should declare her genuine and she was eventually detected in fraud we would be the laughingstock of the world, and in the meantime hundreds of fraudulent mediums would have taken advantage of the error."

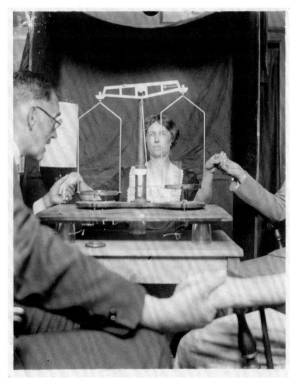

At this séance held on June 8, 1924, Margery the Witch of Lime Street attempts to have Walter tip the scales.

So on July 23, 1924, Houdini headed to Boston to meet Margery face-to-face, hand-to-hand, and foot-to-foot. That night's séance found the magician seated next to the medium, holding her left hand and placing his right foot against her left. He'd heard much hullaballoo about an electric bell that rang inside a box whenever pressure at its lid completed the circuit. The box, placed in front of Margery, rang in previous séances despite her hands and feet being secured by the committee members. The bell, it was believed, had been rung by Walter. Houdini suspected that Margery had been able to leisurely and slyly free her foot enough to ring the bell. He came prepared.

"All that day I had worn a silk rubber bandage around that leg just below the knee. By night the part of the leg below the bandage had become swollen and painfully tender, thus giving me a much keener sense of feeling and making it easier to notice the slightest sliding of Mrs. Crandon's ankle or flexing of her muscles," he said.

The plan worked, as Houdini slowly but surely felt the movements. As the evening progressed, he detected other tricks. She freed her right hand, for example, to place a spirit trumpet on her head, and then "Walter" would fling it in any direction requested. Houdini called it the "slickest ruse I have ever detected, and it has converted all skeptics."

Moving forward, Houdini and the committee decided to devise a restraint that would prevent any of the tactics that the magician detected after one sitting. Houdini informed Margery of his plans in a letter, stating, "I know that with your willingness you are ready to try any of the various controls and assure you that I will be agreeable to anything, where eventually no one can question the control. At no time would I permit the committee to harass or put you to an inconvenience of physical discomfiture. Harmony must reign, but the control at all times, should be satisfactory to all present."

That comfortable, satisfactory control came in the form of a wooden box with a hole on top for Margery's head and holes on the sides for her hands. It looked like she was wearing a secretary desk, but looks weren't important. Results, or lack of results, were.

Once Houdini had Margery secured inside the box, with her hands being held by himself and Prince, the manifestations ceased to exist—except for the voice of Walter. The spirit accused Houdini of trying to deceive the committee by sneaking a carpenter's folding ruler into the cabinet before Margery entered, giving her a tool that could be used to create telekinetic effects.

"Houdini, you goddamned son of a bitch, get the hell out of here and never come back," Walter shouted. The outburst intensified with a threat. "I put a curse on you now that follows you every day until you die."

Margery felt betrayed by the magician and saddened to see this battle of minds resort to dirty tactics. Houdini, of course, denied placing the ruler there and discounted the threat and insults, chalking it up to the medium's frustration. "She knew I had her trapped," he said of the incident. The folded ruler measured just six inches—a size Houdini believed Margery was entirely capable of smuggling in.

Dr. Comstock, trying to play peacemaker, suggested it might have been left by an assistant who'd helped build the cabinet, but given the thoroughness of the examination such an oversight seems unlikely. That being said, he might have been correct about an assistant being involved. William Lindsay Gresham's 1959 book, *Houdini, the Man who Walked through Walls*, claimed that years after Houdini's death, his assistant Jim Collins was asked about the ruler controversy. According to Gresham, "Collins smiled wryly. 'I chucked it in the box meself. The boss told me to do it. He wanted to fix her good.'"

Planted or not, Houdini felt confident he'd finally stumped the Witch of Lime Street. He determined that she'd combined her skills as a secretary and musician and her athletic build to become a "shrewd, cunning woman, resourceful in the extreme, and taking advantage of every opportunity to produce a 'manifestation.'" He also believed her husband helped by holding his wife above suspicion and thus letting go of her hand without thinking anything of it. Crandon's collection of books explaining the methods of mediums may have offered a few lessons to build on as well.

By February 1925, *Scientific American* determined that Margery would not receive the prize. Only Hereward Carrington remained a believer—though emotions may have given him a bit of a bias.

A resentful Le Roi Crandon later said the entire investigation was "largely a period of comedy." He took issue with each of the members, noting that Houdini "came with his mind made up before he started."

Margery may have lost out on the prize, but she wasn't done. Séances carried on and Walter remained angry with Houdini. In August 1926, he expanded on his threat by declaring "Houdini will be gone by Halloween." Oddly enough, Walter was right (and provided specificity that Doyle's spirit friend, Pheneas, did not).

Others continued to study Margery's mediumship. Doyle, of course, had never lost interest and continued to champion her. In 1927, after another study exposed her as a fraud, he countered by declaring her genuine to the press.

"He and his brave wife have had to fight the narrow pedantry of scholars, the cunning tricks of conjurors, the jeers of the humorist, the malice of the prejudiced and limited scientist," Doyle said of the Crandons.

The Sherlock Holmes creator made his own journey to the spirit world in 1930, but had he lived a few more years, a new finding from the Boston Society for Psychic Research may have shaken his confidence. Ectoplasmic fingerprints of Walter, once believed genuine, were proven by a dermatologist to belong to Margery's dentist, who was still alive.

Surely this disappointed those who still believed, yet one had to admire Margery's resourcefulness and creativity. Houdini may have been right about her husband's books informing her abilities and his assistance during the séance, but it hardly seems like a strong enough explanation for Margery's impressive showmanship. How did she master such intricate and convincing effects? Magicians typically learn from other magicians, but Margery had no such apprenticeship. Perhaps Crandon helped more than Houdini suspected. Carrington, blinded by passion, likely partook in the ruse. Even Bird was rumored to have assisted in the séances. Thurlow suggests Margery knew her audience and knew how to manage the room. Maybe one day she told Bird she didn't feel well and might need his help, and another day shared the same message with Carrington or someone else so that no one person was helping at all times. "She had different levers she could use if she needed them," Thurlow says.

It's also possible that another unseen accomplice could have aided in the production of her effects. In this case, the butler literally might have done it. Thurlow believes Noguchi may have helped, particularly because in Margery's early séances she performed automatic writing in Chinese and Japanese. "That seems like an obvious connection," Thurlow said with a laugh. Even if a spirit wasn't doing the calligraphy, Margery proved to be a quick study in complex languages.

As for why she got herself into this in the first place, Thurlow believes her great-grandmother may have simply been fulfilling a need. "I think for her it was fun—I honestly think that was part of her secret," she says. "The intellectual challenge. If you're an intelligent person and you're not given a lot of outlets to express that, you're going to take whatever you get."

But these are all theories. The real whys and hows went to the grave with Margery in 1941 at the age of fifty-three, following a bout with alcoholism. All the unwanted fame combined with a consistent need to perform on the spot and defend herself from skeptics might explain her downward spiral. No table raps, automatic writing, slate writing, Ouija board messages, or other manifestations of Mina Crandon have offered the real truth.

Try as we might, answers from and about the afterlife remain the struggle of the living.

# GHOST SIGHTINGS
# AND PARANORMAL
# PHENOMENA

FROM FAMOUS HAUNTINGS TO
LESSER-KNOWN UNKNOWNS

"Whatever it eventually turns out to be would appear to us today as strange, unbelievable and impossible as, say, the idea of an Internet would have appeared to Newton or even Einstein."

—Guy Lyon Playfair,
Enfield investigator and
author of *This House Is Haunted*,
on poltergeists in 2011

Every town in every country has a creepy old house. A house no one dares to enter. A house that rejects mortal owners. A house built of local lore as much as bricks and mortar. A house said to be occupied by ghosts. We can't be sure if they're trapped within its walls or if they've chosen to stay, whether to protest an unjust death, to right a wrong, or for other reasons unknown to the living. We can only guess why the dead dwell among the living—but if the following stories are to be believed, there's no doubt that they do, indeed, dwell.

## The Winchester Mystery House

In San Jose, California, the Winchester Mystery House is distinct from other haunted houses. After all, it was never meant for people; it was built and designed specifically for its ghostly occupants.

The aptly named house was built by Sarah Winchester, the heir to the Winchester rifle fortune. It took 38 years of around-the-clock construction to turn the home into the expansive rambling mansion it became. Sprawling across 2,400 square feet, it hosts 160 rooms and includes 10,000 windows, 2,000 doors, 40 staircases, and 47 fireplaces. The construction came to an end only when Winchester's life did. Death, however, is where the legend of this extraordinary home begins.

Sarah's husband, William Wirt Winchester, was the son of Oliver Fisher Winchester, the inventor of the Winchester repeating rifle. Oliver's revolutionary new design allowed riflemen to reliably fire numerous shots before having to reload. The days of watching a target escape while tediously loading another bullet were over. Between Wild West frontiersmen, Native Americans, outlaws, and the military, the guns sold by the millions and the money poured in as the bodies piled up.

Life looked good for the young Winchesters—until death had something to say about it. Sarah and William's infant daughter tragically succumbed to a nutrient deficiency on July 25, 1866, just months after the Winchester Repeating Arms Company was born. The couple had no other children but death wasn't done with them yet. In 1880, it claimed Sarah's mother, William's father, and—months later—William from tuberculosis. He left his thirty-year-old widow a $20 million fortune.

"You shall have gold without stint," William reportedly told her in the days before his passing. "You shall build yourself a house—any kind of a house that you desire." With her sizable inheritance, not to mention an extra thousand dollars a day in royalties from rifle sales, she could do exactly as he wished.

Sarah thought building a dream house was an excellent suggestion but sought additional guidance from a medium following William's death. Echoing her husband's message to an extreme degree, the psychic directed Sarah to build a *big* house. So big, in fact, that it could house the ghosts of the thousands, or perhaps millions, of lives that had fallen victim to the Winchester family business. These ghosts would only be appeased if she kept building onto the house. As the story goes, by continually adding to the home she would ward off her own demise. The medium directed her to move out West, far from her current home in New Haven, Connecticut. Sarah didn't resist; moving far away from the death that had surrounded her life must have been appealing.

Sarah's search for the perfect site ended in San Jose when a drive led her to a thirty-acre lot with an eight-room home under construction. This was it. With nearly limitless means, she convinced the owner to sell her the home and the surrounding land. The construction crew stayed on but Sarah took charge of the design, directing the constant building, tearing down, and rebuilding efforts. Her life became an endless barrage of hammers and saws.

The work was hectic and surely a bit confusing to the carpenters, not to mention the neighbors. A local high-society woman once attempted to reach out to Sarah for a visit but her request was reportedly denied with a request of the widow's own: mind your business and leave me alone. It was also reported that Sarah was so "annoyed" by her neighbors' "revelry" on one occasion that she bought their property the next day.

On the other hand, people in her employ were generally treated well. Sarah did whatever she could to treat them fairly and to help improve their work

An example of the switchback staircases with two-inch-high risers in the Winchester Mystery House.

conditions. Gardeners, for example, benefited from her innovative zinc sub-floor and window drip pans in the north conservatory that cleverly directed water runoff from the plants to the garden below.

Over time, the house became a mishmash of architectural oddities. Several doorways lead to nowhere or, even worse, lead to a fifteen-foot drop to the ground below. Staircases are equally as strange, with some heading straight to a ceiling and others requiring an excessive amount of walking to ascend just a few feet. In one instance, a switchback staircase running a hundred feet in length takes seven turns with forty-four steps, each with risers no higher than a couple inches, just to climb a mere nine feet to the second floor. Ascending or descending from one floor to another introduces occasional upside-down support posts. Adding to these curiosities is the prevalence of the number thirteen throughout the estate. There are thirteen subpanels in the grand ballroom ceiling panels, thirteen windows in the thirteenth bathroom, thirteen steps on a staircase, and thirteen panes of glass in certain windows. Thirteen other examples could probably be found as well. All these architectural anomalies beg the question: why?

No one knows for sure, which is how the Mystery House earned its moniker. Even Sarah's own name for the house is a mystery. She called it Llanada Villa, which translates from Spanish to "house on flat land." If she had a special reason for the name, she kept it, like most things, to herself. Aside from her niece, who served as her secretary, and the maid staff, Sarah lived in the home alone. Unless, that is, the ghosts moved in. Some believed the home's many oddities were designed to confuse evil spirits, as if they wouldn't know how to navigate the circuitous staircases or be too befuddled by superfluous doors to stick around. The numerous chimneys were thought to have been tailored to life with ghosts as well, based on a theory that spirits like to escape through them. "When the clock tolled the hour for them to return to wherever it is they came from there was no need of undignified jostling and bumping of elbows," explained one newspaper. "It is doubtful if ever in the haunted castles of Europe ghosts could get such service." The same paper also noted that while the number thirteen is typically considered unlucky, ancient tales about the number consider it unlucky for evil people only. It suggested that bad ghosts would steer clear of those areas.

This line of thinking also explains the privacy of Sarah's séance room, located right near her bedroom. It seemed Sarah went to great lengths to ensure no one but her—including unwanted ghosts—could get there, even if they wanted to. According to one report, she weaved her way through an "interminable labyrinth of rooms and hallways" on her way to a button that opened a secret panel leading to another room, like the original Batcave, "and unless the pursuing ghost was watchful and quick, he would lose her." The description goes on to suggest she climbed out of a window onto the top of a staircase that took her down one story, where another flight brought her right back upstairs. "This was supposed to be very disconcerting to evil spirits who are said to be naturally suspicious of traps."

Considering the séance room is located right near her bedroom, making it easy to spend her evenings chatting with the spirits, this convoluted path may have been a colorful exaggeration. Then again, much of the speculation may have been embellishments designed to stir up excitement and deepen the mystery.

Some of the strangeness might have straightforward explanations. Take the switchback staircases with the unusually low risers, for example. It's far more likely that these were built to accommodate Sarah's debilitating arthritis than to confuse malevolent spirits.

In researching her book on Sarah Winchester, *Captive of the Labyrinth*, author Mary Jo Ignoffo suggests that other oddities, like the stairs and doors to nowhere, are simply a result of damage that occurred during the 1906 San Francisco earthquake, which preceded the creation of the Richter scale but was later estimated to be around a 7.9. Wreckage may have just been sealed off and landings may have collapsed. Ghosts, Ignoffo believed, had nothing to do with it. As for the rest of the unusual designs and construction quirks, she chalks it up to Sarah's interest in architecture and having the cash flow and space to experiment.

Maybe Sarah did take up architecture as a hobby, but given the prominence of Spiritualism, it's not unlikely that she dabbled in communications with the dead, too. Her home may have ultimately represented an amalgamation of both interests. If she truly believed her life depended on nonstop construction, she was prepared to live another forty to fifty years at the time of her death, based on the stockpile of materials she'd stowed away in three large storehouses. Ghosts or no ghosts, heart failure claimed Sarah's life on September 5, 1922, at the age of eighty-two.

The house she'd spent more than $5 million building (that's roughly $75 million today) was emptied and auctioned off. After all her efforts and investments, the home was valued at a bargain basement price of $5,000. Auctioneers didn't think such a meandering architectural behemoth would be desirable.

The Winchester Mystery House lives on as a popular tourist destination.

Fortunately the purchaser didn't share their myopia. The new owner, Thomas Barnett, had the good sense to lease his new home to John Brown, who had the even better sense to open the house to the public. After all these years of whispers and gossip, people could finally see inside this weird and wonderful place.

On June 30, 1923, just over a year since Sarah's passing, the newly named Winchester Mystery House was open for business. Curious neighbors coughed up a quarter to roam the lonely corridors, climb the strange steps, and watch for doors with sudden drops. For a couple extra coins, they could do it all with a hot dog and an ice cream cone in hand.

"Brown was looking to run it like an amusement park," said Natalie Alvanez, director of marketing and sales at the Winchester Mystery House. "He wanted a Ferris wheel and a carousel and all this other stuff on the land.

Then he realized quickly that the house was the star."

Regardless of the ghosts it might or might not have been truly designed for, people claim to see them today. In fact, the mansion has earned a reputation as possibly the most haunted in America. Ghost-hunting shows galore have explored its cavernous innards, as have numerous psychics and swarms of paranormal fans. The mediums agree that any spiritual energy they've sensed has been positive. Were the ghosts pleased with the house Sarah built them? And willing to forgive that whole getting-shot-by-a-Winchester-rifle thing? Or were some of the spirits Sarah's former maids, gardeners, and other domestic helpers who were treated well and happy to stick around?

Whoever the ghosts are, people have detected their presence in different ways and places. Footsteps have been heard on the main staircase when no one is there. Cabinets have opened on their own. Loud bangs have sounded with no cause. Various apparitions have been spotted, including many of a man pushing a wheelbarrow in the basement as he works on the furnace or in the grand ballroom as he tends the fireplace. A recent employee filmed a video of her last goodbyes to the house. As she left Sarah's séance room, she heard the door creak and a faint voice say, "We're all here."

Who they are, why they remain in the house, or if they're even there remains a mystery. But regardless of the answers, the questions and widespread curiosity sparked by the never-ending construction have given Sarah the immortality her medium allegedly promised. Just in a different form.

The Winchester Mystery House has its history, its lore, and clearly a peculiar appearance inside and out. But what is it about other places that give them the appearance and feeling of being haunted? If you were to picture a typical haunted house, it would likely be a large, slightly decaying Victorian home outlined against a gray October sky. The air would be cool and crisp, and dying leaves would pepper the lawn beneath naked tree branches. As you walk inside, you would sense the echoes of generations of stories, cracked and stained like the home itself. Stories about the terrible things that happened to the people who once lived there. We can't help thinking this way. Movies, books, and TV shows have trained us to conjure this specific image—and to read all manner of spooky things into it. It's how we process and control something we know very little about.

But hauntings happen in perfectly normal places, too—and even in broad daylight.

## The Ghosts of the Battle of Gettysburg

Just before the Winchester repeating rifle began its reign as the "gun that won the West," Union and Confederate soldiers waded through a bloodbath across the North and South for four years during the Civil War. All told, 750,000 people died, with an average of over 500 deaths a day. Death collected its highest three-day body count during the Battle of Gettysburg, July 1 to 3, 1863, with roughly 50,000 soldiers losing their lives. If ghosts hang around because they're unhappy or not ready to go, then it's no wonder the small southern Pennsylvania town seems to be overpopulated with them. The battlefield was littered with bloodied bodies left without proper burials.

Whatever you believe about ghosts, visiting a place where so much trauma occurred leaves an impression. As I stood where the soldiers once did on a recent trip to Gettysburg, it was hard not to let the image of thousands of mercilessly slaughtered men enter my mind. Some visitors have reported seeing apparitions and hearing phantom groans of wounded soldiers. As such, Gettysburg has no shortage of ghost tours—and most of them got their start at one of the most haunted locations in town: the Farnsworth House Inn.

Farnsworth House Inn is the center of many Civil War–era ghost stories in Gettysburg, Pennsylvania.

Riddled with bullet holes still visible in its brick wall beneath the garret, the bed-and-breakfast is located near Cemetery Hill and the historic battlefield. When new owners purchased the inn in the early 1970s, their eldest daughter, Patty, discovered she had a sensitivity to ghosts and began hearing their stories in her dreams. She invited the paranormal investigator Lorraine Warren to inspect the inn and give her a crash course in the supernatural. Warren detected a malicious presence in the basement and painted a cross on the door to keep it contained. Perhaps Patty saw this cursed space as a blessing. She opened a séance room in the cellar, dressed as a Confederate widow, and started sharing the stories she'd gathered. And thus, a Gettysburg ghost tour industry was born.

"There are a lot of reasons for this place to be haunted," says Niki Saunders, a paranormal investigator and employee at the Farnsworth. "I mean, there was literally blood rolling down the street. A lot of bodies and piles—a lot of death here."

Of the tens of thousands who died in the battle, one of those bodies belonged to the lone civilian casualty. Jennie Wade was minding her business, kneading dough in her kitchen, when a Confederate sharpshooter perched in the Farnsworth's attic fired a shot that pierced two doors and zipped through the twenty-year-old's kitchen, striking her dead. Wade is known to haunt her own house—in fact, visitors can still see a floorboard with her blood on it—but she has also appeared before guests at the Farnsworth. Perhaps she's been looking for the man whose rifle took her life; the soldiers who holed up at the inn are allegedly still there. The sight of blood and its coppery scent have been experienced by guests, as have the sounds of gunshots, bodies dragging across the floor, and soldiers stomping back and forth through the hallways. Their ghosts have even been known to tie people's shoelaces together to make them fall. It sounds immature for a soldier, but those soldiers weren't much older than boys. Or maybe they learned from the ghost of a little boy who died at the inn.

Jeremy, age six or seven, found out the hard way that playing chicken in the street with a horse and carriage is a bad idea. After a devastating accident, he was picked up by an adult on the scene and brought to the Farnsworth's main bedroom, where a staff nurse, Mary, cared for him. Someone fetched his father, who raced over and held his son in his arms as he passed away. There at the inn, as the tale goes, he stayed forever.

"Jeremy is one of our most beloved ghosts," says Vivian Vega, the housekeeping supervisor and ghost tour guide at the Farnsworth. "Everybody likes to bring him toys."

He's been known to move objects, knock on doors, throw things in the room to get people's attention, and, yes, play with the toys people bring him. Vega has had her own interaction with the ghost by giving him a ball and some blocks.

"'Okay, Jeremy, if you're here go ahead and jump those blocks,'" she has told him. "And three times that ball jumped over blocks. So I know that he's here and loves to play. People seem to enjoy communicating with him."

Nurse Mary, who attended to Jeremy, might've stuck around too. Guests with headaches have felt a soothing, massagelike feeling on their temples. Another guest felt a similar sensation on his foot shortly after having surgery on his leg.

At least fourteen known entities are believed to haunt the Farnsworth, and

"People say it doesn't happen, but yeah, it does. They're here. I can tell you that. Clanking in the kitchen when no one's in the kitchen, apparitions appearing and walking through walls. Images of shoes and boots appearing on the main entrance stairway. *Yeah*, it happens."

—Vivian Vega, housekeeping supervisor and tour guide at the Farnsworth House Inn, in July 2020 so the site has attracted eager ghost hunters who expect some form of experience. For the most part, the ghosts at the inn are known to be a little nosy and prankish, but they're not malevolent. Not unless you give them a reason to be.

Vega recalled two particularly disrespectful guests, a man and his wife, who ran a blog about paranormal activity. During a late-night tour the man had antagonized the ghost of a former owner of the inn, Mr. Sweeney, in hopes that he'd make an appearance. The tour guide grew so disgusted with the guest's behavior that she ended the excursion and suggested he and his wife both return to their room.

"The next morning I'm waiting for him to come for breakfast. I was going to give him an earful," Vega said. "He comes in through the front door, from outside, not down from his room. I said, 'You were up early?' He said, 'No, we didn't stay here last night.' I said, 'And why not?' 'Well, we went on the tour, and I was being a dick to Mr. Sweeney. When I came back to my room I tripped over the doorway and fell on the floor and my face hit the floor on top of a rug. For ten minutes I couldn't get up, like my head was being pushed into the floor. My wife started to scream. As I looked up, my wife was being yanked by her legs like someone was pulling her. It scared the crap out of us and we went to stay with a friend an hour away."

Ghosts don't like rude people. Tour guides don't either, particularly when guests complain about a lack of sightings.

"I always tell people when I'm doing my tours here, we don't have a contract with the entities," says Saunders. "It's not like a TV show. If they choose to do something, we feel like we're getting a gift."

The appeal of seeing, hearing, or sensing the paranormal continues to support a robust industry of ghost tourism. Though results aren't guaranteed, sometimes a place's morbid history is enough to entice lovers of the paranormal.

## LaLaurie Mansion

For those with a dark curiosity, the LaLaurie Mansion in New Orleans's French Quarter does not disappoint. Louisiana aristocrat Madame Marie Delphine LaLaurie purchased the three-story Creole home at 1140 Royal Street in 1831 and outfitted it with elegant furniture, fine art, plenty of gold and silver, and a veneer of evil. It was said her manners were "sweet, gracious and captivating" as she played host to frequent parties, where lavish meals and flowing champagne made the house the social headquarters for the upper crust. But when the guests went on their merry way, the beautiful host turned into an ugly human who took pleasure in whipping and flogging slaves in her attic. There, she kept them chained to walls, wearing iron collars with spiked linings, and left them to starve. As an 1883 article described, LaLaurie would "amuse herself by cutting off their ears, tearing out their nails, and cutting out their tongues." I've spared you some of the other horrors.

Murmurs of Madame LaLaurie's sadistic ways spread. After all, how could people not hear or see the depravity through the ostentation? Sadly, guests and neighbors were afraid to interfere. The horrific stories were revealed only after a fire sent the house up in flames in 1834 and volunteer firefighters found seven of her tortured slaves dead and chained to the wall. LaLaurie fled the scene and escaped to France, where she lived out the rest of her days.

The home briefly became a school for girls later in the nineteenth century. Students complained of scratched arms and bruises. After the structure was reinvented as tenement apartments, horror struck again with the murder of a tenant in 1894.

Now known simply as "The Haunted House," the mansion is believed to be plagued by the restless spirits of the house. Moans and screams from the attic, along with a discomfiting presence, have been reported for more than two hundred years.

In 2007 these paranormal reports became selling points for the actor Nicolas Cage, who purchased the home for $3.4 million. "You know, other people have beachfront property; I have ghost front property," he said in a 2009 interview. He grew up a fan of Disney's Haunted Mansion and bought the New Orleans version to live out his childhood fantasy. Cage didn't experience any ghost encounters, but he did go bankrupt shortly after his purchase. Of course, that may have been due more to splurging on two European castles and a private island than to malevolent spirits.

Today the house is a fixture on New Orleans ghost tours and has gained renewed interest since becoming the subject of *American Horror Story* season three.

## Eastern State Penitentiary

If hauntings seem to happen in places where bad things have happened, it's no surprise that prisons have their fair share of paranormal activity. It's also not a shock that America's oldest penitentiary, Eastern State Penitentiary in Philadelphia, is considered the most haunted of them all. Standing outside its imposing thirty-foot stone walls and medieval-style turrets—complete with battlements designed purely for show—it's not hard to see why. Covering eleven acres and consuming a full city block, it's a step into a dark and evil past.

The prison began with the best of intentions. Before its grand opening in 1829, criminals were subjected to pillories, whippings, and other methods of reform that should've fallen under the "cruel and unusual" category of punishment. It's why Benjamin Franklin, Benjamin Rush, and Bishop William White founded the Philadelphia Society for Alleviating the Miseries of Public Prisons in 1787.

Eastern State Penitentiary was going to revolutionize the prison system. The big idea? Place all the prisoners in solitary confinement. Each would get their own tiny claustrophobic cell, allowing them all the time in the world to reflect on their wretched deeds and be penitent. Hence the name *peniten-*

Eastern State Penitentiary in Philadelphia was known for innovating solitary confinement in the nineteenth century—and torturous punishments that gave the prison its dark reputation.

*tiary.* A single skylight in each cell served as God's peepholes to his penitents. Guards got a good view, too, through Eastern State's innovative radial design. It allowed the spoke-like corridors to be easily visible at all times from a central rotunda.

The first prisoner in this system was a farmer who dared to steal a watch from the local magistrate. He, and each of the prisoners that followed, entered the penitentiary with a hood placed over his head to prevent him from gaining any sense of his surroundings. There was no talking to other prisoners and no visitations. Inmates stayed in their cells twenty-three hours a day. Despite the Philadelphia Society's efforts to alleviate misery, plenty of it remained.

Placing hoods over the heads of prisoners was just one of several extreme disciplinary tactics at Eastern State Penitentiary.

Beyond the hoods and isolation, there were disciplinary tools like the "iron gag" that made things even worse. One prisoner died in 1833 from the iron gag pressing on his jugular vein. The device, as described in 1835 by a Pennsylvania legislator, was "a rough iron instrument resembling the stiff bit of a blind bridle, having an iron palet in the centre, about an inch square, and chains at each end to pass round the neck and fasten behind."

The "mad chair" was another form of torture. It looked like something you'd sit in at the barber shop or dentist's office, but instead of merely getting a bad haircut or a root canal, inmates were strapped in tightly for days until their circulation was cut off. Sometimes it led to the amputation of limbs; other times, to insanity.

When Charles Dickens visited the United States in 1842, he made two stops: Niagara Falls and this place. He got a glimpse at nature's sheer beauty and man's utter ugliness all in one trip. Though the establishment of the prison aimed to fix the system, Dickens was not impressed, stating "those benevolent gentlemen who carry it into execution, do not know what it is that they are doing." Regarding the individual prisoners he stated, "He is a man buried alive, to be dug out in the slow round of years, and in the meantime dead to everything but torturing anxieties and horrible despair . . ."

Disease was its own form of added torture. In 1886, of the 1,713 convicts at Eastern State, hundreds suffered from bronchitis, syphilis, tuberculosis, or gonorrhea. Thirty-nine were writhing from "masturbation to injury." No further details were offered on the latter, aside from part of the "injury" being mental. The other ailments may have started from activities outside prison, but in time led to thirty-four deaths that year.

Suicides were not uncommon. In 1940, a prisoner hanged himself in his cell after he and nine other long-term convicts were caught digging a thirty-eight-foot tunnel when they were just two feet shy of its completion. An escape from life seemed preferable to further punishment.

In addition to aforementioned causes of death, murders, life sentences, and death row pushed the count to thousands of inmates within the twelve-foot-thick perimeter walls before the penitentiary's closing in 1971. If tales of ghostly figures and disembodied phantom heads seen by inmates and guards are to be believed, many prisoners were never freed from Eastern State Penitentiary, even in death. Then again, some of those sightings may have been influenced by the levels of insanity that were prevalent. But since the prison's reopening as a historical site in the early nineties, tourists have had similar experiences.

Eastern State Penitentiary prisoners were strapped to "mad chairs" for several days until their circulation was cut off, occasionally resulting in amputations and madness.

The penitentiary's gruesome history and decaying corridors lined with rusting metal and flaking plaster make it the stuff of nightmares. Visitors who believe in ghosts are primed to attribute anything out of the ordinary here to spirits. Shadowy forms on the walls and echoes of women's laughter in the dirt-filled cells have been frequently reported. A prison locksmith, though, allegedly experienced the most powerful paranormal activity during restoration work in Cell Block 4 in the mid-nineties. While trying to remove a 140-year-old padlock, he sensed an evil presence and eerie energy in the cell, as if he'd been caught in a swirl of souls that froze him in his tracks. Hundreds of tormented faces appeared on the walls and a mysterious fog seemed to draw him in, almost like he was suddenly having an out-of-body experience. The locksmith never got the padlock off, but ghosts of the prison's macabre past, it seemed, had been freed.

## Trans-Allegheny Lunatic Asylum

The inmates at Eastern State Penitentiary led rough lives within the prison's walls, but their lingering spirits might feel better if they could swap stories with the ghosts of the Trans-Allegheny Lunatic Asylum in Weston, West Virginia. Spanning nine acres of long, staggered wings and four floors, it's believed to host many ghosts. The psychiatric hospital opened in 1864 and, like the penitentiary, owns a rather repulsive history. The insanity of its patients was matched only by the insanity of the conditions and treatments administered during their stay.

Let's start with syphilis. Before the invention of penicillin, patients dealing with the disease were treated with malaria. Introducing this second illness to a patient would trigger a fever high enough to kill off the syphilis bacteria. Other patients were treated with hydrotherapy, wrapped tightly in their bedsheets and submerged in hot or cold water. Some were strapped in a chair and spun around to increase the "good" blood flow to the brain. Bloodletting and electroshock therapy were common, as were orgasms for women patients administered by the asylum's own brand of vibrators. And then there were the lobotomies. Too many lobotomies.

Walter Freeman, the father of the lobotomy, had a field day at the asylum—and at many others across the country, in fact. In 1954 he toured West Virginia's institutions and by the end of the year ensured the state could boast more lobotomized patients per capita than any other in the country. With his trusty ice pick in hand and a little electricity to knock patients out, it only took him a few minutes to go in through the eye socket, give the handle a firm tap with a hammer, and pluck out a chunk of brain. Sometimes he tapped too hard and the transorbital lobotomy left patients forgetting how to speak or use the bathroom.

Among these poor souls were the types you might expect to fill an asylum: schizophrenics, epileptics, and the criminally insane, to name a few. But it seemed most anyone could be discarded from society and dumped into the asylum's many wards. A list showing the "Reasons for Admission" from 1864 to 1889 included such maladies as "seduction & disappointment," "marriage of son," "over study of religion," and "parents were cousins."

No matter their supposed disorder, they all shared the struggle of wretched living conditions. In 1938, for example, there were 1,641 patients being treated by just five physicians, six assistants, and nine nurses. For much of the asylum's existence the patients had little heat, no air-conditioning, and insufficient clothing, lighting, and furniture. Even a condemned building continued housing male patients for five years. Needless to say, thousands of patients died there, surely with little to no sanity left.

The Trans-Allegheny Lunatic Asylum in Weston, West Viriginia, was the scene of many horrors, including bloodletting, electroshock therapy, and lobotomies.

Like at Eastern State Penitentiary, both staff and patients experienced the paranormal within the asylum's walls, whether it was strange lights or shadows, or just spooky energy permeating the wards. Some patients enjoyed stringing up a bedsheet across a hallway and watching for shadow forms to appear. Others refused to sleep, believing they were being haunted. The asylum closed its doors in 1994, but was purchased and reopened for historical purposes in 2007. People visit to learn about the asylum, but many come for the ghosts that remain active.

Night event manager Valarie Myers has experienced a lot of them. But the encounter that was "all of the above as far as a terrifying, confusing, mind-blowing, holy-shit-what-was-that sort of situation" happened on consecutive nights in 2017. It started with Myers suddenly feeling dizzy while observing a group of ghost hunters on the fourth floor. She assumed it was nothing but then she felt a burning sensation on her lower back to the right of her spine. It grew so intense she finally had a coworker inspect the area. Myers discovered that she had an abrasion or burn about four inches long and nearly an inch wide. The next night during a tour in the same part of the building, her right arm started burning.

"I shifted my flashlight onto my right arm and both my assistant manager and myself watched three welts develop down my arm," Myers recalls.

She's hardly alone in experiencing strange phenomena. Spirits have been both seen and heard by many. Numerous guests on the second floor, for example, have caught the name "Jane" on recordings and perceived it whispered in their ears. Records showed that a Jane Harvey was a patient in that ward in the 1890s. She hanged herself in her room with a pillowcase.

Over in the children's ward, spirits have been known to get playful during ghost tours. One night as a group of eighteen made its way through the corridor, a ball rolled out of a room on the left side, about three-quarters of the way down the hallway. It stopped in the middle of the path. Just as the tour guide calmed the startled group, a second ball rolled out of the same room and stopped just beyond the first. The first ball then rolled a few feet back toward the room from where it came. No one was in the room. The guide checked for drafts and tested the floor to see if there was an uneven spot that might have caused the balls to roll, but there was nothing to explain the event. Attempts to recreate the phenomenon failed.

If the soul can survive death then surely some of these former patients are causing some of the disturbances at the asylum. Myers suspects some of the experiences may also be due to what's known as the "stone tape theory." The name comes from the title of a 1972 British TV movie, which was inspired by ideas put forth in a 1961 book called *Ghost and Ghoul* by English archeologist and parapsychologist Thomas Charles Lethbridge. In the film, a research team sees a ghost in an old Victorian house and determines it's a psychic impression recorded in a stone wall. A "stone tape," if you will. Lethbridge never used the term but he had suggested that apparitions might be nothing more than a recording of an event in an environment. Through "a sort of surrounding ether" he believed these moments could be stored in rock and other substances and might capture electrical discharges from especially traumatic or emotional moments. This residual energy is like a memory captured in a place that gets replayed and perceived by others. Parapsychologist and paranormal investigator Loyd Auerbach describes it as being similar to watching an old movie from the thirties. All those actors still look the same on film today, even though they've since aged and passed on.

"It may be that certain people have more sensitivity to the recordings so the phenomena may not be observed every time the physical conditions are met," Auerbach explains. "Throw in the possible influences of mood and belief of the observers, and the perceptions can be affected even more."

No one knows how, if at all, these recordings might actually work, but if Lethbridge's supposition is correct, Myers may be in the middle of a massive ghost media center. She notes that the asylum is made from blue sandstone—it happens to be the largest hand-cut stone masonry building in North America—and that there's a high concentration of quartz in the ground in the Weston area. Both contain silica, which is known to be a good semiconductor and might be capable of capturing human energy. "Take that as you will, as far as stone tape goes," Myers says.

This type of residual activity is believed to explain hauntings in general. Ghosts don't create them; the living do. Shadowy forms and ghostly figures could be these types of historical imprints.

The dark, dank conditions around the asylum, along with the overall creepiness of the place, might also lead to experiences people believe are paranormal. "Being primed for it is an environmental cause," Myers says. "But it doesn't explain the welts on my skin or the ball rolling."

This paranormal stew of dark history, environmental conditions, and spirits extends far beyond asylums, prisons, and other ominous places. It even happens at the residence of those who devote their lives to God.

An illicit affair between a twelfth-century monk and nun, and their torturous deaths in a monastery that once stood on the property, led to centuries of terror at Borley Rectory in England.

## Borley Rectory

Across the pond in England, one of the country's most famous hauntings mixes poltergeists, a twelfth-century monastery, the ghosts of an executed nun and her beheaded husband, and a house that committed suicide. Welcome to Borley Rectory, which renowned ghost hunter and psychical researcher Harry Price called the "most haunted house in England."

Like any good haunted house, it has its lore. In this case, it began in 1863 when Reverend Henry Dawson Ellis Bull allegedly built the infamous rectory on the site of the aforementioned monastery in rural northeast England. In the seventeenth century, so the story goes, one of the monks got distracted from prayer and contemplation by a rather fetching nun from a nearby convent. The two fell for each other and rendezvoused in the woods for a little clandestine canoodling. Their scandalous affair led to an elopement with the help of a friendly coachman, but the pair were soon missed. The sweethearts were quickly found, brought back, and severely punished. For the sin of falling in love and breaking her vows, the nun was walled up alive in the convent and her beau, as already noted, was disposed of much quicker by beheading. So was their coachman accomplice.[7]

With their deaths, a legend was born (and perhaps embellished over the years).

In 1929 a *Daily Mirror* reporter invited Price to join an investigation of Borley's current rector Reverend Guy Eric Smith's claims of shadowy figures, spooky noises, and other paranormal phenomena. Price accepted with reserved enthusiasm.

---

7    History later revealed that there was no monastery on the site of the rectory, though monks may have been in the area. When they were, however, it was at a time before the era of coaches.

"My experience told me to look for a mischievous adolescent, rats, practical jokers—or the village idiot," he later wrote. "I have wasted very many weeks in acquiring this knowledge."

Upon his arrival, Price unloaded his ghost-hunting kit and began exploring the large two-story Victorian house situated on nine acres of land.[8] Interviews with the staff revealed that at least one of the maids had seen the spectral nun in her flowing white veil walking near the house. Others claimed to have been awakened by movements in their bedrooms and witnessed wraiths reclining next to them. Price also learned that Reverend Harry Bull, son of Henry Dawson Ellis, had died at the rectory in 1927 and a few others had stayed more than a few months since then. Mrs. Smith, the rector's wife, said that shortly before Bull's death, he often spoke of a "remarkable experience" while walking outside the rectory. "Suddenly he heard the sound of horses' hoofs, and on looking round he saw an old-time coach coming up the road driven by two headless men," she recounted.

That evening at dusk, Price and the newspaperman waited outside in hopes of catching a glimpse of the notorious nun and her decapitated lover. After an hour the reporter excitedly grabbed the ghost hunter's arm and whispered that he'd seen her.

"Sure enough there appeared to be a shadowy figure gliding down the path under the trees," Price recalled. His co-investigator ran after it for a better look, but it "melted away" before he reached it. As the two reentered the house a pane of glass came crashing down from the roof, narrowly missing them. Other phenomena followed, just as advertised. Bells rang randomly. A candlestick flew down the stairs. Books, stones, and bricks were thrown. Throughout it all, Price found no signs of rats or rapscallions. The troublemaker, it seemed, was something much more unusual. All of it was enough to make the Smiths move out a month later.

Reverend Lionel Foyster and his wife, Marianne, were next in line to take on the rectory in 1930. Right on cue, the weirdness started on day one, including a voice calling Marianne's name, the sounds of footsteps, an apparition of Harry Bull, and disappearing jugs. As the days and weeks passed Foyster documented his experiences in a diary and managed to fill 180 pages. Though most were just creepy oddities, at times the phenomena became violent, like the time Marianne got yanked out of bed and suffered a black eye after getting socked by an "invisible assailant."

---

8    What's in Harry Price's ghost-hunting kit, you ask? He didn't have fancy gizmos with blinking lights and buzzers, but he did have a ball of string, a stick of chalk, a pair of soft felt overshoes, a steel measuring tape, white tape, dry batteries and switches (for secret electrical contacts), a camera, film and flashbulbs, infrared filters, a notebook, red, blue and black pencils, bandages, iodine and surgical adhesive tape, matches, a flashlight and candle, a bowl of mercury to detect tremors in room or passage, and, in case things got really out of hand, a flask of brandy.

Price returned to Borley in 1931 to meet with the Foysters, eager to hear their latest strange tales. His obsession with the rectory continued with visits throughout the decade, most notably in 1937 when he leased it for a year to facilitate a more thorough investigation. The ghost hunter found plenty of help after placing a classified ad titled "Haunted House" that sought "responsible persons of leisure and intelligence, intrepid, critical, and unbiased." Between Price's want-ad helpers and more than a hundred observers and two hundred witnesses over the years, he built up a pile of evidence, including scents of perfume stinking up the rooms, keys rotating in locks, red wine turning into ink, white wine turning into cologne, and scribbled pleas for help appearing on paper and walls.

Following Price's adventurous and fruitful ownership, the Borley Rectory was purchased by a retired army officer, Captain R. G. Gregson, who happened to enjoy psychical research. His new home would become his new hobby. Little occurred at first, but then one evening a lamp began to flicker. Was it faulty wiring or a bad bulb? Or was Gregson finally getting a peep of the paranormal?

"Ah," he exclaimed jubilantly, "a poltergeist at last! Let's see if you can do something spectacular." So it did. The lamp exploded, sprayed burning oil around the room, and ignited a fire that consumed the rectory. The "most haunted house in England" became known as the "house that committed suicide."

The "death" of the rectory, however, didn't mean the death of the ghosts. After all, they're already dead. When Price visited Borley in the aftermath of the fire he spoke with numerous witnesses who claimed to have seen "figures moving amongst the flames" near the window. Captain Gregson reported seeing them as well, stating two cloaked figures had exited the rectory during the fire and that the figure of a girl and a "formless figure" could be seen in the upper windows. He also stated he was alone in the house when the blaze began.

Price, who was an amateur magician and had exposed many mediums throughout his ghost-hunting adventures, found himself at a loss with the Borley case. There was no one answer for all the phenomena. He attributed the "stone-throwing, furniture-moving, bottle-dropping, hair-ruffling, bell-ringing, belt-raising, soap-pitching, and door-locking annoyances" to poltergeists, but believed other occurrences were caused by "the persisting remnants of the egos or personalities" associated with the rectory or the land it sat on. Ultimately, he summed up his theories by stating, "I can only say that I do not know. But I will also add that *no one knows.*"

In the mid-1950s, years after Price's passing in 1948, a new investigation by members of the Society of Psychical Research determined that their predecessor might have embellished a few stories and too often accepted hearsay as fact.

A reporter who'd once been silenced came forward in agreement. One night, during his own investigation alongside Price, he got suspicious of the ghost hunter after being hit on the head with a large pebble.

"After much noisy 'phenomena,' I seized Harry and found his pockets full of bricks and pebbles. This was one 'phenomena' he could not explain," the journalist said. His attempt to expose Price was stifled by lawyers who threatened to sue the newspaper for libel. So the story died.

In 1978 another team of investigators tracked down Marianne Foyster, then in her late seventies and living in Canada. She admitted that she and Lionel made up many of their stories, though she added some unusual things did occur that she didn't believe Lionel was behind. Marianne suspected that Price might have turned the ink into wine through sleight-of-hand magic. But while she questioned the ghost hunter, her own believability has been called into question.

"Marianne Foyster has never ever told the same story twice," explains English paranormal historian and writer Paul Adams.

Marianne, who was some thirty years Lionel's junior, had at times claimed there were no ghosts and that her husband was just a forgetful man who'd blame spirits for moving things around. In addition, graphologists determined the writings on the wall were done in Marianne's hand, possibly because she was simply bored there and liked stirring up excitement. Aside from ghosts, she also found entertainment in the form of an affair with a man closer to her age. Lionel knew about the relationship and may have participated as a voyeur. Shortly after leaving Borley—and taking their hanky-panky away from the church—the Foysters needed money, so Marianne began a new affair with a wealthy commercial trader and married him bigamously. Lionel pretended to be her father, and all seemed to be going just fine until the new husband learned the truth and had a nervous breakdown. Considering Marianne's proclivity for mischievousness and ever-changing stories, Adams understandably considers her an unreliable witness. But her antics certainly add to the intrigue of Borley Rectory.

"It's absolutely mad," Adams says of the entire crazy cast of characters. "It's like a soap opera. Not even *Eastenders* would dream up something like this. It really is bizarre, but that's why we love it."

Perhaps Price got caught up in the excitement, or maybe the rectory was a bit of a golden goose for him. The investigations led to numerous books and articles, along with appearances on the radio and television. If there's any truth to him being sneaky with a few pebbles and magic tricks to help keep the public's interest alive, maybe it was worth it.

Why are we so fascinated with visiting old prisons, asylums, and other haunted locations? And why do we revel in standing in the very spot where horror took place? Sociologist and author Margee Kerr suggests it might have something to do with how we see ourselves in comparison.

"People like opportunities to feel a sense of righteousness in a way, that they're on the right side—they're the good guys," she says. "They're not like these evil people that did horrible things. They would never do that. You can feel good that you're on the right track."

That righteousness comes with the thrill of possibly experiencing the unknown and opening your imagination to what might be possible. Not to mention evoking a bit of teenage rebellion. "You feel a little edgy for trying to contact the supernatural or just being in places you're not supposed to be," Kerr adds.

For many who seek out such thrills, there's also just a simple love of being scared. As the founder and owner of Boroughs of the Dead: Macabre New York City Walking Tours, Andrea Janes shares ghost stories with these folks for a living. "They want to experience fear because it's a delicious feeling," she says. "It's a delightful little shiver when you get all that luscious exquisiteness of feeling horror in a setting that is completely safe and completely controlled and doesn't actually threaten or imperil you in any way."

Those feelings aren't just a reaction to morbid curiosity; we're actually wired to feel this way. Fear releases dopamine. This might sound strange given that dopamine is a chemical that plays a role in feeling pleasure. In the case of fear, its release might be the brain's way of letting us know we're surviving a fright. That makes us feel good, so dopamine is just doing its job. Combine that with a dose of adrenaline, and wandering through a haunted house that *probably* isn't haunted gives us a good rush.

Sometimes, though, the scariest phenomena don't revolve around places. They revolve around people. Not understanding how or why the paranormal is happening leads to real feelings of danger. For these victims, the frights are not fun at all.

# THE REAL HORROR
# OF AMITYVILLE

In the wee hours of the morning on November 13, 1974, Ronald DeFeo picked up his high-powered rifle, marched through his two-story home, and brutally slaughtered his parents and four siblings as they slept in their beds. During his trial he claimed voices told him to do it, but the jury didn't buy his insanity plea and sentenced the troubled twenty-four-year-old to six life sentences. DeFeo's life, for all intents and purposes, was over. But the horror in Amityville was just beginning.

Thirteen months later, George and Kathy Lutz moved their family into the Dutch Colonial house in the quiet village situated on the south shore of New York's Long Island. Their dream home quickly became anything but. Strange noises, disconnected telephones, mysterious flocks of flies, a phantom flying pig with glowing red eyes, drops of green slime, and other spooky phenomena were enough to send the family fleeing after twenty-eight days.

The Lutzes shared their story with the press and attracted paranormal investigators, most notably Ed and Lorraine Warren. As self-proclaimed "demonologists," the Warrens inspected the house and found something unsettling.

"In our judgment, there was a spirit that had plagued the Lutzes in the house," Ed said. "But, no ghost was present. The 'spirit' was inhuman." By inhuman he meant a spirit that "has never walked the earth in human form" had caused all the commotion.

Another paranormal investigator, Hans Holzer, visited the home in 1977 accompanied by a trance medium. The psychic claimed an angry Native American chief was responsible for the trouble, allegedly because the home had been built on a sacred burial site. Holzer believed in his medium and worked with the local historical society and librarian to find evidence of a chieftain in the area.

The Amityville Horror house is one of the most recognizable haunted houses in pop culture. Its legend was stoked by former owners George and Kathy Lutz and famed demonologists Ed and Lorraine Warren.

Local Native Americans, however, disagreed with the suggestion and said there were no records of burial grounds in Amityville.

These explorations fueled hype building up to *The Amityville Horror*'s book release and subsequent movie adaptation. Suddenly, Amityville became America's scariest place. Especially for the neighbors. Curiosity seekers made the pilgrimage to Long Island from all over the country. One group came dressed in hooded black robes carrying crosses and candles, totally prepared to face evil, and then marched around the wrong house. A do-gooder brought a goat on a leash to eat the house's nefarious spirits. And then there was just about everyone else: executives, teachers, cops, doctors, you name it. They came day and night, roaming the street in their cars, asking for directions, clogging traffic, taking photographs, and building up the blood pressure and anger of residents trying to just live peaceful lives. The horror in Amityville was real.

One woman responded to a stranger's plea for help finding the house by calmly telling him,

"You're a stupid, gullible, ignorant, pea-brained boob!"

Another remarked that "the only true thing in that book is the address."

The Lutzes' lawyer would've agreed. He claimed the whole affair was nothing more than a commercial venture. "We created this horror story over many bottles of wine that George was drinking," he told the Associated Press in 1979. "We were creating something the public would want to hear about."

Barbara and James Cromarty, who bought the home just months after the Lutzes skedaddled, were especially disgusted by all the hoopla. When they heard the book was coming out they knew the invasion of morbid tourists would only get worse.

"We begged them not to print it," Barbara said after the publisher sent them galley proofs, "and they told us, in legal terminology, to go to hell."

As far as the Cromartys and the rest of the neighbors were concerned, they were already there.

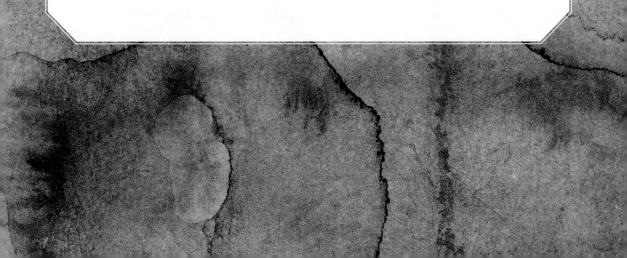

## The Telekinetic Temper Tantrums of Living Poltergeists

In the fall of 2013, a family in rural North Carolina sought medical help for their eleven-year-old boy. He didn't seem ill; he just happened to make electronic devices go haywire whenever he was near. The doctor didn't have a prescription for that, so he reached out to parapsychologists at the Rhine Research Center in Durham, North Carolina, for help.

By the following January, John Kruth, executive director of the Rhine, assembled an investigative team and visited the boy to witness the claims for themselves. The phenomena proved just as odd and wondrous as described.

"The electronics in his house would go wild whenever he went near them," Kruth says, certain that trickery could not explain all the observable disturbances. "The phone would ring when he walked by it, over and over again. He couldn't touch cell phones. Smoke alarms would go off when he walked by them. The TV remote would do strange things whenever he was holding it."

The boy's peculiar relationship with electronics followed him wherever he went. At school he'd walk by a printer and it would spit paper out all over the floor. Tests administered on computers would malfunction, forcing teachers to make him take exams only after his classmates finished. Those same teachers thought he was a prankster determined to sabotage the school's computer system.

Kruth considered the case to be a poltergeist. The term is German for "noisy ghost" and dates back to the mid-nineteenth century. These strange happenings are often thought to be provoked by some sort of mischievous spirit, as experienced at Borley Rectory. But parapsychologists distinguish these types of cases from others. Instead of being caused by the dead, the occurrences are believed to be induced by the living. To be more specific, where there's a poltergeist, there's typically someone going through some form of emotional, psychological stress. That stress is rooted in the subconscious mind and gets manifested through psychokinetic abilities. Since it happens repeatedly during these stressful periods, it's been termed recurrent spontaneous psychokinesis (RSPK). In Loyd Auerbach's words, "You can think of a poltergeist scenario as a telekinetic temper tantrum."

As the North Carolina boy's experiences continued, he became sensitive to how they affected people around him and the resulting comments directed toward him. He developed anxiety, and the whole situation caused the family distress. Plus the bills were piling up from all the damaged electronic devices. They didn't care why or how it was happening, they just wanted it to stop.

So Kruth sought to ease the anxiety. "I taught him some relaxation techniques, some breathing exercises, some mindfulness, and within a week things subsided."

"The strange thing about PK is you can feel it happening. You can feel the pressure. It builds and it builds and it's almost like your ears are popping. And then it builds to a point where it has to build so far, something has to give in the atmosphere. I felt that and a light bulb popped above my head."

—Robyn Wilson, a paranormal investigator with psychic abilities, describing an example of a psychokinesis experience in 2020

The family was relieved, and Kruth considered the treatment a success from a psychological point of view, though from a scientific parapsychological point of view he would've liked to study the activity in a lab, run some tests, and understand more about how it worked. "But that wasn't my purpose here," he notes, "my purpose was to try to help the family."

The idea of poltergeists typically conjures visions of moving chairs and randomly thrown objects, not malfunctioning printers. That's with good reason. After all, those types of cases have been recorded for nearly two thousand years. In his 1951 book, *Haunted People*, Hereward Carrington documents more than 360 of them, dating back to a German case in 355 AD. And that's just in one chapter. Charles Fort, author of the 1919 *Book of the Damned* and several other books compiling tales of anomalous phenomena, reported his fair share of poltergeists as well. One example from 1921 involved a family in London with an unfortunate situation involving exploding coal. When police were called to investigate, Fort reported that the volatile coal also "hopped out of grates and sauntered along floors" and "fell in showers in other rooms, having passed through walls, without leaving signs of this passage."

Though "telekinetic temper tantrums" can be thrown by all types of people, frequently they're linked to mental stress and the physical changes of puberty. Yes, teenagers are often at the center of poltergeist cases, just like Stephen King's *Carrie*—only these cases aren't works of fiction. Well, depending on what you choose to believe, that is. Some of these kids might just be clever mischief-makers.

Dr. Nandor Fodor, a psychoanalyst and psychical researcher, studied many poltergeist cases in the early- to mid-twentieth century, often involving teens, and could not chalk it all up to hoaxes. In 1960 he proclaimed, "Psychic phenomena do exist. Biology will have to revise some of its concepts. It will have to admit to a force in the human body that can move objects at a distance without muscular contact."

It all sounds fantastic, but Fodor saw what he saw and saw no other explanation. In 1958, for example, he investigated the Herrmann family on Long Island, New York, where the strange happenings included an assortment of flying objects: sugar bowls; a seventy-five-pound bookcase (full of books); a dresser; a record player; and, much to the family's chagrin, their collection of eighteenth-century ceramic figurines. The Herrmanns had not one, but two teenagers in the house—a situation that's usually stressful enough without inanimate stuff randomly springing to life.

Fodor didn't have a scientific explanation of how exactly this psychic force worked, but he believed that within adolescents, "a side-tracking of the sexual energies in a maturing body may be responsible for the explosive manifestation" and added that such episodes could include a "schizophrenic character." In other words, teenagers exhibiting RSPK might have a part of their minds or personalities dissociating during their poltergeist moments, all stemming from repressed frustrations or desires.

The family dealing with the exploding coal conundrum included three children, and though Fort didn't research explanations for his cases, he certainly unearthed many accounts of poltergeists involving adolescents. He topped his burning coal story with that of a twelve-year-old California boy who, in 1886, caused a stir by setting things on fire "by his glance." His antics, whether through RSPK or sneaky mean-spiritedness, led to a swift expulsion from school. Fort noted a similarly infernal story that occurred a year later in a town in New Brunswick, Canada, concerning a family with four children, two nieces, and forty fires blazing within a few hours. "The fires can be traced to no human agency, and even the most skeptical are staggered," one newspaper reported.

Extraordinary as these poltergeists seem, a few cases over the past two centuries have levitated to the top of the list in the world of paranormal phenomena. We'll start in the early 1800s, with the one Nandor Fodor called "the greatest American ghost story": the Bell Witch of Robertson County, Tennessee. Like many poltergeists, it began with knockings, scratchings, and other strange noises. But unlike other such cases, this one ended in murder.

## The Bell Witch of Tennessee

John Bell was "an honest, God-fearing" Christian farmer who tended hundreds of acres of land as he and his wife, Lucy, raised their five sons and two daughters. All was well until 1817, when their family was joined by a mysterious presence. The manifestation quickly progressed from creepy sounds to creepier physical contact to the ability to speak in a whispery voice. Though the Bell family had initially kept the disturbances private, the town eventually heard about the phenomena and visitors came to experience things for themselves. Whatever it was, it became known as the Bell Witch.

Much of the entity's malicious activity began to focus on the Bell's youngest daughter, Betsy, who was fourteen at the time. She was described as "fit and proper for a tall, pretty girl with eyes blue as the sky, skin like cream and rose leaves, and the finest yellow hair." Everyone

THE BELL WITCH

Strange Doings of a Talking Goblin

UNSOLVED MYSTERY

Facts Authenticated by Living Witnesses

Sustained by the Evidence of People of Unquestioned Integrity in This County.

The *Democratic Herald* chronicles the legend of the Bell Witch, a poltergeist-like entity that initially haunted the Bell family in early-nineteenth-century Tennessee. She would later inspire *The Blair Witch Project*.

liked Betsy, except, of course, the Bell Witch. It didn't approve of her relationship with a neighborhood boy and showed its disdain by pulling her hair,
pinching her, and slapping her face with enough force to leave fingerprints
on her cheeks—all while shouting "I tell you, don't marry Joshua Gardner!"
The witch, it seemed, had an affinity for getting involved in people's personal
business. Not only did it shame Betsy in front
of her parents, but it dished out secrets about
all the local townsfolk. Accusations of ventriloquism were lobbed at Betsy, but a witness
placed his hand over her mouth as the voice
spoke and had no effect.

The witch continued to plague the young
girl by sticking her with invisible pins until
she shrieked and throwing her into spasmodic
trances that lasted up to an hour. Physicians
who examined her said she was perfectly
healthy.

As the months passed, the entity only got
louder and behaved in increasingly bizarre
ways. According to early published reports on
the case, the witch could "quote scripture in a
way to astound the most learned minister" and
it "became profane and ribald, howled, sang and
swore, and, worse still, became a fearful toper,
filling the room with her tipsy breath."

This illustration of the Bell Witch appeared in a 1935 edition of the *Des Moines Register*.

All the commotion caught the attention of
General Andrew Jackson, under whom one of
Bells' sons fought in the Battle of New Orleans. The future president arrived
with his entourage and joined the family for a lovely dinner and delightful
small talk, but he grew impatient when the Bell Witch failed to show up. One
of his men took responsibility for the peace and quiet. Armed with a silver
bullet in his pistol, the man considered himself a "witch tamer" and thought
the entity wouldn't dare make an appearance in his presence. The seemingly
omnipresent Bell Witch heard his braggadocio and swiftly let him know
it didn't care for it. The man suddenly jumped from his chair, grabbing his
behind, and shouted, "Boys, I am being stuck by a thousand pins!"

"I am in front of you—shoot!" the voice said. The witch tamer tried but
his pistol wouldn't fire. The Bell Witch, it was said, slapped his face repeatedly
as it shouted, "It's my night for fun!" Crying in pain, the man made a run for
it and escaped the house. General Jackson loved it. He told John he'd never

encountered something so amusing and mysterious and asked if he could stay another week. The Bell Witch told him to go to bed and promised to attack another of Jackson's men the next evening.

Over time the witch introduced itself as several different entities, ranging from the spirit of an evil stepmother to a Native American spirit whose bones had been disturbed to an early settler who'd buried gold and silver on the Bell property and wanted to give it to Betsy. Eventually a minister got the entity to admit to, or settle on, being the spirit of an eccentric neighbor whom John had once quarreled with, known as Old Kate Batts. And it intended to torment John to death.

Betsy's father was already mentally agonized by the Bell Witch's mischievous antics, but its wrath soon affected him physically with a series of odd ailments beyond what others had experienced. It began with a strange swelling of his tongue that rendered speech and swallowing nearly impossible, which was exacerbated by twitchings throughout his whole body. This went on for about a year—and then things took a sharp turn for the worse. One fall morning John stepped out of the house and had his shoes suddenly snatched from his feet. According to a newspaper retelling, "he was beaten and twisted until there came upon him a seizure so violent that when at last he got home he had to take to his bed."

Pleased with its work, the Bell Witch exclaimed, "I have got him this time, he will never get up from that bed again." True to its word, he didn't. John Bell eventually slipped into a coma and succumbed to death on December 20, 1820. The Bell Witch celebrated with "bloodcurdling shrieks of triumph" and claimed to have finished the job with a dose of poison. The next day a small dark vial with a strange liquid was found in the medicine cabinet. Puzzled by the potion, the doctor gave the family cat a taste and it dropped dead within minutes.

Afterward the Bell Witch calmed down, but it continued to pester Betsy about her love for Joshua Gardner. She eventually broke off her engagement in fear of the entity's wrath.

The story of the Bell Witch wasn't written down till thirty years after the fact, at which time Richard Williams Bell, who was six when the events began, recorded the manifestations in a diary he titled "Our Family Trouble." His account was published in 1894, after the last of John's children had passed away. Naturally, the facts might be a little fuzzy, but the story has held intrigue for two hundred years and the true cause remains a mystery.

Nandor Fodor saw several possibilities. Either the whole thing was a hoax, the witch was a spirit using Betsy as a medium for contact, or it was a split in Betsy's personality, a "Betsy-X on the rampage." He ruled out the first option, claiming "if human testimony has any value, hoax or imposture cannot be considered as a serious explanation." That, of course, left him with the more-difficult-to-explain notion of a spirit or unknown force capable of producing phenomena from the subconscious mind. He opted for the latter: "As the physical manifestations seem to be closely linked with the biological upheaval caused by the onset of Elizabeth's puberty, John Bell's illness looks like a strange echo of the psychic tempest that was being loosed from his daughter's unconscious."

The Bell Witch, Fodor concluded, was part of Betsy Bell. Accepting this meant recognizing that "we have to revise our notions regarding the scope of activity and powers of dissociated personalities, and the very nature of this dissociation."

Assuming he was correct, why was Betsy's subconscious dead set on killing her father? Fodor suspected sexual abuse. If it occurred when she was very young, she may have successfully repressed it "until the shock of puberty produced a regressive earthquake." Fodor admits this is pure speculation, as no allegations of abuse were ever made. But then, speculation is all anyone has to piece together how a violent, murderous, Bible-quoting, gossiping entity bullied the Bell family.

Though the trigger of Betsy's experience remains unknown, a century later a Romanian teenager traced the beginning of her living nightmare to buying a piece of candy. That night, in 1925, fourteen-year-old Eleonore Zügun discovered what appeared to be a demonic spirit possessing her. She had paid for the sweets with a silver coin found in the woods, despite her grandmother's wishes.

"If you spend that coin may the devil haunt you!" the elder woman threatened.

And so, it seems, it did. Shortly after the curse Eleonore and her mother watched red welts appear upon her arm, forming letters that spelled *Dracu*, the Romanian word for "devil." Things only got weirder from there. Dishes fell off shelves and zipped across rooms, and tables would suddenly jolt off the ground. Wherever Eleonore went these occurrences followed—all of which made her a rather unpopular girl in the village. Neighbors closed their windows and shut their doors whenever they saw her coming, echoing her grandmother's taunts of the devil. Just in case Eleonore had in fact been possessed, the village priest attempted an exorcism but had no luck. Out of ideas, he sent the poor "devil girl" off to an insane asylum. The villagers rejoiced and freely opened their doors and windows again. Eleonore, on the other hand, did not share in their joy and continued producing paranormal effects at the asylum until an Austrian parapsychologist, Countess Zoë Wassilko-Serecki, heard of the case and rescued Eleonore from the institution. The staff, like the

# Scratches on Her Face Left by the Evil Spirit's Claws

## Perplexing Case of Little Eleanore and Her "Poltergeist" That Smashes Dishes, Throws Things Around, and Marks Her Skin With Its Unseen Fingers

*Frequently Little Eleanore Complains That Her "Devil," or "Dracu," as She Calls It, Is Scratching Her Face With Its Invisible Claws. And, Sure Enough, in a Moment or So Scratches and Welts, Like Those Which Would Follow Contact With Sharp Talons, Appear Upon the Child's Skin Without Any Visible Reason to Account for Them.*

LONDON, Dec. 5.

A LITTLE fourteen-year-old Rumanian peasant girl named Eleanore Zugun has thoroughly mystified a number of sober scientists who have been trying to find out why furniture dances, small metal objects whiz through the air and plates smash themselves on the floor and walls when she is around. Also why needles jump out of workbaskets and are, apparently, stuck in her arms and cheeks by an invisible hand.

Even stranger than all this, welts suddenly appear on her face and arms, and now and then these curious markings assume the shape of letters. Sometimes the welts are red and scratchy, just as though they were made by talons of a claw or long fingernails scraping the skin.

All these curious happenings take place in full sunlight or in the glare of electric.

The committee which examined Eleanore at the National Laboratory for Physical Research here included Professor William MacDougall, of Harvard University; Professor A. C. Baskine and Hans Thirring, of Vienna; Doctors R. Y. Tillyard and Alfred Eddows, distinguished English scientists, and Dr. Henry Price, the director of the laboratory. They were able to find no trace of trickery, either conscious or unconscious, and while they decidedly do not believe that the strange happenings are caused by any "poltergeist" or malicious spirit which has attached itself to little Eleanore, they are inclined to think that she has demonstrated the possession of some force within her which is able to move objects beyond the reach of her hands.

Nor do they believe that the marks which appear upon her body are made by the unseen claws of any demonic attendant. They say that they belong to a class of little understood mental phenomena whereby the mind is able of itself to cause "stigmata" or marks to appear upon the skin without the use of any instrument. History has recorded a number of such cases, among the most notable of which are the wounds of the Crucifixion which are said to have appeared on the hands and feet of St. Francis of Assisi.

But Eleanore is firmly convinced that she is accompanied wherever she goes by a playfully malicious demon, a "poltergeist," as the Germans call it. Eleanore is not afraid of "it," whatever it is. When "it" is good she leaves out food at night which she believes it likes. When "it" is naughty she leaves out food which she thinks it detests as a punishment.

The devil, according to her story, was saddled on her by a grandmother's thoughtless "curse." Up to about eighteen months ago she was a perfectly normal child with no more "spook" to make her conspicuous. Then one day, while she and her brother were on their way to visit their grandmother, she found a silver coin in the woods near her home. She showed the grandmother the money and told her that she was going to buy some candy with it.

"You must not do that. It does not belong to you!" ordered the old woman. "But I want to," said stubborn little Eleanore. The man had a quarrel about it, and at last the grandmother, thinking to frighten her, exclaimed:

"If you spend that coin may the devil haunt you!"

But Eleanore was not to be frightened. On her way home she spent the money.

She had just returned to her home and was undressing to go to bed when she turned to her mother and said:

*The Countess Wassilko-Serecki, Who Took the Little "Devil Girl" From the Asylum Where Her Frightened Parents Had Sent Her.*

"Mother, I feel a hand on my arm. It is cold and has long nails and it is scratching my skin."

The mother began to laugh, but stopped as she watched with amazed eyes what appeared to be red welts rising on the little girl's arm. They were exactly like those which appear on tender skin after a scratch from a blunt fingernail.

"Dracu." It is the Rumanian word for demon, or devil.

"A dracu! A devil!" the horrified mother cried. "Our Eleanore is possessed by a devil!"

From that time on all sorts of queer things happened in the Zugun household and everywhere else the child went. A heavy chair would begin to dance ponderously, a table would rear up like a frightened horse and lift off all it held to the floor, dishes fell from the shelves or hurtled across the room. Eleanore was not a pleasant visitor to have and all the superstitious villagers were frightened half to death. They shut the doors and closed the windows when they saw her coming.

She was no more welcome in her own home. The village priest tried his best to exorcise the "devil," but failed. And at last Eleanore was sent away to a home for the insane, and everybody was so terrify glad to be rid of the poor little "devil child," as they called her.

The great lady of the district is Zoe, Countess Wassilko-Serecki. She heard about Eleanore and quivering with the force of the impact.

So the Countess took the little girl out of the insane asylum. They, too, were glad to get rid of her, because she had made it seem even crazier than such an institution is supposed to be. Little Eleanore went to her titled rescuer's home in Vienna.

The Countess Wassilko-Serecki gives this account of some of the strange things she has watched happen:

"When Eleanore was safely established in my home in Vienna, the first thing I noticed was that she herself was entirely unable to control the manifestations. They appeared to be connected only with her presence in the room and in no way actuated by her will.

"Eleanore has been with me now for twelve months and during that time I have observed as many as 1,200 examples of the mysterious powers that she unwittingly possesses.

"I was in the room with her one day with Dr. Harry Price, and we were both observing her closely. She was winding up some wool into a ball, a perfectly harmless occupation which kept both her hands busy.

"Suddenly we were transfixed with horror.

"On the opposite wall hung a stiletto, a long gleaming dagger of steel, and before our eyes we saw it move, point toward, and with the speed of a hurricane come whizzing past us. It launched itself without any human help right across the room and plunged into the door near which we had been standing. There it remained deeply imbedded and quivering with the force of the impact.

"Eleanore was aware of this uncanny incident, and she was frightened and came running to my arms. She had dropped the ball of wool on the table. Next moment we were further astonished to see the ball of wool vanish into the air. On opening the workbox later we found the identical ball of wool again. Ten minutes later it reappeared on its bright light. Yet, while Eleanore's hands and feet were

"It is not unusual for rings, money and other small objects to disappear when Eleanore approaches, but they are never permanently lost, reappearing again at some other time and place. Metal objects such as brooches seem to be attracted to her. They are never actually found in her possession, but appear to drop from the ceiling of the room she is in or to slide down the wall until they reach the floor.

"Pins and needles thrust themselves into her cheeks, inflicting painful wounds. I have seen the needles jump out at the work basket and project themselves at her, and when I have looked at her I have seen her face a mass of pins, as if she was one of those Indian fakirs who inflict all sorts of tortures upon themselves.

"On our way over from the Continent, when we were in the train between Folkestone and London, there was a continual hanging upon the windows of our compartment as though some invisible body outside was trying to gain an entrance. I was more frightened than the child.

"'It is the devil trying to get in to me,' she said.

"I listened again. Crash! Crash! The blows rained outside the train, which was then traveling at nearly sixty miles an hour. If it really was the devil, he must have borrowed some wings to help him fly along with us."

held fast by the investigators, coins, weights up to a pound and rings were moved about without any visible agency on the table. Letters about two inches high and cut from metal arranged themselves into words while the girl was sitting in a chair, bound, and an foot from them.

Nets were arranged around the laboratory so that no threads or strings could be used by the child to move objects on shelves. Nevertheless, these objects did move. Once a pair of jars were hurled to the floor and another crashed through the net.

At another time, while Eleanore was standing at the end of a passage and Dr. Price was standing at the door of the room where the experiments had taken place, a marked coin which had been placed on top of a cabinet leaped off it and rolled to the window. A second marked coin "jumped" from the inside of the door.

Again, a ring which had been lost by the secretary for a few hours rolled off a shelf while Eleanore was being held fast in her chair by Professors Thirring and Baskine. An investigator accounts for the mark by the claws of her "evil spirit" made by the claws of her evil spirit is thus grown by one of the investigators.

"Eleanore was sitting at the table trying up in its box the toy I had given her the day before when she suddenly winced violently as if acute pain.

"'Do look!' as her face we found long 'scratches,' which gradually developed into white wealx.

"A few minutes later, when she was standing near the window in a corner of the laboratory to be photographed, she winced again and pointed to her arm. What looked like teeth marks quickly formed. Other clearly defined marks, including two that seemed like attempts at the letters B and O, also appeared.

"Within fifteen minutes Eleanore looked, indeed, as if she had been tattooed all over her face and arms.

"At the time the markings appeared

## Little Eleanore and investigators at the Psychic Laboratory.

*Little Eleanore and investigators at the Psychic Laboratory. The Shelves Were Covered With a Net to Prevent Her From Using Trickery to Make Objects Upon Them Move. But Nevertheless, Two Jars Were Thrown to the Floor and Another Hurled Through the Net While She Stood There.*

*Eleanore Zugun With a Little Statue of an Evil Spirit, Similar, She Says, to That Which, Like Mary's Little Lamb, Goes Everywhere That She Does.*

*A Photograph of Eleanore Showing the Marks Upon Her Face, Which She Says Are Made by the Claws of Her Attendant "Evil Spirit"—And They Do Appear Like Marks of Long, Sharp Fingernails.*

those present in the room were Mr. H. W. Seton-Karr, F. R. G. S., the well-known explorer, big game shooter and author; Colonel Hardwicke, a member of the council of the laboratory and an experienced and skeptical investigator, and Miss Kaye, secretary of the laboratory.

"All agreed that there was no sign of trickery. Mr. Seton-Karr and M. Robert Blair, entirely independent inquirers, both insisted that they had Eleanore under the closest observation and were satisfied that she did not cause the marks by her own physical action."

What is known as the "poltergeist" phenomenon has been observed for many centuries by writers in all countries. The word itself means "rocket," or, better, "polting ghost." The "manifestations" consist of furniture being moved and broken, objects picked up and thrown around rooms, dishes being broken and strong noises. These take place as much in daylight as at night. Although some have translated the word "poltergeist" as hobgoblin, this is not strictly true. The hobgoblin belongs to the realm of fairyland and is a partner of the elves, gnomes, fays and the court of Queen Titania. The "poltergeist" belongs to the realm of demonology.

The word "geist" is not to be taken in the sense of "ghost" or "spook," but in the older sense of evil spirit or devil. It is considered to be more mischievous than malignant, although legends tell of it inflicting serious injury by pelting out chairs from under people and biting those with plates and even heavier objects. Old Martin Luther tells in a rare book of his of an encounter with a "poltergeist" that threw walnuts at him, and Ben Johnson, back in the seventeenth century, mentioned a notorious case of a "poltergeist" in London.

It is a fact that while investigators has shown that almost every case has been due to trickery on the part of some person—usually, strangely enough, young girls about the age of Eleanore—there is a considerable residuum of cases that have never been found. But, of course, this may be due to the superior cunning of the afflicted person in such cases.

The unusually unfortunate or unusually gifted little Eleanore, having been given up by the English investigators, is now in Berlin for similar experiments. Perhaps the Germans may have sharper eyes.

---

Eleonore Zügun of Romania claimed to be possessed by a demonic spirit after she paid for candy with a silver coin she found in the woods. Her condition baffled scientists, even in laboratory conditions.

villagers, said good riddance. According to a 1926 article in the *San Francisco Examiner*, "They, too, were glad to get rid of her, because she had made it seem ever crazier than such an institution is supposed to be."

The countess spent a year observing Eleonore, both at her home in Vienna and in London, where Harry Price investigated the case at the National Laboratory of Psychical Research. Wassilko-Serecki recorded 1,700 examples of poltergeist activities, including one at her home that nearly killed her.

"On the opposite wall hung a stiletto, a long gleaming dagger of steel, and before our eyes we saw it move, point towards us, and with the speed of a hurricane come whizzing past us," the countess told a reporter. "It launched itself without any human help right across the room and plunged into the door near which we had been standing."

Tests at the laboratory were highly controlled to prevent any attempts at fraud. Eleonore's hands and feet were tied and nets were arranged around the testing room to ensure no strings or threads could be used to surreptitiously yank objects. Still, coins, rings, and jars were all moved despite Eleonore being seated six feet away from them. If that didn't spook investigators enough, scratches suddenly materialized on her face, teeth marks formed on her arm, and stigmatic markings appeared on various parts of her body.

"Within fifteen minutes Eleonore looked, indeed, as if she had been tattooed all over her face and arms," one of the investigators said.

Price and his team at the lab concluded that Eleonore "was not consciously responsible for the production of the marks" and "that under scientific test conditions movements of small objects without physical contact undoubtedly took place."

Beyond these acknowledgments, the best they could offer was a theory as to how Eleonore's poltergeist phenomena began:

What has happened to Eleonore is apparently this: During her early childhood when the so-called "poltergeist" phenomena became first apparent, the simple peasants threatened her so often with Dracu (the Devil) and what he would do to her that her subconscious mind became obsessed with the idea of whippings, bitings, etc., which the ignorant peasants said would be her lot at the hands—or teeth—of Dracu. Remove the Dracu

complex and the girl would probably be troubled
no further with stigmatic markings.

---

From London, Eleonore headed east to Berlin to give German investigators a chance at a better conclusion. But by this point she was nearly fifteen—
perhaps over the hump of puberty—and the move to Germany coincided
with the end of her phenomena.

# FAKE MEDIUMS AND
# THE MANIFESTATION OF ESP

Among the thousands of people attending Sir Arthur Conan Doyle's lectures on Spiritualism in the 1920s was University of Chicago PhD student Joseph Banks Rhine. Inspired by the talk, he later wrote, "The mere possibility of communicating with the dead is the most exhilarating thought I had had in years."

Rhine moved to Boston to study psychology with Professor William McDougall at Harvard University. There, he joined the investigations of Mina "Margery" Crandon and believed he saw instances of fraud. But still, the idea of mediumship was fascinating. By 1927, McDougall left Harvard to help establish Duke University and invited Rhine to join him and pursue psychical research at the new school. The young researcher happily accepted.

During the drive to Durham, North Carolina, perhaps as a sign that it was the right move, Rhine saw a sign for a talking horse called Lady Wonder. This allegedly psychic animal could answer questions about math, personal information, and even the future by pressing her snout on the keys of a large, horse-size typewriter. Rhine set up camp outside Lady's stable and began a weeklong study involving five hundred tests. His parapsychology career was off to an interesting start. He published his findings in the *Journal of Abnormal and Social Psychology*, stating that Lady Wonder seemed responsive to telepathy and possessed a degree of psychic power. However, Rhine concluded that she

didn't possess independent thinking because she could only give a correct answer if someone else in the room knew it.

Horses aside, Rhine pursued his studies of human psychics and found many of them to be similar to his séance experience with Margery—riddled with theatrics and fraud. Yet he recognized that some mediums were getting information that they seemingly had no access to. Were they getting it from spirits or, he wondered, was there another way they could be receiving it?

"That's where he started to develop the theory of ESP, and talk about telepathy, clairvoyance, and precognition," says John Kruth, executive director of the Rhine Research Center. "He discussed how people could get information that way and started to test it."

The idea of survival after death remained an interest, but Rhine's main focus shifted to studying the limits of human abilities within living beings. His work led to a book on extrasensory perception in 1934 and the establishment of the Duke Parapsychology Labs the following year.

Thirty years later Rhine retired from the university, but with generous funding from Chester Carlson (the founder of Xerox), he established the Foundation for Research on the Nature of Man. Renamed the Rhine Research Center in 1995, it continues to research and explore the answers its late founder may have since discovered.

## The Enfield Poltergeist

Those who believed the devil possessed Eleonore may have believed he struck again in the fall of 1977. This time, though, he was throwing Lego bricks and marbles in a seemingly ordinary English public housing unit at 248 Green Street in Enfield, a suburb just north of London. Peggy Hodgson had recently separated from her husband, but that nightmare was nothing compared to one just beginning to engulf her and her four children: Margaret, twelve; Janet, eleven; Johnny, ten; and Billy, seven.

Their once peaceful home seemed to have suddenly been hit by a poltergeist earthquake: beds shook and jolted; heavy furniture overturned and slid across the floor; and Janet levitated in her sleep.[9] The Enfield haunting was particularly unusual because the story went well beyond the family's account of its experiences. There were numerous witnesses throughout the haunting, including neighbors, reporters, the mailman, and even police officers who were called to the scene after a chest of drawers attacked Peggy. During the police investigation one of the constables, Carolyn Heep, stated, "A large armchair moved, unassisted, four feet across the floor." She uncovered no wires or other devices that could've rigged the chair to move. Because police don't arrest ghosts, Peggy looked to the Society for Psychical Research for help. Maurice Grosse and Guy Lyon Playfair arrived and began documenting what would become 2,000 paranormal instances or, in Grosse's words, "practically every known phenomenon in a poltergeist case."

Janet tended to be in the middle of the action, but she took center stage for good once the voices started. The preteen had moments when a raspy-voiced seventy-two-year-old man named Bill Wilkins spoke through her. He claimed he had once lived in the house and died downstairs in a chair that remained in the same spot. Grosse and Playfair discovered that what the voice said was true—a Bill Wilkins did live and die there, just as he described. Further verification came from Bill's son, who was played recordings of the voice and recognized it as his father's.

Ed Warren, the famed demonologist who'd just been busy investigating the horror in Amityville, New York, visited Enfield toward the end the poltergeist activity. During his interview with a ghost being channeled through Janet, Warren claimed other boisterous spirits disrupted his chat: "Chairs and tables were lifting and dropping. Small, little objects would whiz across the room and bounce off the wall. In the dining room, the wallpaper was peeling away from the walls as we watched." But those juvenile hijinks turned dangerous when a butcher knife materialized in the lap of his assistant and became

---

9   If this sounds familiar, you can thank *The Conjuring 2*. The 2016 horror flick wasn't exactly accurate, but it was indeed based on real people and some really strange happenings.

downright disgusting when, according to Warren, "the spirits left a pile of excrement on the mother's bedroom carpet upstairs."

Between the ghost poop and all the other paranormal activity that carried on for more than a year, Warren said the case "makes Amityville look like a playhouse."

Decades later, Janet told England's Channel Four, "I felt used by a force that nobody understands. . . . I knew when the voices were happening, of course, it felt like something was behind me all of the time. They did all sorts of tests, filling my mouth with water and so on, but the voices still came out."

Part of those tests included a visit by a ventriloquist, who determined the girls were creating the voices and enjoyed the attention that came from it. Grosse and Playfair caught Janet faking certain instances, like bending spoons, banging the ceiling with a broom handle, and hiding Grosse's tape recorder. But the investigators nonetheless believed much of what they'd seen couldn't have been faked. At one point Grosse described Janet's levitation as "going from horizontal to vertical in a sixth of a second," and Playfair recalled her violent convulsions, exclaiming, "We had everything *The Exorcist* had except the green slime and the head spinning round." The latter helped them rule out demonic possession.

Given these seemingly real occurrences, why would Janet fake a few of them? The answer might be the same as believers of Eusapia Palladino and Margery Crandon accepted—the intense media attention and sudden celebrity created pressure to perform. If the press wanted poltergeists, Janet would make sure they got them.

In October 1978 reinforcements were summoned in the form of a Dutch medium, Dono Gmelig-Meyling, and the haunting appeared to go away as mysteriously as it started. He couldn't speak English, but, according to Playfair he "went up and sat in the bedroom on his own, and came down and implied that was it. And it was."

Skeptic and magician Joe Nickell examined Playfair's full account of the commotion and in a 2012 issue of the *Skeptical Inquirer* and concluded that the phenomena "are best explained as children's pranks." Margaret and Janet later admitted to faking "about two percent" of the paranormal phenomena and insisted everything else was real. But Nickell thinks her estimate might be low: "The evidence suggests that this figure is closer to 100 percent."

But given all the witness accounts, could a young girl really have fooled them all? Is it possible the stress of her parents' separation and the onset of puberty unleashed a case of RSPK? Robyn Wilson, a paranormal investigator and spirit communicator who grew up near Enfield, believes the manifestations may have been partly produced through paranormal phenomena combined with other factors, including some degree of fraud. "I think [RSPK] lays dormant," she said. "There's something that activates it, like the contact with spiritual energy."

Without being there to personally experience the phenomena, one can either accept Nickell's view of a rational explanation through trickery and perhaps a willingness to believe on the part of the eyewitnesses, or accept that it's a mystery and that there are still things we simply don't know. If you need a little more justification in keeping an open mind, it might help knowing that even a court of law has accepted the idea of ghosts.

# THE HAUNTING
## OF *POLTERGEIST*

The set of *Poltergeist* was plagued by misfortune. Some believe it was all coincidence, but many claim the cast and crew were supernaturally cursed.

"They're heeere!"

When actor Heather O'Rourke's character, Carol Ann, spoke those now classic words, they were only meant to refer to spirits in the movie. Yet, looking back at the tragedies that followed the 1982 blockbuster release of Steven Spielberg and Tobe Hooper's film *Poltergeist*, it seems some evils spirits escaped the actors' own TV screens and caused what's become known as the *Poltergeist* curse.

It began just weeks after the film's premiere when twenty-two-year-old Dominique Dunne, who played Carol Ann's older sister in the film, was strangled by her boyfriend following an argument at her home. Suffering from brain damage and lying in a coma, she died five days later in a hospital.

Before the launch of the sequel, actor Julian Beck (who played Kane, the malevolent preacher) succumbed to a long battle with stomach cancer, and months after its release Will Sampson (who played Taylor the Medicine Man, and, most famously, the Chief in *One Flew Over the Cuckoo's Nest*) passed away after complications from a heart and lung transplant. Neither death was shocking, given the actors' personal circumstances. As rumors of the curse steadily grew, it hit its peak with the untimely passing of Heather O'Rourke.

During the filming of *Poltergeist III*, abdominal pains and a supposed bout of flu hospitalized the twelve-year-old star. Sadly cardiac arrest struck during an operation. The cause of death was listed as "septic shock due to congenital stenosis of the intestine."

Coincidence is the logical cause of the cast's misfortune, but when a film's subject revolves around the supernatural, there are always those who suspect something more sinister might be at work.

## The Greenbrier Ghost and Other Landmark Moments of Supernatural Law and Order

Those who believe ghosts stick around to seek justice might point to the spirit of Zona Heaster Shue as proof. Known as the Greenbrier Ghost, it holds the unique distinction of being the only known specter to help a court convict a murderer.

On January 23, 1897, Edward Stribbling Shue, known by folks as Trout, was busy working a shift at the local blacksmith shop. Tall and muscular, the thirty-six-year-old had moved the previous fall from Droop Mountain in Pocahontas County, West Virginia, to nearby Lewisburg in Greenbrier County to take the job. Soon after, the dashing new stranger had met Zona, a comely twenty-year-old maiden. The two lovebirds had married in October.

The ghost of Zona Heaster Shue, known as the Greenbrier Ghost, gave testimony about her murder to her mother, resulting in the first conviction based on supernatural evidence in US history.

While Trout was sweating over the forge that January day, he asked a neighborhood boy to stop by his house to help Zona with some chores. The boy obliged, only to arrive at a gruesome scene with a trail of blood leading to the young woman's lifeless body on the dining room floor. Her head was tilted to the side. Terrified, he raced home and told his mom. She called the coroner, Dr. George Knapp, and broke the news to Trout.

The sudden widower rushed home and began making the proper arrangements. Proper, that is, for his purposes. Trout placed Zona on her bed and dressed her with a high, stiff collar covering her neck, held by a large bow, and covered her face with a veil. By the time Knapp arrived he could hardly inspect the body since the grieving husband clung to her, sobbing and blocking access to Zona's neck and head. Achieving nothing more than a cursory examination, Knapp officially recorded "everlasting faint" as the cause of death. In normal speak, Zona had a heart attack. He reportedly later changed his mind and claimed the real culprit was childbirth. In the weeks prior Knapp had been treating her for some unknown malady, which might or might not have been a pregnancy.

Zona's mother didn't agree with either of the doctor's assessments, and neither did the surrounding community. Trout's behavior at the scene of her death was fishy. So was his past. Zona was wife number three. Trout had divorced the first and the next one died, also under mysterious circumstances, after he accidentally dropped bricks on her head while repairing a roof. Rumor had it that he already had a new Mrs. Shue eager to try her luck. As if his history with women wasn't bad enough, he was also an ex-con who'd done time for stealing a horse. To top it all off, he wouldn't let anyone near Zona's neck at the funeral. All these suspicions weren't enough for authorities to take action, until Zona spoke up from the dead.

A short while after the burial, Mary Heaster prayed for an explanation of what had happened to her daughter. She wanted the truth, not Dr. Knapp's sloppy, fickle-minded medical reports. In all, Mrs. Heaster had four visions over the course of several days. By the last one, Zona did a full Linda Blair head spin and spilled her phantom guts through her snapped neck, saying it "was squeezed off at the first joint."

When local officials heard the stories of Zona's ghost, they decided to exhume the body to take a closer look at her injury. With the widespread acceptance of Spiritualism, maybe detective work from a ghost wasn't so far-fetched. Or maybe the prosecutor took pity on a grieving mother and had his own lingering doubts about Trout's innocence. Regardless of the true reason, what Dr. Knapp found on Zona's unearthed corpse matched her mother's story. Her neck had been broken at the first vertebra. While other ghosts were busy rapping on tables and writing on slates, Zona's was putting her husband on trial for murder.

Trout wasn't worried. How could they prove he'd done the deed? Maybe they'd just pin it on the kid who'd found the body. Trout's lawyer planned to discredit his mother-in-law by positioning the whole apparition thing as nothing more than a dream or the whims of a superstitious woman, but Mary assured him it was no such thing.

"I was as fully awake as I am at this moment," Mrs. Heaster explained to the court. "She told me that Shue had come in from the shop very hungry and was furious when he found that she had not prepared any meat for supper.

She had replied that there was plenty of supper without meat, including applesauce and preserves, and that it was a very good supper. She said he had come over to her, had taken her head in his hands and lifted her, and with a sudden wrench he had dislocated her neck, and she died."

The grieving mother further explained that Zona shared physical descriptions of the house and surrounding neighborhood to help prove the apparition was real. When she shared these details, a neighbor confirmed their accuracy. Mrs. Heaster had never been to Zona's house prior to her death.

The jury considered all the circumstantial evidence and the eyewitness account from the ghost. An hour later it came back with a guilty verdict of murder in the first degree. Trout was sentenced to life in prison. His sentence lasted three years, after which point he fell victim to an "unknown epidemic"—or maybe Zona found a way to finish her revenge.

With justice served, the Greenbrier Ghost lived on as a claim to fame for the small town. By the 1970s the story had been so embraced by locals that a sign commemorating the event was erected along Route 60. About a decade later, historian Katie Letcher Lyle read the curious marker and began researching the case. She eventually uncovered an article in the January 28, 1897, edition of the *Greenbrier Independent* that announced the death of Zona—and also happened to include a story on the front page about a ghost. But not just any ghost. The story was about the ghost of a murdered man in Australia who came back from the grave to tell authorities about the crime against him. Years later, as the article reported, the man who shared the ghost's story confessed that he'd made the whole thing up. He had witnessed the crime, but death threats prevented him from telling the police. So he let a "ghost" handle it.

"As soon as he started the story, such is the power of nervousness that numerous other people began to see it," the story recounted, "until its fame

Zona Heaster Shue's identification of her murderer from beyond the grave is commemorated by a plaque on Route 60 in West Virginia.

reached such dimensions that a search was made and the body found, and the murderers brought to justice."

Had Mrs. Heaster read the local paper that day? It seems highly likely she saw her daughter's name in print and would've caught the ghost story on page one. She knew natural causes hadn't taken her daughter's life, but if no one was going to listen to her pleas, maybe she believed they'd listen to a ghost.

Decades later, and a couple hundred miles directly south, another ghost spoke up and forced the legal system to listen. But before James L. Chaffin became that particular ghost, he was an eccentric but well-off farmer in Davie County, North Carolina, who'd inexplicably willed his property to just one of his four sons, Marshall. By September 1921, a fall down a staircase led to Chaffin's death. Marshall inherited everything and shared nothing with his brothers and mother. With no bad blood between the father and the rest of his family, the whole situation was baffling and left everyone but Marshall angry and confused. But rather than fight the legitimacy of the will, the family went their separate ways and got on with their lives. In a twist of karma, Marshall died shortly after the ugly affair and so the estate was passed along to his widow and son, who were perfectly happy to keep all of it.

Unlike Zona, who wasted little time trying to make things right, Chaffin's ghost took four years to come to his senses and fix his inheritance mess. It began on a night in June 1925, when his son, James, woke in fear from a nightmare. There, standing beside his bed, was an apparition of James's father wearing his favorite old black overcoat. Tugging at the inside pocket, the ghost told his frightened son, "Look in the inside pocket of this coat and you will find my will."

James was convinced this was no dream. He shared the tale with his wife, who laughed at him and told him to forget about it. But he couldn't. That overcoat had been so vivid, and the message about the pocket so specific. His mother searched her house high and low before remembering that his brother John had the coat. James drove to John's house in a nearby county and, sure enough, found what his father's ghost had pointed him to.

"I looked in the inside pocket and found that the lining had been sewn together," he recalled. "I opened the lining and discovered in the inside a small piece of paper rolled up with a piece of string around it. I opened the paper and written on it in my father's handwriting was this line: 'Look in the 27th chapter of Genesis.'"

The spectral scavenger hunt continued with a reference to a large Bible that had been in the family for generations. Recognizing the whole ghost thing might sound suspect, James brought a neighbor as a witness to whatever might be found inside the Bible. Together, they tracked down the well-worn book in a bureau drawer at his mother's home, and there at the designated location was a sheet of paper with his father's handwriting:

"After reading the 27th chapter of Genesis, I, James L. Chaffin, do make my last will and testament, and here it is. I want, after giving my body decent burial, my little property to be equally divided between my four children, if they are living at my death, both personal and real estate divided equal." This updated will, dated January 16, 1919, also stipulated that his children were to care for their "Mammy" if she was still alive.

Genesis 27, if you're not up on your Bible studies, is the chapter where Jacob poses as his elder brother, Esau, to secure Isaac's blessing. Chaffin seemed to be suggesting that Marshall had pulled a Jacob. Chaffin may have been more to blame for that than Marshall, but James was about to put all that behind him.

Anyone who knew the late farmer agreed that the handwriting was his, as did a handwriting analyst. Armed with a new will, apparently written after the Marshall version, and a host of witnesses, the inheritance-less Chaffin boys prepared to go to court and fight for their long overdue share. By December 1925, a jury had been sworn in. It was suggested that perhaps Chaffin had mentioned the coat-pocket-Bible will at some point and that James subconsciously was aware of it, but he adamantly claimed neither he nor anyone else in the family knew anything about it. As the case went on, even Marshall's widow acknowledged the new will appeared to be in her father-in-law's handwriting. The court agreed and the second will was probated, meaning Davie County had officially accepted into its records a message from beyond.

"Many of my friends do not believe it is possible for the living to hold communication with the dead, but I am convinced that my father actually appeared to me on these several occasions, and I shall believe it to the day of my death."

—James P. Chaffin, in December 1925, after the jury returned a verdict in his favor

## Friendly Ghosts

When Michael and Stephanie Romano (last name changed for privacy) bought their house in New Rochelle, New York, a paranormal experience was the last thing they expected in their new suburban neighborhood. This was a town best known as the idyllic home of the Petries from *The Dick Van Dyke Show*, not ghosts. For the most part, life was more Petrie than paranormal, until their two-year-old daughter, Isabelle, started talking about an "angel" who would come into her room to care for her and just be with her. The young girl called her Rebecca. "She was never scared of her," Stephanie recalls. "She was super matter-of-fact. It wasn't like an imaginary friend."

After a few years Isabelle stopped talking about Rebecca. The spirit, whatever it was, seemed to have gone away. Then the Romanos had a second daughter.

"We'd joke that Rebecca was back because Amelia would track like she was looking at someone, but there was no one there," Stephanie says.

As the newborn appeared to be seeing something, Isabelle began having dreams about a monster climbing the stairs and heading to her room.

"It felt like it wasn't a dream the way she talked about it," Stephanie says. "I got to the point where I put up a cross in her room and a St. Benedict's medal. I don't know, but whatever it is, it's upsetting her."

Stephanie, a New York City lawyer, found herself researching what to do to get rid of a ghost. One answer suggested the solution was as simple as asking the ghost to leave.

"I'm up with the baby in the middle night, and I said, 'Rebecca, I think you're here taking care of my babies, but I've got this. I'm taking care of them and they're okay, and I need you to leave now because you're not taking care of her, you're scaring her. So I need you to leave.'"

After that Isabelle stopped having the bad dreams, and Amelia's eyes stopped tracking movements that weren't there.

The previous and only other owner of the home had been a woman who'd passed soon before the Romanos purchased the house. She was the mother of two daughters.

There are often reports of children reminiscent of that creepy kid in the

1999 film *The Sixth Sense*. They see dead people. Fortunately the ghosts they're seeing aren't like the ones believed to be haunting places like the LaLaurie Mansion or Eastern State Penitentiary. Ghosts, after all, aren't always trapped in places where their living selves suffered gruesome torture or other terrible misfortunes. The ghosts children see might be perfectly friendly; comforting, even.

While working at the American Society for Psychical Research years ago, Loyd Auerbach had colleagues working a case in Brooklyn regarding a "doting grandmother" who'd recently died. Her daughter had two young boys who claimed the grandmother appeared in their bedroom at night to tuck them in and watch over them. The experience was a pleasant one, not a scary one. At one point their father was quoted as saying, "If we could leave them with her legally as a babysitter, without getting into trouble, we would've done it." The family had no issues with the ghost; they called the ASPR purely out of curiosity.

These types of stories happen often enough to cause wonder. Sure, kids are known to have imaginary friends and their tales of "ghosts" might be nothing more than some phantasm of their own creation or even just a dream.

"I think, on occasion, kids do mix up imagination and reality to have something like a hallucination-like experience," said Charles Fernyhough, a psychologist at Durham University, in a 2019 interview with the *Washington Post*.

Then there are occasions where something else seems to be happening. Jason Lambert, an advertising creative director, shared a story from his childhood that would appear to fall squarely in the "something else" category. His ghostly encounter happened at the age of eleven while visiting his aunt's late-eighteenth-century farmhouse in Cheshire, Connecticut. Lambert and his younger sister were staying for the weekend, and being the older sibling, he took the larger of the two guest rooms. It had a single window and just a few pieces of antique furniture as décor. A large closet held linens but was mostly empty.

"I'd be lying if I didn't say I was a little freaked out when I went to bed that first night—clearly a combination of my eleven-year-old imagination plus the fact that a house over two centuries old will no doubt take on a different feel at night," Lambert says. "Regardless, though, I managed to fall asleep easily."

All was well until just after midnight when he woke with a feeling that he wasn't alone. It wasn't a noise. No knockings or rappings on walls, as mediums so often claim.

"There was a weird energy. A heaviness, really. Like there was somebody in the room with me . . . specifically, in the closet—and even more specifically, an old man who was really angry. Out of all the things that an eleven-year-old's mind could conjure, I don't why I felt that it was angry old man, but I did."

He got out of bed and moved into his sister's room for the rest of the weekend. Lambert didn't speak of the event until college, when he made another visit to his aunt's house. By then she had a dog. The pooch, like eleven-year-old Lambert, felt an uneasiness around the closet. He'd sniff at it and bark.

"You know we have a ghost in the house, right?" Lambert's aunt told him. He explained that he couldn't sleep in the guest room as a kid, and she responded saying that she couldn't either.

"She had slept in the room once herself and had experienced an incredibly vivid nightmare that an enraged old man came out of the closet and was standing over her with a knife," Lambert says. "She said it had felt so real that

she immediately switched rooms and never slept there again."

Another guest tried sleeping in the room and had a similar nightmare, claiming an angry old man was at the foot of his bed trying to pull the sheets off. He woke up and saw the comforter slowly being pulled off the bed. Not slipping off, but being slightly lifted and pulled.

Lambert's aunt eventually learned from a neighbor that the previous owner was a "nasty old man who everyone on the street utterly despised."

He had died of a heart attack in the house years before Lambert's aunt moved in.

As imaginative as eleven-year-old Lambert may have been, the old man who multiple people experienced was no hallucination-like creation.

Hans Holzer, who's been called the "Father of the Paranormal" and wrote 140 books on the subject, believed that oftentimes ghosts don't realize they're dead and have unfinished business on earth. Lambert's angry old man may have been such a ghost. The living, however, can help a ghost resolve a conflict so it can get on with its afterlife. These types of cases show up often in movies, such as *The Changeling* (1980), in which George C. Scott's character helps the ghost of a child murdered in the attic get the truth out. The aforementioned *The Sixth Sense* explores the same theme, with Haley Joel Osment's psychic child helping Bruce Willis's character eventually see that he's dead.[10] Some-

---

10    Apologies for the spoiler, but if you haven't seen *The Sixth Sense* by now, that's on you.

times, it appears they happen in real life, too.

Artist and spirit communicator Philip Wilson described his experience with helping a ghost in conflict find peace at his family's Montana house. The phenomena began one night in the mid-1990s after his sister brought home an antique freestanding mirror covered with dark spots. His mother, who had exhibited psychic abilities in the past, saw an apparition of a woman in a ball gown walking up the stairs. The following evening she heard sounds of a party in the kitchen. Philip had yet to witness any of this until he looked in the mirror one day and saw a woman's face in his reflection, albeit fuzzy and unfocused. The family got together to understand what was happening, when suddenly his mother and sister began chan-neling a conversation between the madam of a brothel in the 1800s and a woman who was her best friend. Adding to the bizarre scene were two antique dolls sitting atop a cabinet, which appeared to cry real tears as the story unfolded. As the conversation grew heated, the two women revealed that the friend had a lover in town and the madam became jealous. Soon after, the man was suspiciously crushed to death by a pile of wood. Before the friction began, the madam had given her friend the mirror, which Philip believes had entrapped the energy of both women.

"They were talking to each other and all of a sudden my mom and sister hugged each other, said they were sorry, the whole entire area lit up, and the marks on the mirror went away," Philip recounts. If the antique had quarreling spirits trapped within, the long-overdue apology seemingly brought closure and set them free.

Other ghosts know they're dead and are ready to go, but just want to say their good-byes. According to Auerbach, ninety-five to ninety-nine percent of people who appear to others as ghosts do so at the moment of death or within a few days. They usually appear only to family members and people they knew well, but not to everyone else who may be around. Such occurrences turned Lady Beresford into a legend and launched a young Andrew Jackson Davis into Spiritualism royalty. More recently, Auerbach experienced this phenomenon himself shortly after the death of his friend, Martin Caidin, in 1997. Caidin, a science fiction author and aviation expert, had fought a long battle with cancer. Among his books were the novel *Cyborg*, which was adapted into the 1973 TV movie *The Six Million Dollar Man*, and *Ghosts of the Air*, a nonfiction collection of paranormal experiences from pilots.

"He constantly kidded me about haunting me after he died," Auerbach recalls. "I challenged him to do it."

Nothing happened within the expected window of two days, but a week and a half later, as Auerbach was driving to the Oakland airport for a morning flight, something unusual happened. His three-month-old vehicle that still had its new car smell suddenly filled with the aroma of cigar smoke—despite the fact that Auerbach doesn't smoke. It was Caidin's brand of cigar smoke specifically.

"It felt to me like somebody was sitting in the passenger seat next to me, but there was nobody there," Auerbach describes. "I just said my goodbyes and it went away."

When he arrived at the airport he called a mutual friend of his and Caidin's and, to his surprise, learned that the aviation expert's spirit could zip across the country in minutes.

"I don't know why you're calling. The timing couldn't be better," the friend told Auerbach. "I just got back from flying my Cessna here in New Jersey, and at 10:10 a.m. my cockpit fills up with the smell of stinky cigar smoke. I swear to God Caidin was with me. It was there for a few minutes, and I was talking to nobody, then it went away."

This had occurred ten minutes after Auerbach's experience in his car. What's more, the friend had just spoken with another pilot in Florida who was also close with Caidin. At 10:20 a.m., the same thing happened to him during a flight.

Auerbach believes ghosts project an image reflecting their appearance in the prime of their lives, since that's how people usually think of themselves. Alternatively, paranormal investigator Greg Newkirk suggests apparitions might appear as the loved ones experiencing the phenomena remember them. "They don't see them as they were when they died—frail and old—they see them as their best memory of the person," he says. "So I think that there's an intelligence out there, whether it's our intelligence or something else, and occasionally it pokes us. I think it needs our minds in order to do that."

Both theories would agree that apparitions occur within the mind, but might appear in different ways. In other words, what you experience is not physically in front of you or around you, it's a mental phenomenon. In the case of Caidin's cigar smoke, the spirit's information was processed in an olfactory sensation. At other times, any given apparition could be experienced uniquely by different people in the same location. For example, if you and some friends were at the Trans-Allegheny Lunatic Asylum, one of you might see and hear an apparition speaking, another might only see it or hear it, and another might smell it—be it the patient's perfume or another aroma associated with the person. One last person in such a group might experience nothing at all and suggest the rest of you get a room in one of the wards.

Capturing evidence of these perceptions isn't easy. If it were, we'd have many more answers by now. But that doesn't mean people aren't trying. The Rhine Research Center in North Carolina and other institutions are engaging in scientific studies to better understand the paranormal. On a less scientific level, countless ghost hunters, from the Roto-Rooter guys on *Ghost Hunters* to Zak Bagans and his crew on *Ghosts Adventures* to Ozzy Osbourne's son on *Portals to Hell*, are trying to record otherworldly chatter and spot spirits in every creepy corner. However, long before parapsychologists began their experiments and plumbers ventured into the dark, others were working hard in the light to develop technology that might connect us to the Other Side.

# WHY DO GHOSTS WEAR CLOTHES?

People have been seeing ghosts since, well, since there've been people. In all the stories that have been passed down, the ones you've watched on reality TV and in the movies or heard about from friends, the ghosts have one thing in common: they're dressed. You don't hear about naked spirits. It's not because the afterlife is fashion conscious or chilly in winter (it seems like a safe assumption). The theory on ghostwear is that apparitions appear to us as they see themselves.

Loyd Auerbach offers a simple test to illustrate this: close your eyes and picture yourself for ten seconds. Go ahead. Now think about how you visualized yourself. Were you naked? Probably not. Did you see your shoes? Most likely you didn't. And when you picture a ghost in your head, it's probably clothed and fading away just before the feet—as if floating in midair.

# GHOSTS IN THE MACHINES

CAN TECHNOLOGY BUILD
A BRIDGE TO THE BEYOND?

"Is it a coincidence that this century–known as the age of anxiety, a time rife with various hysterias, the era that gave birth to existentialism–is also when we stepped inside an electromagnetic bubble and decided to live there? . . . We have never quite comprehended that we walk about in a sea of mild electromagnetism just as we do air. It is part of our atmosphere, part of the containing bath our consciousness swims in."

–Jack Hitt, writing for *Wired* in 1999, on electromagnetism as a possible explanation for paranormal phenomena

Imagine what it must have been like to be alive in the early twentieth century when something called "radio" first yanked distant voices right out of the air and played them in your living room. Or, even more amazing, seeing moving pictures from faraway places suddenly appear on another newfangled device called "television." We take it all for granted today, but back when these technologies exposed an invisible world bristling with data all around, people surely found them to be as magical as they were scientific. So is it any wonder that technology would offer the hope of uncovering another aspect of our world that remains unseen? If there were one person who might unlock a scientific door to the realm of spirits, it was the man known as the Wizard of Menlo Park: Thomas Edison.

## Thomas Edison's "Spirit Phone"

Edison had proven his genius with the ability to capture the human voice in 1877, starting with the words, "Mary had a little lamb, little lamb, little lamb . . ." The famous nursery rhyme was transferred to a tinfoil-coated cylinder and became the first recording of a person. Forty-three years and countless inventions later, Edison set out to create a device that would once again capture a human voice and change everything. Only this time, that voice would come from the dead. The wizard was going to build a telephone to the afterlife.

The inventor had heard enough about séance tables, rappings, spewing ectoplasm, Ouija boards, and other effects that mediums offered as means of communication with the afterlife. If Edison was going to talk to the dead, it was going to be done through science. As he told B. C. Forbes of *American* magazine in 1920, "The methods and apparatus commonly used and discussed are just a lot of unscientific nonsense."

Why, he wondered, would any personality in the afterlife bother communicating in such prankish and primitive ways?

Edison didn't offer Forbes specific details of how his device would work, but he explained, "I am proceeding on the theory that, in the very nature of things, the degrees of material or physical power possessed by those in the next life must be extremely slight; and that, therefore, any instrument designed to communicate with us must be super-delicate—as finely responsive as human ingenuity can make it.

# EDISON AT WORK ON MACHINE TO TALK WITH DEAD

Inventor Hopes To Perfect His Apparatus Within Few Months.

## BELIEVES IDEA WILL BE SUCCESS

Methods Commonly Used Unscientific Nonsense, Wizard Says.

Among Thomas Edison's lesser-known inventions was a prototype for a telephone to the afterlife—one of many attempts by scientists to prove the existence of ghosts.

"For my part, I am inclined to believe that our personality hereafter will be able to affect matter. If this reasoning be correct, then if we can evolve an instrument so delicate as to be affected, or moved or manipulated—whichever term you want to use—by our personality, as it survives in the next life, such an instrument, when made available, ought to record something."

He added that, should he succeed, the first spirits to take advantage of the device would likely be telegraphers or scientists or anyone else with experience in the use of delicate instruments and electric currents.

Was Edison making a joke? Was he merely looking to grab headlines during the Spiritualism craze? Many believed this was the case, but a 1933 article in *Modern Mechanix* magazine reported on a secret demonstration the inventor held one winter night in 1920 in his darkened laboratory with several scientists present. According to the article, "Edison set up a photo-electric cell. A tiny pencil of light, coming from a powerful lamp, bored through the darkness and struck the active surface of this cell, where it was transformed instantly into a feeble electric current. Any object, no matter how thin, transparent, or small, would cause a registration on the cell if it cut through the beam."

The team of scientists spent hours closely watching Edison's prototype for any sign of movement from beyond. But none came. Still, Edison maintained his belief that some form of afterlife might exist. Months after his announcement, the modern-day wizard added to his theories on what constitutes life in an interview with the *New York Times*. He explained that he believed the human body to be composed of 100,000,000,000,000 (that's 100 trillion) infinitely small life units, beyond microscopic, and beyond what the human mind can conceive.

True to his nature, Edison took a very pragmatic approach to how the life units might operate. They, much like him, maintain a strong work ethic by constantly rebuilding our tissues to replace any that might be wearing out. They also monitor the functions of our organs, "just as the engineers in a power house see that the machinery is kept in perfect order." When all of our internal machinery finally breaks down beyond repair, the life units move on and leave our broken bodies behind.

"Being indefatigable workers, they naturally seek something else to do," Edison said. "They either enter into the body of another man or even start work on some other form of life. At any rate, there is a fixed number of these, and it is the same entities that have served over and over again."

In the final chapter of the posthumously published *Diary and Sundry Observations of Thomas Alva Edison*, the great scientist expanded on his thoughts and even postulated that human life is alien in its origin. "I cannot

believe for a moment that life in the first instance originated on this insignif-
icant little ball which we call the Earth—little, that is, in contrast with other
bodies which inhabit space," Edison wrote. "The particles which combined to
evolve living creatures on this planet of ours probably came from some other
body elsewhere in the universe."

Edison died in October 1931, having never completed his spirit phone.
Sadly, this meant he couldn't call the living from the Other Side to share
new inventions, which he surely would be working on if possible. He said it
himself four years earlier after a reporter asked how he'd spend his afterlife,
answering with a smile, "Experimenting."

Though Edison's spirit phone never materialized, many Spiritualists
believed technology had already started building a bridge between the living
and the dead more than half a century earlier. Like the phonograph capturing
sound, the introduction of the camera sparked wonder with its ability to preserve images on paper. Could the lens see what the eye couldn't? In 1861,
it appeared the answer was a resounding yes.

## William Mumler and the
## Rise of Spirit Photography

William Mumler, a jeweler and photographer working in Boston, had just
finished developing a self-portrait when he noticed an image of someone
behind him. At first he assumed he just hadn't cleaned the plate properly,
so he cleaned it again, took another photo, and still saw a faint figure. He
recognized it as a deceased cousin and decided to show it to a Spiritualist
acquaintance.

"Not at that time being inclined much to the spiritual belief myself, and
being of a jovial disposition, always ready for a joke, I concluded to have a
little fun, as I thought, at his expense," Mumler wrote years afterward in 1875.

The joke went well beyond their visit and quickly reached the Spiritualist
newspapers, like Boston's *Banner of Light*. Enthusiastic believers proclaimed
that Mumler had opened a new door to the afterlife—and taken the world's
first spirit photo. Mumler rolled with the wave of excitement and decided
that perhaps the "wonderful phenomenon" was worthy of investigation. That
would be up to others, though. His role involved taking more photos of
people eager to fork over ten bucks. Mumler never promised a spirit would
appear, but one often did.

William Mumler defied skeptics with his spirit photographs. In portrait settings, ghosts can be seen over the shoulders of their living loved ones.

Naturally, there were skeptics. People assumed trickery was involved and various photographers wished to investigate his process. Mumler didn't shy away. He allowed the respected Boston portrait photographer William Black to examine his methods. Black was so confident he'd uncover shenanigans that he offered fifty dollars if Mumler could produce a spirit photo in his presence. So Mumler let Black inspect his camera, plate, dipper, and chemical bath and observe every step of the process, from preparation to development. Sure enough, Mumler's photo produced a hint of a man leaning against Black's shoulder.

The seemingly legit photographer of the spirits gained further credibility after a peer, William Guay, conducted his own investigation. The *Banner of Light* printed this letter on November 18, 1862:

Mr. Editor—Having been informed by Mr. William H. Mumler that you desire to publish the results of my investigation into the possibility and genuineness of Mr. M.'s photographic impressions of spirit forms, it gives me much pleasure to detail to you what I have seen. As I have been commissioned by Messrs. J. Davis and Co., you can rest assured that I was resolved, if permitted, to allow nothing to slip my utmost scrutiny. Having had ten years' continual practice in this particular branch— that is, negative on glass, and positive on paper from negative—I felt competent to detect any form of deception. Having been permitted by Mr. Mumler every facility to investigate, I went through the whole of the operation of selecting, cleaning, preparing, coating, silvering, and putting into the shield, the glass upon which Mr. M. proposed that a spirit form and mine should be imparted, never taking off my eyes, and not allowing Mr. M. to touch the glass until it had gone through the whole of the operation. The result was, that there came upon the glass a picture of myself, and, to my utter astonishment—having previously examined and scrutinised every crack and corner, plate-holder, camera, box, tube, the inside of the bath, &c.—another portrait. Having since continued, on several occasions, my investigations, as described above, and received even more perfect results than on the first trial, I have been obliged to endorse its legitimacy.

Respectfully yours, Wm. Guay.

Mary Todd Lincoln with the ghost of Abraham Lincoln, as captured by spirit photographer William Mumler.

The newspaper was quite pleased with Guay's report. Mumler surely was, too, given that the dead were helping him make a good living. As with the Spiritualist mediums we met in part two of this book, the great loss of life during the Civil War translated to more business from grieving family members. Over the years, Mumler developed thousands of photographs. One of the most famous was taken of Mary Todd Lincoln and showed the assassinated president and her recently deceased son, Thomas, behind her. As the story has been told, however, Mrs. Lincoln entered the studio wearing a black dress and a veil and gave a false name. Perhaps she just wasn't sneaky enough to fool the clever photographer.

P. T. Barnum, always one to enjoy a good humbug, was intrigued as well and displayed several Mumler photographs in his American Museum in Manhattan. But with growing success came more skeptics. And eventually some of them recognized several spirits as people who were still living.

By 1869 the police were on the case and claimed Mumler was swindling his clients. The spirit photographer went to court, supported by the Spiritualist community, who maintained the belief that he was innocent and genuine.

P. T. Barnum, however, wasn't buying it. In fact, he had planned to include Mumler in a book about humbugs.

"I went yesterday to Mr. Bogardus's gallery, and asked him if he could take a spirit photograph, telling him that I did not want any humbug about it,"

Barnum testified.[11] "He said he could do it. I examined the glass, and discovered nothing in it. I saw the process of pouring over the first liquid, and afterwards the pouring over of nitrate of silver, and then saw it placed in the camera. When done it had my likeness and the shadow of Abraham Lincoln. I saw the ghost of Lincoln as soon as it was developed in the dark room. I was unconscious of any spiritual presence."

Others testified in Mumler's defense, swearing the images were real. "I have had a photograph of my deceased daughter, who died in August, 1863," a believer, Paul Bremond, told the court. "She told me when she died that if it were permitted she would return to me from the spirit land. By this photograph I see that she has returned."

Another photographer, William Slee of Poughkeepsie, New York, testified that Mumler produced spirit photographs in his own gallery and had no idea how he'd done it.

Ultimately, no proof was given that Mumler had been deceptive in his techniques and he was acquitted. Despite the win, Mumler's business suffered afterward and he faded into obscurity. Spirit photography, however, did not. In fact, it spread across the pond to Europe.

---

11  Barnum referred to Abraham Bogardus, a daguerreotypist and photographer who had a gallery on Broadway, not far from where the showman's American Museum had stood until it burned to the ground in 1865.

# PASS THE GHOST, PLEASE

Séances were all the rage in the late nineteenth century, but if you were having guests over on short notice and couldn't book a medium, you could still see plenty of ghosts—guaranteed—all thanks to another craze that spread through Victorian parlors: stereoscopy.

Long before evenings of Netflix and chill, friends passed around stereoviewers and stared at three-dimensional photos of spirits flying over sleeping children, ghosts drifting through rooms, and people shrieking in fear of phantoms.

The two images seen on stereoview cards look identical but are slightly different, representing the views from the left and right eye. Seen through a stereoscope, each eye views its corresponding image and the brain merges them into one miraculous 3D image. The remarkable rich effect allows you to see right through the ghost, transporting you directly into the room with it, but without any pesky fears of being haunted.

Today the same technology still works but is presented in shiny new wrappers. You know it as Google Cardboard and virtual reality headsets.

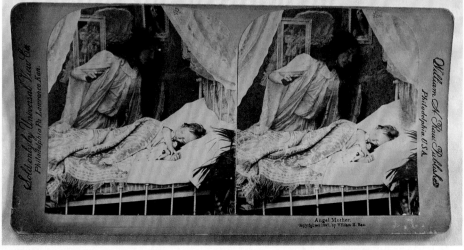

Édouard Buguet was a Parisian photographer who made a name for himself capturing ghosts in London. Picking up where Mumler left off, Buguet's images were sharper, more defined, and often recognized by his eager customers. The devout Spiritualist William Stainton Moses hailed Buguet's work as "very decidedly the gems of spirit photography" and lauded their lifelike appearance. After studying 120 of his images, Moses concluded that forty of them featured recognizable dead people.

With such high praise, the future looked bright for Buguet. Well, at least, for about a month. That's when the French government cracked down and had Buguet arrested for fraud. During his trial, like Mumler's, many came to support the photographer and testify to his mediumship. Buguet, however, confessed that he'd simply been creating double exposures.

Buguet initially employed a team of three to four assistants to play the parts of ghosts. As his success grew, he had to get more creative to avoid

Édouard Buguet's spirit photographs captured the imaginations of devout Spiritualists but ultimately landed him in hot water.

repetitive apparitions. Two headless dummies were constructed to serve as the bodies of the spirits. The assistants would meet with the clients first, gather information, and then select an appropriate visage from a large stock of heads tucked away in the studio. These props were shown to the court. Still, witnesses swore the figures in their photos were the real deal. One instance of testimony went as follows:

> **WITNESS:** The portrait of my wife, which I had specially asked for, is so like her that when I showed it to one of my relatives he exclaimed, "It's my cousin."

> **COURT:** Was that chance, Buguet?

**BUGUET:** Yes, pure chance. I had no photograph of Mme. Dessenon.

**WITNESS:** My children, like myself, thought the likeness perfect. When I showed them the picture, they cried, "It's mamma." A very fortunate chance! . . . I am convinced it was my wife.

Double exposure plus desire plus a dash of coincidence proved to be the perfect formula—until, of course, it landed Buguet in prison for a year and cost him a five-hundred-franc fine.

Despite all the evidence, Moses didn't take kindly to looking like a fool. He denounced the trial, accusing the judge of being biased and declaring that Buguet had been forced to confess or had been bribed. This alleged ruse included conjuring up the collection of dummies and heads shared as evidence.

# WANT TO SEE A GHOST IN THE NEXT TWENTY SECONDS?

In the mid-nineteenth century, author J. H. Brown didn't bother with séances or spirit photographers to see ghosts. He believed each and every one of us already has a perfectly designed machine capable of seeing ghosts. Our eyes.

His 1864 book *Spectropia, or Surprising Spectral Illusions Showing Ghosts Everywhere* hoped to put to rest "the absurd follies of spiritualism" through the brilliance of the eyeball.

"With perhaps the exception of the ear, the eye is the most wonderful example of the infinite skill of the Creator," Brown wrote. "A more exquisite piece of mechanism it is impossible for the human mind to conceive."

He then went on to explain that mechanism in exquisite detail—complete with illustrated diagrams—giving the reader a scientific, rather than a Spiritualistic, explanation for why people might see ghosts. For example, people "startled by what they fancy an apparition" could simply be seeing a glimpse of a retinal artery. Or it could be an afterimage, which leaves a brief retinal impression of a visual after the stimulus has gone away. *Spectropia* demonstrates how this works through a series of sixteen color images of spooky ghost figures. Well, fifteen ghosts and one rainbow to end the book on a cheery note.

Try it for yourself. You can see the Creator's infinite skill in action by staring at the black asterisk on the ghost featured here for twenty seconds (inside the skeleton's nose). Then turn your head and look at a white wall or ceiling in your newly haunted house. You'll see the image float by in front of you and then vanish into nothingness, beyond the veil.

Other Spiritualists weren't dissuaded by Buguet's case either. After all, they loved their spirit photos. A letter in the November 1883 issue of *Gallery of Spirit Art*, for example, praised the spirit photography skills of New York City's Dr. William Keeler. The author, J. L. O'Sullivan, showed his support by proclaiming that the medium's "genuineness as a spirit photographer is beyond all question" and had sat for him seven times in one day for just a dollar a photo. Six images successfully showed a ghost of his mother. In each she held a cross, which he said was the way she always announced her presence to him through other mediums. As a result, O'Sullivan claimed, "it would be impossible for the photographic art to have produced these by fraud or trickery." He urged the Spiritualist readers to share the photographer's gift with all their non-Spiritualist friends. Decades later Keeler was exposed after a thorough examination by the American Society for Psychical Research.

Sir Arthur Conan Doyle sits for a spirit photo with his photographer of choice, William Hope. More of Hope's spirit photos can be found on page 206.

Not surprisingly, Sir Arthur Conan Doyle raved about spirit photos. His favorite shutterbug of the spirits was William Hope. Like Mumler, Hope's career started by accident. An Englishman from the town of Crewe, he snapped his first miraculous photo in the early 1900s while taking pictures of a friend. Upon developing the film he noticed the figure of the subject's sister in the print—his recently *deceased* sister. Hope embraced his newfound mediumship and embarked on a career that would last nearly thirty years.

It certainly helped that Doyle swore by his authenticity. Just looking at Hope, the Sherlock Holmes creator could hardly conceive how he could be deceived. "His hands with their worn nails and square-ended fingers are those of the worker, and the least adapted to sleight-of-hand tricks of any that I have seen," Doyle noted in his 1922 book, *The Case for Spirit Photography*.

Doyle's first experience with Hope came in 1919 with a visit to Crewe with two Spiritualist companions. Like his Holmes character, he played detective and tracked Hope's process throughout the sitting. As was often the case with Doyle, everything looked kosher.

"There is a hazy cloud covering us of what I will describe as ectoplasm, though my critics are very welcome to call it cotton-wool if it eases their feel-

ings to do so," Doyle wrote. "In one corner appears a partial materialization of what seems to be the hair and forehead of a young man."

The next day Doyle went back for more. Eventually he got a photo with a spirit that he claimed resembled his son eight years before his death. Doyle was sold.

Harry Price didn't share the same confidence in Hope. A few years after Doyle's first experience, Price caught the photographer changing his plates, which had been specially marked beforehand. "Arthur Conan Doyle and his friends abused me for years for exposing Hope," he wrote in *Confessions of a Ghost-Hunter*.

Another Doyle favorite was Alexander Martin of Denver, Colorado. He told Harry Houdini that Martin was "a very wonderful man in his particular line." So the magician paid him a visit, and once inside the studio he attempted to explore the dark room.

"Now don't you go in there, just wait a minute," Martin said.

The photographer proved to be quite particular. Houdini had to stand where Martin wanted him. "This led me to think he was keeping that side of the plate clean for something to appear," Houdini reported. After further secretive photographic tomfoolery, Martin finally shared some ghosts. Houdini's conclusion: "I have not the slightest doubt that Mr. Martin's Spirit photographs were simply double exposures."

Houdini also noted the lack of creativity not just in Martin's photos but in those of his peers and predecessors. The spirits always posed and appeared as they were in life. "How much more interesting it would be and how much more such photographs would add to our knowledge and aid the advancement of science if once in a while the Spirits would permit themselves to be snapped while engaged in some Spiritual occupation."

## Hippolyte Baraduc: Capturing the Mind and Soul on Film

The camera allowed for wondrously creative images, but not every spirit photographer tried capturing ghosts of friends and loved ones. French physician and parapsychologist Dr. Hippolyte Baraduc took the concept one step further: he claimed to take photos of thoughts and emotions—and even the soul.

In 1896, he informed the Paris Académie Nationale de Médecine that he had successfully photographed ideas. According to reports, Baraduc's method was simple: "The person whose thought is to be photographed enters a dark room, places his hand on a photographic plate, and thinks intently of the object the image of which he wishes to see produced."

Most of the images Baraduc supplied as evidence were very cloudy, but some, according to reports, offered distinct "features of persons and the outlines of things." He even claimed it was possible to produce thought photos from a distance, simply by willing an image from the mind to the photographic plates.

The doctor, along with others, believed we all exhibited auras. That our emotions produced energies. These too, Baraduc claimed, could be captured on film.

Two years after his announcement to the Académie, the doctor addressed the Society of Psychical Sciences in Paris. Newspapers reported that he informed the group that photography could "measure and register the volatile matter of which every living thing is constantly ridding itself."

Baraduc explained that he experimented on himself for ninety days by photographing himself whenever he felt his soul was particularly active. This early pioneer in selfies said the luminous points of images were full of light and vitality when he was happy and dim when nervous or sad. He found similar results with other people.

But he didn't just perform tests on humans: "I have experimented on pigeons, as well as on fresh milk. Moreover, there is evidence that even plants possess a sufficient amount of sensibility to render them fit subjects for such experiments. A Portuguese whom I know photographed some plants which he had just gathered, but obtained no result. Thereupon he tore them to pieces, crushed them in his hands and otherwise tortured them, and this time he was not disappointed. The plate contained fluidic impressions very similar to those which are obtained when a sickly person is the subject."

In April 1907, Baraduc took his studies to another level. His son, André, passed away at the age of nineteen. Nine hours afterward, Baraduc photographed the coffin and discovered a misty cloud emanating from all around it. Six months later, on October 15, Baraduc sadly had a chance to continue his studies with his wife, Nadine, on her deathbed. With his cameras all set up for the event, he captured a photo twenty minutes after her passing, which he claimed revealed her departing soul. The image appears to show three misty luminous clouds over her body. A photograph taken about thirty minutes later exhibits one larger cloud. Soon after, it left the body and floated into Baraduc's bedroom, creating an icy breeze before leaving entirely.

Hereward Carrington covered the phenomena in his 1921 book *The Problems of Psychical Research*:

There is no inherent absurdity in the idea, as many might suppose. Of course the spiritual body would have to be material enough to reflect light waves, but where is the evidence that it is not? There seems to be much evidence, on the contrary, that it is. It must be remembered that the camera will disclose innumerable things quite invisible to the naked eye, or even to the eye aided by the strongest glasses or telescopes. Normally, we can see but a few hundred stars in the sky; with the aid of telescopes, we can see many thousand; but the photographic camera discloses more than twenty million! Here, then, is direct evidence that the camera can observe things which we cannot see; and, indeed, this whole process of sight or "seeing" is a far more complicated one than most persons imagine. As Sir Oliver Lodge has pointed out, there is no reason why we should not be enabled to photograph a spirit, when we can photograph an image in a mirror—which is composed simply of vibrations, and reflected vibrations at that! We are a long way from the tangible thing, in such a case; and yet we are enabled to photograph it with an ordinary camera. Any disturbance in the ether we should be enabled to photograph likewise—if only we had delicate enough instruments, and if the "conditions" for the experiment were favourable. The phenomena of spirit-photography, and especially the experiments of Dr. Baraduc, to which I shall presently refer, would seem to indicate this.

---

Many think all these photographic effects could've come from tiny pinholes behind the camera lens, though Carrington's theory is much more exciting. So was Baraduc on to something? Could evidence of the soul—an afterlife existence—be proven? At the same time Baraduc was using a camera to find out, Dr. Duncan Macdougall of Haverhill, Massachusetts, was using a simpler tool: a scale. Macdougall theorized that the human soul occupied the entire physical body. If it had weight, then upon death and the soul's departure, the body would weigh less.

Sir Walter Raleigh had the same idea in the sixteenth century. Not about souls, but about smoke. Raleigh believed he could weigh smoke and, as the story goes, he made a bet with Queen Elizabeth I to prove he was right. She made the wager and then watched as Raleigh weighed a cigar, smoked it, and carefully tapped the ashes back onto the scale. The ashes and butt indeed weighed less, proving that smoke accounted for the before-and-after difference. The queen paid up. Macdougall hoped for similar results by weighing a body just before death and again at the moment of death.

He'd been working secretly on the experiment for six years with the help of a sanitarium. There, he found a dozen test subjects on the verge of death, usually from tuberculosis. The dying patients gave him the results he sought. With each death, the scale showed an immediate drop in weight of three-quarters of an ounce to one ounce. Thus, he proclaimed, the soul weighed roughly three-quarters of an ounce. Macdougall, it seemed, had scientific evidence of the soul's existence. Though the testing preceded Edison's spirit phone project, the concept aligns with the inventor's theory of tiny life units moving on to a new life. Macdougall wasn't interested in talking with the souls, just acknowledging their existence. Problem solved, right? Well, not so fast.

Carrington, who kept up on all the latest psychical goings-on, got involved with the project and recommended Macdougall continue his experiments with a better brand of patients: criminals. More specifically, murderers facing execution. They could be weighed before and immediately after facing the chair. As reported in the *Washington Times*, this would allow Macdougall to test his theory on men dying "in the full vigor of their manhood" and as a bonus, the doomed prisoners would be "made of some use to the world in this way."

Carrington loved the results Macdougall had gotten in his sanitarium studies but had concerns that they were flawed because the patients were all in the midst of death. "Decomposition, some types of which in a very short space of time, might have taken place at the instant of death," he said. "How much more satisfactory it would be if the subjects were normal men in perfect health?"

There are no recorded incidents of Macdougall following through with Carrington's suggestion, perhaps because bigger skeptics started weighing in. For example, Anton J. Carlson, an associate professor of physiology at the University of Chicago, offered a different explanation for the change in weight: "It is probably that the loss of weight was due to the passing out of carbon dioxide gas, which is a very natural result. Every time a man breathes a certain amount of weight is lost by the passing out of a certain amount of water and also of carbon dioxide gas."

Carlson's dean of the medical school, John M. Dodson, was less scientific in his analysis: "Such a statement about the weight of a man's soul is absolutely silly."

But outside the medical field, Macdougall found appreciation for his hard

# THE WEIGHING OF A SOUL

## What Is a Soul?

Dr. Macdougall asserts that it has the same shape as the human body, and that it weighs three-quarters of an ounce. He claims to have proved this by experiments.

CAN the human soul be weighed? Is it a material substance which has a definite shape and weight?

Dr. Duncan Macdougall, of Haverhill, Mass., answers yes, and says that he has proved it beyond all question.

He claims to have done this just as Sir Walter Raleigh first proved to a doubting audience that smoke has weight.

RALEIGH first weighed the tobacco, and, after he had smoked his pipe, weighed the ashes. The difference, he said, was the weight of the smoke.

**Weighs Three-quarters of Ounce.**

Dr. Macdougall has been weighing human bodies just before death and immediately following. He claims that he has found a difference of about three-quarters of an ounce.

Three-quarters of an ounce is therefore, the weight of a soul, according to Dr. Macdougall. He has been conducting the experiments for a period of six years.

In order to test the theory still further, Dr. Howard Carrington, of New York, suggests that murderers be weighed just before and just after they are electrocuted.

At the Ohio penitentiary in Columbus executions are being made. It

is said, to make the first experiment in this way. The man whose death will thus be made of interest to science and to the world in general is Dr. Oliver Haugh, of Dayton, who will be electrocuted next month for the murder of his father, mother, and brother.

**Same Shape as Body.**

Dr. Macdougall's theory is that the soul occupies the entire physical body during life, in shape and proportion, therefore, the soul, which goes out at the moment of death is the same as the body. But it is much less dense, for it only weighs three-quarters of an ounce. It is even less than air, he says, and upon going out into the air rises. But where it goes is something that no one knows.

In addition to the experiments which he made with human beings Dr. Macdougall also tried to find out for the same means whether dogs have souls. Some people claim that these intelligent and much-petted animals have souls as surely as be human beings.

The device used his ascertain the facts about soul. Grant and Sprouls, selected thirteen

dogs weighing from fifteen to seventy pounds. "Each one of these died," he says "as scales balanced to weigh the fraction of an ounce, and in each case the weight, even in the heaviest of them, remained exactly the same.

**Death Caused Scales to Drop.**

In the case of human beings," he adds, "the very second of death was determined by the instant dropping of the opposite scale."

The famous French astronomer, Camille Flammarion, says has weighed.

"If is my own belief," he says further, "that the soul of most exists at an entity, independent of his body, and

it survive the destruction of the same.

"It is certain that one soul can influence another soul at a distance and without the aid of the senses. There is not the slightest doubt in my mind that the soul acts not as a dynamo.

"The soul by its interior vision and not only what is needed at a great distance, but it may also have at influence what is to happen in the future.

"Positive observation proves the existence of a psychic soul, as real as the world knows it our physical sense.

"And now, because the soul acts at a distance in some power that belongs to it, as are authorized to conclude that it exists or something real. I think that the soul exists, and that it is endowed with faculties at present unknown.

"For many years," says Dr. Macdougall, "I had given much thought to the subject of death, and especially to the nature of the soul doing after the separation from the body. I reasoned that personal identity to be retained without a space-occupying body, it could not be, therefore, that nothing, I thought,

be something. If a soul is a space-occupying body, I thought, it must have substance. Then I thought, what kind of substance has it? Does it possess weight?

It was this last question which led him to undertake the experiments which he has carried on for six years in the Cuillo Free Home for Consumptives.

It was because Dr. Macdougall's experiments were made with persons who died when worn out with disease that Dr. Carrington suggested making similar experiments with men who die in the full vigor of their manhood, and he said that murderers who are put to death might be made of some use to the world in this way.

## Thrilling Moving Pictures Quicken Pulse But No Excitement in Making Them

## Hidden in Sauerkraut Revolutionist Escapes

GREGORY GERSHUNI, first leader of the fighting organization in Russia, has come to America.

work. One minister hoped the doctor was correct, noting that science would have "done more for the church than it has ever succeeded in doing before. The conversion of the world would be made easier, for it would establish beyond controversy the truth of life beyond the grave."

Since Macdougall's results were not "beyond controversy," those seeking evidence of the afterlife would just have to find new ways to get it. Technology, after all, had plenty of other new tricks up its sleeve.

## The Original Ghost Hunters

By the early 1920s a whole host of new contraptions were being developed by the crafty investigators of the American Psychical Institute and Laboratory in New York to either snatch a ghost or record evidence of one. These early ghostbusters were led by our friend, the always-curious and ever-prolific Hereward Carrington. His "Psychic Howler" was likely on par with other machines but certainly boasted the best name.

The psychical researcher hoped the howler—technically called the ululometer—would force haunted houses to at long last give up their secrets. So what was this seemingly magical machine? Carrington described it as an "intensely sensitive coil of three thousand finely turned copper wires" which could be set up wherever one suspected a ghost might be lurking. When, for example, the ululometer sat in a room believed to be haunted, wires would connect it to a receiving apparatus in another room where investigators would listen for a signal—like waiting for a spirit to answer the phone. Its delicate sensitivity could record radiating energy from the hearts and lungs of the living, so Carrington theorized that energies radiated by a spirit creeping around would be detected as well simply by causing a variation in the electric current passing through the coil. When that happened, it would set off a loud howling noise. He'd record and preserve these ghost calls on a phonograph record.

In case the ghost howls weren't caught on shellac, Carrington also armed himself with an oscillograph. This type of instrument could register the vibrations emanating from the human body—imperceptible to the human senses, like ultraviolet rays.

Picture this oscillograph as having a glass cone with a small opening at the top, standing on a circular graduated disc. The opening is covered by a flat nickel disc, from which a fine thread hangs inside, and a small ball is suspended from the string. If a person were to place their hands on top of this device and keep them steady, the ball would start to swing. Carrington believed the motion of the ball would vary based on the gender, temperament, electric, and psychic nature of the subject. Most important, the ball would move without the subject applying any discernible force.

"If, as so many reports indicate, spirits are capable of exerting physical force, then it is reasonable to believe they can influence this exceedingly delicate instrument," the *Washington Times* wrote in 1922. "Furthermore, there is a hypothesis that the vibratory force is that part of the body which survives after the tangible portion dies."

If Carrington or another investigator couldn't sit around all night waiting for a ghost, a psychic Dictaphone could help. This handy tool was just what it sounds like—an instrument that takes dictation from ghosts. As described by a reporter in 1921, "A spirit capable of producing the faintest impression on a sensitive disc can leave a message when there is no one in the laboratory at any hour of the day or night, which can afterward be amplified." No need for a medium to hear raps, knocks, whispers, and footsteps from the Other Side.

None of these fancy devices were known to have registered the presence of a dead person. But Carrington, ever the optimist, found new hope in two well-respected Dutch doctors, J. L. W. P. Matla and G. J. Zaalberg van Zelst. Twenty years of intense research led them to what they believed demonstrated proof of a physical existence after death. This miraculous achievement that promised to solve humankind's greatest question once and for all was made possible by a piece of cardboard.

(This page and page 211) Ghost technology made headlines throughout the early twentieth century, including attempts to weigh the soul and detect the presence of ghosts with air displacement.

To use the doctors' more scientific terminology, this cardboard was a twenty-inch-tall cylindrical chamber called a dynamistograph. Its capacity was about twenty-two liters, which equated to about two-fifths of an average-sized man. Matla and van Zelst placed it inside a room seven feet long, six feet wide, and nine feet high, with a concrete floor to prevent the earth's vibrations from affecting the data. A controlled temperature and atmospheric pressure helped guard against other natural interference. The cylinder was then hermetically sealed at the top and bottom and fitted with a thermometer-like device to register displacement of air. This "manometer," as they called it, used a drop of alcohol instead of mercury, and its slightest movement would indicate a displacement and measure the volume of a man's spirit, or a "man-force." To put it simply, the plan was to call for a spirit to enter the chamber and determine its weight based on the amount of space the spirit occupied in the cylinder.

As the doctors waited outside the sealed-off room, all measurements had to be observed through a small window in the door, often with the aid of opera glasses to get a closer look at the fluctuations of the instruments. The last piece of the puzzle, of course, was a cooperative spirit. Lucky for them, all they had to do was ask. As Carrington tells the story, a man-force immediately entered the chamber and a bubble inside the manometer proved that a portion of the air had been displaced by a "solid or semi-solid body." Next the doctors asked the spirit to leave the chamber and then reenter. The bubble ran back and forth across the scale accordingly.

"The fact of coincidence was thus quite excluded," Carrington noted. Matla and van Zelst were enthused by their results but believed they needed a bigger piece of cardboard to fine-tune the data. Cylinders ranging from forty to sixty liters in capacity were tested, and after a series of man-force observations they determined that the human spirit weighed 2.25 ounces—about triple the weight of the soul that Macdougall had calculated. The afterlife entity's molecules, they believed, were held together by some unknown "x-force."

This breakthrough led them to the development of a new and improved dynamistograph that would enable the man-force to communicate without a need for a human intermediary. Think of it like a mash-up of a Ouija board and a typewriter. The Ouija-like part consisted of a wheel with twenty-eight spaces, one for each letter of the alphabet along with a period and a blank space. A motor turned this wheel one space every five seconds. If the man-force wanted to "type" a letter, it would press its tiny weight against an electric "key" designed to be ultrasensitive to any amount of pressure. If touched ever so slightly, electricity would course through the wires and jolt a typewriter-like hammer forward, striking a ribbon and printing the letter on a strip of paper.

This dynamistograph, as Carrington described, was kept in a cupboard at a constant temperature and barometric dryness. If spirits wanted to play with it, they simply moved through the doors by a form of osmosis. The doctors

"The man who discovers such an energy—common to the two worlds—and learns how to direct and utilize it for the purpose of communication, will assuredly be hailed as the greatest scientist of all time; one beside whom Newton and Galileo and Darwin and Archimedes will shrink into insignificance, and their discoveries appear small and trivial when compared with this great cosmic truth!"

—Hereward Carrington on the eventual discovery of an instrument that successfully communicates with the dead, in *Modern Psychical Phenomena* from 1919 ran experiments for a year and claimed to have received messages daily. As you might expect, they learned a lot. First of all, since the spirit was physical in form, it had a shape. By Matla and van Zelst's estimation, these ghosts drifted about like invisible heads and shoulders while the rest of their bodies faded away.

"According to the accounts given by this entity, it does not have by any means a 'fine time' of it in the next life," Carrington reported, "but is destined to wander about aimlessly, unable to do anything, having no useful members until it disintegrates in the same way that the physical body does here! It undergoes a 'second death;' and then, annihilation!"

This outlook was far less cheerful than the messages received by Spiritualist mediums. But even if an afterlife annihilation awaits us all, a third state of existence could follow. So maybe things will eventually look up. Regardless of our ultimate fate, Carrington was excited by the preliminary results and the potential of making contact beyond the veil through instrumentation alone, noting that if Matla and van Zelst's experiments proved conclusive, "then some form of electricity would seem to be the intermediary between the two worlds. We may then have a wireless direct to the spirit world!"

Harry Price opted for a more low-tech approach to ghost hunting. His kit, as mentioned in part three, was packed with felt overshoes to ensure quiet footsteps, flashlights with extra batteries, a notebook to record potential events, a camera loaded with infrared film for night shots, a thermograph to detect temperature changes in a room, mercury in a bowl to detect tremors, fingerprint brushes, a portable telephone to communicate with other researchers, and more. On March 10, 1936, he added a BBC broadcast to his goodie bag during an investigation of an old haunted house near Meopham in Kent, England. "There was no reason to hope that we should broadcast any actual phenomena, which, as is always the case in haunted houses, are so very spontaneous, rare, and sporadic," he acknowledged.

The only thing Price could promise listeners was a detailed journey alongside his team as they explored and prepared the house. He rigged up four microphones to cover the attic and the cellar and coated floors with powder to detect ghostly footsteps (do they leave footprints?), but none were detected. However, at about 9:45 p.m., one minor phenomenon did occur in the "haunted cellar." Price's thermograph transmitted a sudden variation in temperature, deviating from its consistent level throughout the day. England's most famous ghost hunter had no explanation for his listeners, other than that, perhaps, the first radio broadcast of a spirit had just occurred. Newspaperman Denny Brown had a different theory, suggesting the temperature fluctuation "may have been caused by perspiration on the brows of the excited radio men on the floor above."

By 1938 Austrian-born Hans Holzer had moved to New York and soon became the first big name in American ghost hunting. In addition to the Amityville case, he investigated thousands of paranormal events around the world, in locations ranging from private residences to motorcycle shops to strip clubs to medieval churches. He believed many ghosts were confused about their state of being and were "caught up in the emotional turmoil of their tragedies." If he could convince them that they were dead and it was time to move on, they could feel free to head off into the spirit world. These poor ghosts just needed a good psychopomp.

Holzer, like Price, didn't rely on the latest technology. Pen and paper, a camera and tape recorder, interviews with witnesses, and research as needed at local historical societies and libraries were enough. That, and a trance medium at his side. In one investigation he even brought Regis Philbin. Price had his radio show, but Holzer would use television and one of its rising stars.

The TV icon was just a young talk show host in San Diego in 1965 when

Ghost hunter and psychical researcher Harry Price uses a low-tech approach to detect ghosts in the cellar of a haunted house in Kent, England, during a radio broadcast for the BBC in 1936.

"The camera has no human foibles and emotions. What it sees, it sees. If ghostly impressions on the ether are emotionally triggered electric impulses in nature, it seems conceivable that a sensitive film inside the camera may record it."

–Hans Holzer, in his 1965 book *Ghosts I've Met*, adding that all his film is developed by commercial houses he suggested that he and Holzer spend an evening at the haunted Whaley House, a two-story brick house built in 1857 in the heart of Old Town. Long before haunted houses were flooded with film crews, the two decided to bring one along to record a séance with Holzer's medium, Sybil Leek, and then discuss the experience on Philbin's show the next day. Regis had been to the Whaley House once before and claimed to have seen an image of a "transparent shape of a woman," which disappeared when he shone a flashlight on it.

As Leek fell into a trance, Holzer conversed with ghosts speaking through her and learned that there were indeed numerous presences in the house: Thomas Whaley, the original owner; his wife; and a few children. Whaley had no intention of leaving his house, despite being dead. Later, Holzer discovered a man known as Yankee Jim Robinson was hanged on the property in 1852 as punishment for stealing a boat. He, too, stuck around the house, as if trapped on the gallows. Much of the information gleaned from Leek was corroborated through Holzer's research. Philbin, however, didn't have a repeat sighting of the presence from his first visit.

In 2019, Holzer's daughter and a current ghost hunter, Alexandra, brought another film crew to the Whaley House to pick up where her father left off for an episode of her show, *The Holzer Files*. Her team's lead investigator, Dave Schrader, found that the spirits hadn't left. And they seemed angry.

"This thing drops me like a sack of potatoes," he said in a 2020 interview with the podcast *Edge of Reality Radio*, referring to a ghostly encounter. "Hits me so hard I practically broke my hip. . . . That was life-altering, because I never believed so much about the physical contact aspect, but now I can tell you wholeheartedly it happens and it's scary as hell when it does."

If it was Yankee Jim, who could blame a ghost for being a little irritable after spending nearly 170 years in the place where he was hanged?

## Electric Voice Phenomena

The electronic voice phenomena (EVP) craze began innocently enough back in 1959 with a group of birds just minding their own business and singing in the woods. On that day, June 12, Swedish artist Friedrich Jürgenson was out and about capturing the sounds of nature with his recorder and made an unexpected discovery upon listening to his reel-to-reel tape. Amid the birdsong was static noise peppered with voices. He initially assumed he'd picked up radio signals from afar, but as he listened closely he found that the voices were discussing "birdsongs at night." This, he felt, was too bizarre to be a coincidence. He headed back out to the forest with his recorder and captured more sounds of birds and spirits. The messages seemed to become more personal. At one point he believed he heard his deceased mother call to him in German, "Friedel, my little Friedel, can you hear me?"

Jürgenson continued making recordings, and after publishing his findings in 1965 he attracted the attention of Latvian parapsychologist Konstantin Raudive. The two began collaborating and recruited German parapsychologist Hans Bender. They started by pulling the experiments out of the woods and putting them into a controlled environment in an attempt to protect against random outside transmissions. Over the next several years they recorded more than a hundred thousand phrases within a controlled laboratory space. During these sessions one of the researchers noted that "Man had very little knowledge of matters concerning life after death, and that neither his understanding, his judgment,

nor his intuition could follow the implications." In reviewing the tapes, a voice responded, "He can."

Chatting with the dead through electronic devices (now called instrumental transcommunication, or ITC) seemed quite promising. Many of these messages from beyond, however, weren't unlike the types of generic communications about faith, friendship, love, and courage that Spiritualist mediums frequently reported. Among the otherworldly nuggets of wisdom and advice were:

"It is the heart that counts."

"We should beware of flattery."

"Tolerance is important."

"Love is necessary."

"Don't talk too much!"

As thrilling as hearing voices from the dead must have been, it's a shame they didn't have more interesting messages to share. Surely the greatest mystery of humankind warrants more enlightening conversation. Nevertheless, Raudive published accounts of these types of recordings in the 1968 book *The Inaudible Becomes Audible* in Germany. A UK publisher, Colin Smythe, was intrigued and consulted with the English psychologist Peter Bander to determine whether or not to proceed with an English translation.

"Although I knew some of Dr. Raudive's collaborators personally and have always respected their scientific work, the thought of dead people communi-

"I am convinced that other-worldly beings are trying to contact the living through audible manifestations via electromagnetic waves. . . . Konstantin Raudive deserves all the credit for having made this phenomenon accessible to us."

–Dr. Wilhelmine C. Hennequin, anesthetist and one of many of Raudive's convinced coresearchers, in 1967 cating through a tape recorder seemed really too silly to be taken seriously," Bander wrote in the introduction to his 1973 book *Voices from the Tapes: Recordings from the Other World.*

Smythe had already carried out his own experiment and shared the tapes with Bander to convince him that maybe Raudive's work wasn't so silly after all. The psychologist humored the publisher and gave a close listen to a particular section Smythe had pointed out.

"I was on the point of giving up when suddenly I noticed the peculiar rhythm mentioned by Raudive and his colleagues," Bander wrote. "After a further five or six playbacks, out of the blue, I heard a voice. It was in German, . . . I believed this to have been the voice of my mother who had died three years earlier. This was the first of a number of remarkable happenings which moved me to change my mind."

The revised English language edition of Raudive's book, *Breakthrough: An Amazing Experiment in Electronic Communication*, hit bookstore shelves in 1971. If EVPs hadn't been a thing before, they were now. But were these recordings, as the title suggested, a breakthrough to the afterlife? Or were the researchers unintentionally identifying stray radio signals as voices of the dead? Parapsychologist Jurgen Keil studied a recording that Raudive considered one of his clearest EVPs and concluded that it had likely been a German radio broadcast of an Easter Sunday service.

A student at Trinity College at Cambridge, David Ellis, began his own investigations in the early 1970s. In one of them, he managed to collaborate with Raudive using a recorder in a Faraday cage to ensure no radio signals could sneak onto the tape. The dead remained silent. Other experiments, conducted with Bander, yielded a mixed bag of results. Some researchers on the team believed they heard voices, some weren't sure, and a few even believed that when voices were captured they originated not from the dead but from flying saucers.

Apophenia is another likely cause of the EVP excitement. This is essentially the audio version of pareidolia, in which the mind makes sense of patterns and draws conclusions. Like finding a shape in a cloud or Jesus on your toast, the mind finds words in patterns of noise. Expectations of hearing something only enhance one's ability to hear it. For example, it's hard not to hear Jimi Hendrix sing "'Scuse me while I kiss this guy" once you've been told to listen for it instead of "'Scuse me while I kiss the sky."

As for Bander's experiments, he felt they were on to something but recognized the results were preliminary and the technology needed refinement to discover if EVPs could lead to genuine conversations with the deceased.

"Our scientists and engineers have yet to invent a machine or discover a method which would yield instant results," he said. "'Dial M for Mother' is still something very much in the future."

That future seemed to arrive in 1979, thanks to a man named George W. Meek, who believed a dead man had recorded the words "Mary had a little lamb." As incredible as Thomas Edison must have felt in 1877 hearing those words in the first recording of a human, Meek might have been even more amazed capturing them in what he considered the first two-way voice contact with the beyond.

Decades earlier, he had earned a fortune as an engineer in the air-conditioning business. In 1970 the now-retired Meek founded the Metascience Foundation to study the nature of life and the afterlife. After twelve years of research, he ecstatically announced his findings at a news conference at the National Press Club in Washington, DC. It was April 6, 1982, just days before Easter. The timing was no coincidence. Meek's announcement was, in his mind, the biggest news in resurrecting the dead since Jesus.

"For many Christians, this may be one of the most significant Easter weeks in two thousand years," he declared in his opening remarks. As he built up to his grand achievement, he acknowledged some of the journalists might be shaking their heads and wondering, "Is this guy Meek some sort of crackpot?"

He hoped his ITC evidence and detailed instructions on how to receive messages from beyond would eventually put such concerns to rest. Meek, along with an electronics whiz and psychic medium named William O'Neil, had built a machine called the Spiricom. As in "spirit communications." It was just the sort of thing Edison was trying to build sixty years earlier. But Meek believed he had succeeded. More specifically, he believed O'Neil had triumphed by combining electronic technology with his psychic energies. Meek merely funded and promoted the effort.

"For the first time we have electronic proof that the mind, memory banks, and personality survive death of the physical body," Meek announced. Then he repeated himself for effect.

"An elementary start has been made toward the eventual perfection of an electromagnetic-etheric communications system that will someday permit those living on earth to have telephone-like conversations with persons very much alive in higher levels of consciousness." He repeated that statement, too. After all, this was the news humanity had been waiting to hear since forever. It'd be a shame to have missed it.

Meek claimed to have several hours of recordings on tape featuring voices from the afterlife. One came from Fred Engstrom, a man who died in rural Maryland in 1830. As Meek shared two minutes of Engstrom's posthumous words, he noted that "records of that area during that time are scanty" and therefore he couldn't verify that Engstrom lived when he said he did, but he did believe that O'Neil had verified facts about his life.

Astral voices from English Shakespearean actress Ellen Terry and American publishing giant William Randolph Hearst were also captured by the Spiricom. But the most robust conversation came from an American physicist, Dr. George Jeffries Mueller, who died of a heart attack in 1967. Mueller was more than a voice on a tape; he became an integral part of the Meek-O'Neil team by offering technical advice on their equipment. Again, Meek played samples from his recordings.

"Near the third transistor in the preamp unit. There is an impedance mismatch, which could be corrected by using a 150-ohm half-watt resistor with a .0047 ceramic microfarad capacitor," Mueller told O'Neil from the land of the dead. His voice sounded garbled and robotic, as if his consciousness had left his body and floated into a pile of microfarad capacitors.

"What better proof could there be that Dr. Mueller's mind, memory banks, and personality are still alive and functioning in a useful and dramatic way?" Meek challenged the reporters.

Mueller's recording also included mundane banter between him and O'Neil that seemed far less scientific. "Oh wonderful, send me a couple of carrots . . . and a nice head of lettuce," the dead physicist told his living inventor, perhaps in a discussion of some type of telekinetic machine in the works.

By now those in attendance must have either been picking their jaws up off the ground or shaking their heads in confusion and skepticism. Most likely the latter, and Meek was fully prepared for such a reaction. This breakthrough was no different than discovering humans could achieve flight. Meek reminded his audience of a 1903 *New York Times* editorial opining that human flight wouldn't happen for another thousand years, just days before the Wright brothers lifted off the ground for the first time. He also drew on Edison's

**SPIRICOM**

An Electromagnetic-Etheric Systems Approach
to
Communications
with
Other Levels of Human Consciousness

COPY NO. *16*

(This page, opposite page, and page 226) George W. Meek and William O'Neil's Spiricom, the spiritual successor of Thomas Edison's spirit telephone, came with a detailed manual. Among the ghostly voices it allegedly captured was that of American businessman William Randolph Hearst.

early experience with the phonograph and an investigation of the device by a member of the French Académie des Sciences who investigated the device and assured his colleagues "that the effect is accomplished by ventriloquism." The Spiricom was just another great milestone for humankind. Still, Meek knew

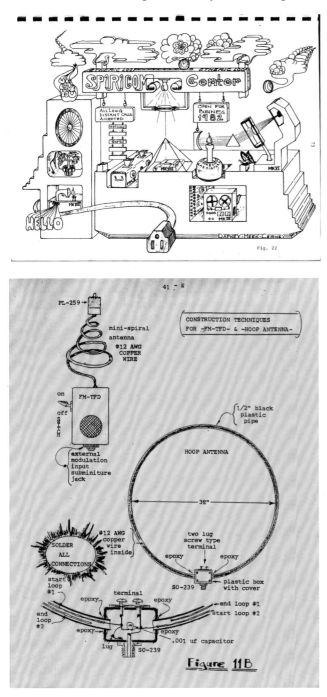

some would cry fraud. But he wouldn't waste his efforts on them, preferring to stay focused on research. There was, after all, lots of work to be done to perfect his machine. Adding to his challenges was the fact that Dr. Mueller had ceased his communications just prior to the news conference. It seemed he had moved on to a higher plane in the afterlife at a rather inconvenient time for the living.

As Meek wrapped up his speech, he stressed there was no motivation for such a "cruel and senseless" fraud. Why would he risk his good name? He wasn't even seeking a patent on the machine; in fact, he was offering a technical manual with full schematics to anyone and everyone who wanted it so the Spiricom could benefit all of humanity. Right or wrong about the device, you had to admire his benevolence.

"Maybe during these days before Easter you can steal some space from stories about murders and wars and rapes and robberies and drugs and natural disasters to share the news that man is far more than the highly trainable pigeon or rat with which he is equated by our behavioristic psychologists," Meek said in closing.

The next day, the press reported on the Spiricom, as Meek had hoped for. One reporter described the voices from beyond as sounding like "Igor responding to Dr. Frankenstein through a closed

◁ ▷ A Very Unusual Notice Regarding
Copyrights, Patents, Suppression and Harassment

All researchers affiliated with Metascience Foundation during
the ten years of world-wide study of problems and potentials of
electronic communication with the so-called "dead" have shared a
common goal. They want the fruit of their labors and financial
contributions to be made freely available to people of all races
all over the world.

Therefore, on their behalf I state that:

1. We have not filed for any patents in any countries on the
   many inventions represented by the equipment presented
   herein.

2. The material in this report has not been copyrighted.

3. The name SPIRICOM has not been trademarked.

But please note! Everything in the cosmos is energy of one
sort or another, and although all energies can be used for good
or for evil, it is our hope that the hundreds of individuals and
organizations which will carry these developments forward in the
decades ahead, will use them ONLY FOR THE GOOD OF ALL MANKIND.

If any individuals acting alone or as part of a corporate
entity endeavor to use these inventions solely for money-making
purposes, or to the detriment of any person, they are herewith
forewarned: They should know that the first step for them, after
they sooner or later shed their physical bodies, will be at the
bottom of the Lowest Astral Plane - as described on the Metascience
diagram entitled, "In Our Father's House There are Many Mansions."

We are gradually waking up to the fact that our universe and
all therein operates on an inexorable law of cause and effect.
None can afford to scoff at the admonition, "As ye sow, so shall
ye reap." And note carefully the contents of Chapter 13!

Any effort by any individual or organization to suppress or
destroy the material contained herein will be useless, and any
attempt to in any way harass or harm any of the Metascience research
team will be pointless: the material contained herein has been
distributed throughout the world to more than one thousand persons
who are dedicated to the ultimate perfection of a clear, static-
free, dependable system for communication with those persons now
living in the higher worlds of spirit who desire to bring enlight-
enment to mankind.

George W. Meek
President and Director of Research
Metascience Foundation, Inc.

door on a windy night in Transylvania."

Several years later a minister from Oklahoma named Terrance Peterson began looking into Meek's tapes and the vocal qualities of the supposed recorded spirits. He noticed a few odd things. Yes, a dead person's voice on a tape is obviously the first odd thing, but looking past that, Peterson was struck by the strange use of language. Dr. Mueller repeated O'Neil's first name, William, fifty-three times, which is unusual in a conversation. He also exhibited poor grammar, and both he and Fred Engstrom said "oh boy" multiple times. That phrase, Peterson noted in an exposé in *Fate* magazine, hadn't come into usage until around 1920. Another curious recording found Mueller calling out for William, wondering if he was there, yet a spirit reaching out to a medium would know if he was there. How would he find his way into a lab and not know if the host was available? But what bugged Peterson more was the computerized quality of the voices. They reminded him of the sound of an electrolarynx—what someone might use to speak after losing their voice box to cancer. Was O'Neil using such a device to create the ghostly voices? Meek's confidence came from the reports of several speech and electronics experts' analysis of the tapes, which indicated the voiceprints came from two separate voices. One was O'Neil, so the other had to be Mueller, or one of the other spirits.

Peterson sought another opinion from an old friend, Dr. David Rivers, who happened to be a speech and language scientist at Texas's Baylor University. Rivers hardly shared Meek's enthusiasm. "Send me your tape and I'll duplicate what Dr. Mueller says with my voice," the professor said.

A few weeks later Peterson had a new tape which, according to the voiceprints, featured two separate voices: that of Rivers, and one with the artificial larynx reciting, "Mary had a little lamb" like Igor in bad weather in again. That was enough for Peterson to conclude that "Spiricom is considerably less than 'one of the most exciting events in the long history of man'" and apparently "no more than a fairly transparent hoax."

Meek did not care much for Peterson's article and let the editor of *Fate* know in a lengthy letter that he had requested be printed for the magazine's readers. In it, he suggested that Peterson should've reached out to him personally to read through his piles of documents before jumping to a "flawed" conclusion. He added, in the third person, "Before charging hoax, he would have first sought to find what possible motive Meek could have had for having spent several hundred thousand dollars of his own savings in the most serious research project of its kind ever assembled. And he would have asked himself why Meek would be so foolish as to gamble an international reputation and saddle his children, grandchildren and great-grandchildren with the disgrace which such a hoax might entail. Was Meek really so diabolic a character that he would perpetrate a cruel and senseless hoax?"

A few more angry comments followed before Meek suggested that "history, not Mr. Peterson, will be the judge."

History is now judging, and what it's learned is that O'Neil's only income came from Meek, so the more results he shared, the more bills he could pay. This cash flow may have motivated him to fool Meek with the recordings. For all of the engineer's excitement, he had truly entrusted O'Neil to all the work. Meek was never actually in attendance of any of the spirit recordings. They were left entirely in the hands of this brilliant mediumistic electronics whiz who wasn't quite what he appeared to be. Though Meek had scoffed at the French scientist who accused Edison of using ventriloquism, it turned out that O'Neil himself was a trained ventriloquist and was in possession of an electrolarynx. Making the case all the more strange, O'Neil was also diagnosed with schizophrenia, meaning that the hoax may have been unconscious and unintentional.

## How Physics Haunts Us

If you had to pick a type of place that might be haunted, a fourteenth-century English cellar would rank pretty high on the list. It's old, dark, underground, and perfectly creepy. What more could a ghost ask for?

Near Coventry Cathedral in the heart of England, such a cellar sits beneath its tourist information center. Once used to store wool, clothing, spices, and other valuable goods, the cellar became inaccessible during World War II when its entrance was blocked off after an enemy bombing. The cathedral was renovated in 1962, and the addition of the tourist center opened access to the medieval cellar once again. And strange experiences followed.

Visitors walking through the long, narrow corridor that led to the cellar would fall ill upon crossing the threshold of the room. Some would turn white as goosebumps quickly spread across their arms. Others felt a chill and the presence of an otherworldly entity. Those were just the normal, everyday globetrotting tourists. Then there were the witches. "White witches," meaning those who practice magic for the purposes of good, to be precise.

Two of these women ventured into the cellar together in the late 1990s hoping to establish contact with whatever ghost might be lurking there. They claimed success, reporting the presence of a friendly spirit belonging to a woman. All those other tourists had nothing to fear. Unless, that is, they listened to the third white witch, who descended into the cellar and ruined all the good vibes. Whatever spirit she detected proved far less friendly and sent her racing away in absolute terror.

With such a plethora of activity, the spooky cellar attracted the attention of a ghost hunter. But this wasn't your typical modern ghost hunter armed with EVP recorders and EMF detectors. This was Vic Tandy, an engineer and technology lecturer at nearby Coventry University. More than a decade earlier he'd gotten into hunting ghosts for a reason no one else could claim: he'd caught one.

It happened by accident in the late 1970s, and unlike other ghostbusters who've claimed to capture elusive evidence of the afterlife, Tandy stirred far less debate with his discovery. That wasn't the headline, though. The big news was the realization that a low-frequency, inaudible sound wave called infrasound affects our senses and creates visions of what can be perceived as ghosts.[12] In other words, Tandy's ghost was born from science, not the supernatural.

The engineer's discovery began late one night while he was working at an English medical manufacturing laboratory that he'd been warned was haunted. Burning the midnight oil, he felt "increasingly uncomfortable" and broke into a cold sweat as he sat at his desk writing. That's when he sensed an apparition.

"I became aware that I was being watched, and a figure slowly emerged to my left," Tandy later recalled. "It was indistinct and on the periphery of my vision, but it moved just as I would expect a person to. It was gray, and made no sound. I was terrified."

Pushing fear aside, he turned to face whatever was there but the apparition faded and vanished. He decided he might be "cracking up" and headed home. Undeterred by whatever might be haunting the laboratory, Tandy returned the next day armed with a fencing foil—not to ward off the ghost, but to make a few minor adjustments to his blade in preparation for an upcoming competition. He placed it in a vice and went to find some oil. When he returned a few minutes later he noticed the free end of the blade vibrating wildly. Given the previous night's episode, the unprovoked movement gave him a "twinge of fright." But then his engineering instincts took over. Vibrating metal granted him a decided advantage over an apparition: he could run experiments to find the source of the energy.

Tandy arranged the foil in the vice as before and moved it along the floor across the room. Near his desk the vibration was intense, but as he slid the blade away the amplitude lessened and eventually the vibration stopped.

---

12  Infrasound also happens to be used by elephants to communicate over long distances. Spending time with chatty elephants would lead to extraordinary memories for anyone. And maybe some paranormal ones too.

"You can't hear it, but it makes you shake. In a good theater with a subwoofer, you may be more scared by the sound than by what's happening on the screen. A lot of people can take the images but not the sound. Those reactions are physical."

—Gaspar Noé, director of *Irreversible*, discussing his use of infrasound in the unsettling film with Salon.com in 2003

This told him there was a "standing wave" next to his desk sending a very low-frequency sound wave through the foil.

"It turned out to be caused by a new extraction fan, which was making the air vibrate at about nineteen cycles per second," he explained. "When the fan's mounting was altered, the ghost left with the standing wave."

Tandy had unmasked the source of the ghost. But what exactly had that frequency done to his vision, and how might it have been affecting others who'd thought they'd been seeing ghosts? Digging deeper, he discovered that the low-frequency sound waves were known to cause severe middle ear pain, persistent eye watering, respiratory difficulties, and sensations of fear—including excessive perspiration and shivering. Furthermore, he found research stating that an 18.9 Hz resonant frequency can cause a vibration in the eyeball, leading to "a serious 'smearing' of vision." Until Tandy, no one had connected that physical phenomena with the idea of "smeared" vision as an explanation for seeing ghostly forms.

After his revelation, Tandy began researching other allegedly haunted places, like the basement in Coventry, to see if reported experiences could officially be blamed on infrasound instead of dead cellar dwellers. Equipped with his own brand of ghost hunting equipment—a precision sound level meter fitted with a microphone sensitive to frequencies down to 1 Hz—he and two fellow researchers analyzed their measurements and found a clear peak at 19 Hz in the cellar. Just as he predicted.

A standing wave was detected in the narrow corridor as well. This was consistent with other findings in similarly skinny hallways—the type one might find in a stereotypical haunted house.

Tandy's results were a win for science, but they didn't exactly explain all types of paranormal activity. Interactions between the living and apparent ghosts, for example, had nothing to do with vibrating eyeballs and sounds that can't be heard. Tandy recognized this, and after he published his experience in the *Journal of the Society for Psychical Research* in 1998, he told reporters, "I keep an open mind. 'Ghosts' is a very broad term really, so I am not suggesting this sort of thing is the end."

John Fraser, a paranormal investigator and member of the Society for Psychical Research, would agree. "By its nature there is little chance that infrasound is present in most paranormal experiences and is therefore no 'magic bullet,'" he says. "Electricity, or more precisely electromagnetic and possibly even geomagnetic, seem to be far more present in some cases."

Studies of the effects of electromagnetic fields have indeed shown evidence that certain levels of electromagnetism could create paranormal experiences not unlike Tandy's infrasound findings. Around the time Tandy was first experiencing the effects of infrasound, Dr. Michael Persinger, a psychologist at Laurentian University in Ontario, Canada, began experimenting with the powers of electromagnetic fields on the brain. When exposed to low frequencies (below 100 Hz) of varying intensity and duration—and when deprived of their senses with eye coverings and a perfectly quiet room—Persinger found that a high percentage of his subjects reported experiences that mirrored paranormal activity, or even sensations of seeing God. This led to the belief that natural and/or human-made EMFs could be what's behind ghost sightings, religious experiences, or even extraterrestrial encounters.

By 1986 Persinger created what looked like a modified motorcycle helmet that could shoot patterns of weak electromagnetic pulses into the temporal lobes. He called it the God helmet. Persinger theorized, in a nutshell, that stimulating the right temporal lobe (the side that processes emotions and aspects of visual perception) would disrupt the notion of self and cause the normally dominant left temporal lobe (the logical side) to understand this new state, resulting in the creation of a "sensed presence." By dialing up or down the frequency, intensity, and duration, he could essentially create artificial experiences.

Jack Hitt, a writer for *Wired*, visited Persinger in 1999 and donned the helmet. By that time the doctor had already tested it on more than nine hundred volunteers. Based on Persinger's results, Hitt was hoping to see God.

"After I adjust to the darkness and the cosmic susurrus of absolute silence, I drift almost at once into a warm bath of oblivion," Hitt wrote, replaying his experience. "Something is definitely happening. During the thirty-five-minute experiment, I feel a distinct sense of being withdrawn from the envelope of my body and set adrift in an infinite existential emptiness, a deep sensation of waking slumber."

The only ghosts he saw were those of his past. The experiment took his mind back to scenes of his childhood, but a dearth of visions of God or other particularly paranormal experiences left him disappointed. Yet there seemed to be something to Persinger's experiments and the effects of EMFs.

"Is it a coincidence that this century—known as the age of anxiety, a time rife with various hysterias, the era that gave birth to existentialism—is also when we stepped inside an electromagnetic bubble and decided to live there?" Hitt wondered. "We have never quite comprehended that we walk about in a sea of mild electromagnetism just as we do air. It is part of our atmosphere, part of the containing bath our consciousness swims in."

As new technologies continue to permeate everyday life, that atmosphere continues to grow thicker. Dan Sturges, a New York City–based paranormal investigator, uses EMF meters as one method of ruling out ghosts as a cause of his clients' phenomena. When a couple in downtown Manhattan complained of paranormal experiences in their apartment, Sturges measured the EMF levels in their bedroom. The woman had mild experiences, but her boyfriend's were much more intense and left him feeling like he was constantly being watched. Sturges discovered her side of the bed had a low reading, but his side "went through the roof."

"It turns out the elevator room was right behind where he sleeps," Sturges said. "He was getting bombarded with EMF."

At the suggestion of rearranging their room, the couple found that the ghosts went away. It would seem that more and more paranormal experiences might be connected to these increasing EMFs, but Persinger's theory has its holes.

"Logically, it makes sense that you can evoke certain experiences when you activate certain parts of the brain," John Kruth of the Rhine Research Center acknowledges. "This technique is used in brain surgery to explore brain topography, but just because I can make you taste a lemon by stimulating your brain doesn't mean that you haven't ever really tasted a lemon."

Though Persinger's experiments might explain some cases, a study conducted in 2016 demonstrated that psychology could have also been the cause of some of Persinger's results. Dr. Christine Simmonds-Moore, an associate professor of psychology at the University of West Georgia, conducted her own experiment with a replica of the God helmet. Her version, however, didn't do anything. No electromagnetic pulses. No frequencies dialed up or down into the temporal lobes. It was a sham God helmet, designed to look like Persinger's version, complete with nifty coils and wires and switches. A group of paranormal skeptics and believers were invited to participate in the study and were informed of the types of results Persinger had obtained. If the helmet *suggested* it would cause exceptional experiences, the study wondered, would it?

After setting the mood with the sounds of Enya, Simmonds-Moore brought subjects to a small, cozy dark room and had them sit in a recliner. As in Persinger's experiment, they wore eye masks and earplugs to deprive the senses. Then they donned the helmet and sat with it for thirty minutes.

Both groups reported experiences, though the majority came from the believers. These included pulsing or tingling sensations, dizziness, alterations in the sense of body size (as if having an enlarged head or hands, or feeling really massive or really tiny), sensing a presence of someone walking in the room, luminous phenomena, and out-of-body feelings.

This study doesn't discount Persinger's results, nor does it discount the possibility of EMF affecting people outside of the lab. "When your whole body's in a space, that might be really different from if you're sitting in a chamber with something on your head," Simmonds-Moore noted.

Personality, as this psychological experiment suggests, is yet another factor in what might cause paranormal phenomena. That, along with infrasound and electromagnetic fields, still doesn't explain everything. But science has other sneaky secrets. Take carbon monoxide. As everyone should know, the sightless, scentless gas can lead to unconsciousness and death. However, if it doesn't reach those extremes it can still cause quite a scare with hallucinations that may lead victims to believe they're living among ghosts.

An example of this was documented in a 1921 issue of the *American Journal of Opthamology*, which detailed the story of a family that in November 1912 moved into a "large, rambling, high-studded house, built around 1870, and much out of repair." Though electricity was available at the time, the home was still lit by gaslights.

The family, identified only by the letter H, began feeling depressed within a few days of moving in. Strange things began happening that didn't help them feel any better. Footsteps were heard when no one else was present, ringing bells that hadn't been touched awakened them, headaches became common, and the children grew pale and lost their appetites. Oh, and they started seeing ghosts.

"On one occasion, in the middle of the morning, as I passed from the drawing room into the dining room, I was surprised to see at the further end of the dining room, coming towards me, a strange woman, dark haired and dressed in black," Mrs. H recounted. "As I walked steadily on into the dining room to meet her, she disappeared, and in her place I saw a reflection of myself in the mirror, dressed in a light silk waist."

These types of experiences grew frequent, occurring in all parts of the house. Mrs. H continued describing the haunting feelings:

"Sometimes as I walk along the hall I feel as if someone was following me, going to touch me. You cannot understand it if you have not experienced it, but it is real. Some nights after I have been in bed for a while, I have felt as if the bed clothes were jerked off me, and I have also felt as if I had been struck on the shoulder. One night I woke up and saw sitting on the foot of my bed a man and a woman. The woman was young, dark and slight, and wore a large picture hat. The man was older, smooth shaven and a little bald. I was paralyzed and could not move, when suddenly I felt a tap on my shoulder and I was able to sit up, and the man and the woman faded away."

This went on for nearly two months, until finally Mrs. H's brother-in-law came over and suggested an alternative explanation. Instead of ghosts, the culprit might be poison. He'd read a recent story about a family poisoned by gas that seemed to suffer similar hallucinations. The Hs decided to have their home inspected and found that their furnace had been sending carbon monoxide fumes into the house instead of pushing them out through the chimney. The gaslights may have contributed to the problem as well, since gas used as that time contained as much carbon monoxide as car exhaust. Once these leaks were remedied, the ghosts went away, and the whole family felt healthy once again.

Albert Donnay, an environmental health engineer and toxicologist, who wrote about the case in 2004, explained that "carbon monoxide poisoning can cause all manner of hallucinations" including auditory and visual perceptions, and feelings of strange things on the skin without cause. "People often report that they hear noises in their ears, bells ringing, rushing sounds," he added.

Because carbon monoxide blocks the absorption of oxygen in the blood, the brain lacks the level of oxygen it needs and the mind can begin to hallucinate. If your brain gets too little oxygen, eventually you won't see ghosts—you'll find out if you can become one.

"Given that carbon monoxide is still the most common cause of toxic poisonings and deaths in America, it is probably still a common cause of haunted houses," says Donnay. It's not as exciting as signs of an afterlife, but it does explain a lot of classic paranormal tropes.

"Many ideas and theories have been proposed in the last hundred years and continue to be advanced. Regarding these I recall the prescient words of researcher Maurice Grosse (1918-2006) in 2003: 'In the past we have had underground streams, ley lines, absorbent building materials, planetary influences, faulty observation, delusions, overactive imaginations, alien visitors, low and high frequency sound, earth tremors, temperature changes, to name but a few of the reasons to account for PK [psychokinesis], haunting and all the other phenomena associated with our subject. I look forward to the next popular and fashionable revelation.' And still new ideas emerge. Even with those proving to be mistaken or complete blind alleys, much can still be learned. On the road to truth, false direction may be a necessary part of finding the truth path in the process of discovery. At the center of the problem we still do not have an understanding of everyday consciousness in the living, so maybe the focus on the environment is the wrong direction. Whatever the case, the quests continue."

–Alan Murdie, chairman of the London Ghost Club, in 2020

## The *Ghostbusters* Effect

In the early 1980s, while Tandy was speculating about the effects of infra-sound and Persinger was wondering if science could elegantly explain the paranormal, Ray Parker Jr. was asking a much simpler question: "Who ya gonna call?"

*Ghostbusters* introduced the general public to the idea of parapsychology and the concept of catching ghosts. With really neat machines. In the end, what most people got out of the movie were laughs and its theme song firmly planted in their heads. But for some, the comedy classic was a revelation. Maybe they, too, could catch a Slimer. Instead of wearing unlicensed nuclear accelerators on their backs and shooting proton streams at spirits, this new generation of Venkmans, Stantzes, Spenglers, and Zeddemores has its various EMF readers and other gizmos that light up, capture noises, sound alerts, and may help find evidence of either the paranormal or just the plain old normal. Yet without the aid of movie magic, how well do all these things work?

It depends who you ask and how the devices are used, but as Sturges notes, "Nothing has been created technology-wise or equipment-wise that can capture a ghost and that can prove that ghosts exist beyond a shadow of a doubt." If such a tool did exist, there'd surely be a bunch of ghost hunters getting rich and famous without the help of a cable television show. Still, aspiring ghostbusters everywhere are trying.

One of the ITC methods that has grown in popularity over the past decade involves an altered radio called a spirit box. The device rapidly sweeps through radio frequencies and generates white noise. It's believed that spirits can thrive on the energy and manipulate it to manifest words, some of which may form intelligent responses. You can't tune in to a regular terrestrial station, but hey, talk radio and oldies stations aren't nearly as interesting as the afterlife. Some models even come with MicroSD cards to record spectral messages and flashlights to seek spirits without becoming a thing that goes bump in the night. They bring a whole new level of convenience to the modern ghost hunter.

The spirit box was originally called Frank's Box, named after its creator, Frank Sumption, an amateur radio enthusiast who developed the gadget in 2002. Figuring out how to tune in to ghost channels took a little help from—who else?—ghosts. Sumption claimed a group of spirit engineers he referred to as "the guys" helped him design the contraption. According to the medium Christopher Moon, an early adopter of Sumption's invention, one of "the guys" was Thomas Edison, who apparently was finally finishing his work on his telephone to the dead. Moon claims to have communicated with Edison through the device, along with many others, including John Lennon, John F. Kennedy, Abraham Lincoln, and even a few extraterrestrials.

Dr. Karen Stollznow, who earned a PhD in linguistics from the University of New England and investigates the paranormal, looks to Occam's razor to help explain Frank's Box. "Is this a paranormal device through which extradimensional entities manifest and harness the signals to communicate with the living," she asks, "or is it a busted radio that produces random noise misperceived or primed for patternicity primates to hear what they want to hear?"

Spirit boxes, as they're more commonly referred to now, might offer nothing more than apophenia, as Stollznow suggests. Yet other paranormal investigators have started using them in a unique way that separates a team into a single listener and one or more questioners. The listener is blindfolded to deprive the senses and wears headphones to receive a direct feed from the spirit box. Whatever that person hears, they announce. Afterward, they find out what questions were asked. This avoids the complications of groupthink in which one person might think they hear something and then everyone else listening suddenly agrees. Isolating the listener from the questioner has occasionally given results demonstrating intelligent responses seemingly carrying on a two-way conversation.

This technique is called the Estes Method, named for Estes Park, the small Colorado mountain town that is home to the Stanley Hotel. The Stanley, of course, is where Stephen King stayed many years ago and found his inspiration for *The Shining*. Paranormal events have been observed at the hotel for decades, and ghost hunters investigate the premises often.

Three of those investigators, Karl Pfeiffer, Connor Randall, and Michelle Tate, spent years leading ghost tours and became familiar with several of the Stanley spirits. Some of them they even considered friends. But when these friendly ghosts grew quiet after nonstop tours, the paranormal investigators

Connor Randall listens for voices of ghosts through the spirit box at the Stanley Hotel in Estes Park, Colorado.

"None of the gadgets being fielded is specifically designed to detect ghosts—despite the claims—because we do not know what ghosts are or what causes them. . . . Even though it might look and sound impressive, having something that beeps does not make a scientific investigation."

—Dr. Leo Ruickbie, a member of the Society for Psychical Research's governing council, discussing the "gadget trap" in his 1988 book *A Brief Guide to Ghost Hunting* decided to try communicating with them in a different way—one that didn't include a group of paying strangers tagging along. Late one night in early 2016, they clocked out and experimented with the idea that became the Estes Method.

In one of their sessions, a friend, Mark, held up four fingers and asked the ghost how many he was holding up. As they all sat in the balcony of the Stanley's concert hall, where spirits are believed to roam, they didn't have to wait long for a response. Randall, acting as the listener, began speaking right away, first announcing "Mark sees it," and "You want numbers now?" and then offering a string of numbers: "six . . . seven . . . nine . . . can't tell . . ."

The exchange continued, and though the ghost couldn't count the fingers, it certainly seemed to understand the challenge at hand.

"The numbers one was the best session we've had because, before that, we'd get two or three direct responses towards what we were asking about," Pfeiffer says, "but to hear a stream of numbers like that—I asked Connor about it later and he said, 'I was hoping you guys asked for the winning lottery numbers.'"

Randall recommends finding a comfortable place to relax while listening to the box, and he noticed that holding the antenna helps create better activity. "It adds into this nice symbology of the human being becoming the antenna themselves," he says. "If you hear something, say something. You don't want to sit and think about the answers. You don't add editorial opinions. You just spout out what is coming across that feed as quickly as possible."

So are ghosts actually coming through the radio waves? That's one theory the team offers. Alternatively, they believe it might be a way for the spirits to communicate through our minds. Perhaps listening to the bits of sound through the radio placates the conscious mind and, as Pfeiffer suggests, "allows the unconscious brain to recognize sounds that aren't there, or manifest them or produce or hear them in a psychical sense."

Over in West Virginia, Valarie Myers of the Trans-Allegheny Lunatic Asylum has gotten "freaky" results using the method over the past couple of years. One of her spookier sessions occurred while she and her assistant manager were in what she called "the notorious bedpost murder room." Of all the places in an old insane asylum to seek out a creepy experience, this would seem to be an ideal candidate. Myers had her blindfold on and was hearing nothing but radio static until a ghost seemed to come through the box.

"All of a sudden I hear a woman's voice say 'evil.' So I spoke up and I said 'evil.' Next thing I know Brandi's flashlight is getting my attention: 'Did you just say evil?' I said, 'Yeah.' She says, 'Time to go! Time to go!' She put her flashlight on in front of her, and she's hauling ass through the violent men's ward and through the violent women's ward, and we got to the nurses' quarters before she'd tell me what happened. While I was hearing nothing but radio static, she was hearing someone walking out in the hallway. She spoke up and said, 'Is that person out in the hallway nice?' And that's when I spoke up and said 'evil.'"

Other ghost hunters use regular recording devices hoping to pick up an EVP. With any luck, after recording an investigation they'll hear something upon playback. Nothing would be heard during the actual recording since ghosts probably can't talk. Without a tongue or voice box it's basically impossible to create a sound wave that can wiggle its way through our ears. Just as Loyd Auerbach spoke of an apparition occurring in our mind's eye in the previous chapter, with an EVP the ghost's voice would be imprinted on the media. Dan Sturges describes it as a psychokinesis process. He's had luck capturing EVPs over the course of twenty years of investigations. Of note were voices captured at the Merchant House Museum in New York City's Greenwich Village. The museum's long history of ghosts has earned it the title of Manhattan's most haunted place.

The four-story brick row house was built in 1832 and purchased by a merchant named Seabury Tredwell. One of his eight children, Gertrude, was born in an upstairs bedroom in 1840 and lived in the elegant Greek Revival home as the neighborhood grew and changed around her for the next ninety-three years. She left this world in 1933 in the same canopied bed where she entered it. No one would ever occupy the Merchant House again. Several years later, in 1936, it became a museum, which ensured all of the original furnishings would be preserved as a Tredwell time capsule. The sheets on the bed are the sheets they slept on. The dishes on the table are the dishes they ate from. They played the pianoforte in the front parlor, where guests were entertained and family funerals were held. The family's DNA is ingrained in every room and stairway. This presents ghost hunters with a unique opportunity to study a house that has a full history of just one family, whom many believe never left. Gertrude in particular has been seen by many visitors over the decades, often in a brown dress drinking a cup of tea. Some have claimed to see her outside the front steps, shouting at kids to be quiet.

A museum volunteer in the mid-1960s recalled a time when her hand was overtaken by Gertrude's spirit: "Suddenly the pencil I was holding started moving. It seemed to be guided by a very powerful force—not me—and it wrote 'Miss Tredwell is here.' The handwriting was not my own. It was very large and flowery, with a lot of loops—like old-fashioned penmanship."

Before Sturges begins any EVP session he records everyone on his team talking and saying their name in order to have a voice print of all present. If something is captured, a digital forensics analyst can use that information to rule out their voices. Sturges acknowledges fakery is still possible—the Spiricom case has proven that—but he's not one to coordinate such antics. The EVPs his team caught at the Merchant House Museum were especially interesting because they proved to be direct answers to their questions. In one instance, a girl asked Ms. Tredwell if she was pretty. The answer they discovered later was "Pleasant enough." Another question asked Mr. Tredwell if he liked to play the piano. "I like to strike the keys in succession," came through on the recording.

"It's crazy!" Sturges exclaims. "And we've had such luck at the Merchant House, sometimes I take it for granted. I'll be talking to someone about it and I'll see their eyes popping open when they listen to it. And I go, oh yeah, this is crazy!"

Crazy is an understatement, based on his experiences at the house. "I think we have lots of things happening there and it's not only Gertrude Tredwell, it's (according to the many mediums I've brought there) various members of the family as well as the servants," Sturges added in an email. "We've also had family members and friends of the people on the investigation pop in for a visit. So, not only is it an imprint or 'place memory' haunting happening but also an apparitional or 'intelligent' haunting as well."

Niki Saunders of the Farnsworth House Inn hunts ghosts with a high-tech tool kit that includes audio recorders for EVPs, spirit boxes, lasers, antennas, and more. She'll use lasers, for example, to set up a grid, as if helping a museum protect an exhibit of rare jewels. If something crosses the line, it'll be clearly visible by a break in the laser's beam.

"We can tell if one of us goes through it, but when something else makes it go off it's pretty interesting," she says. "In video you just see something crossed the force field. We've had it go off [at the Farnsworth]."

Another go-to device is the REM Pod. It features an antenna that radiates its own electromagnetic field. The base has lights and noises that go off if anything should come close or make contact with it. Ghost hunters can leave it in a room and, in theory, invite a ghost to interact with it in an attempt to communicate.

"If we're sitting here and it's over there

and it starts going off, we're not touching it, we're not close to it, so something is making that happen," Saunders said.

Working at the Farnsworth led her to develop her own version of the device called the Seeker. It gives investigators the ability to turn the sound off yet still have the lights alert observers.

"If you're here in the bed-and-breakfast where the walls aren't so thick, you can turn the volume down but still have the lit-up validation, so it won't wake up the guests," she explains. "Those tones from the REM Pods are deafening."

Despite the explosion of ghost-hunting tech, paranormal investigators like Sturges and Auerbach prefer a simpler approach, not unlike earlier ghost hunters Harry Price and Hans Holzer. Their main tool: humans.

Witnesses are key to an investigation. Auerbach stresses the importance of conducting extensive interviews with them to find out where, when, and what paranormal events happened.

"We really go over the testimony a number of times," he says. "Sometimes asking the same questions in different ways, in different spots of the house, with different combinations of witnesses just to get a fuller picture."

Auerbach will employ psychics and mediums as well, but only after fully vetting them and feeling confident they might be able to provide useful information. Alexandra Holzer works in a similar manner by following her father's techniques—the Holzer Method—which she describes as "the scientific method for collecting data minced with a medium in tow as another tool to get as much information as to what's going on." That includes digging up the history on any residence under investigation, finding out when it was built, and learning about who lived there before and what happened on the land prior to the construction of the house.

As for technology, audio and video recorders are useful for their intended purposes of preserving interviews—not for capturing EVPs and apparitions. EMF detectors can be useful in attempting to debunk reported phenomena.

"We're always looking for ways to separate the things in an environment that could cause us to conclude something is paranormal or psychic from the things that might genuinely be paranormal or psychic," Auerbach explains. "I

"I know a couple magicians who work with ghost hunting shows to create subtle special effects to wig out ghost hunters. They have an hour with nothing to go on. They have a beep on a device. . . . I do talk to one executive producer who said, 'You know, I really thought there was something out there, but by the end of the first season, no.'"

–Todd Robbins, performer and historian, discussing in 2020 the proliferation of ghost hunting shows and their validity had a case early on where people were talking about footsteps in their attic and it turned out the attic acoustics were such that the squirrel that got into the attic and pushed a nut across the floor sounded like footsteps. I caught the squirrel. Then I tested it out. I scared the hell out of the people, I grabbed a bunch of the nuts that I'd found and rolled them across the floor and they were screaming because they thought that I was taken by the army of darkness or something."

It doesn't take much more than a level head to debunk ghostly visitors by seeking out rodent offenders in the attic or walls, or even creaky floors or old pipes that like to make noises whenever they feel like it. Once you get past the normal, you can start to explore the possibility of the paranormal.

But until technology provides some form of indisputable proof of the afterlife, belief in ghosts comes down to the basics: reason, personal experiences, and faith. Thousands of years after humankind's earliest recorded ghost sightings, these are the very same things that have always formed our opinions. Sometimes reason perfectly explains a personal experience, and sometimes faith wrestles reason to the ground and wins us over. At our core, it's human nature to wonder what's next for us—and to hope for something more. Yet for all our desire to solve the mystery of ghosts, perhaps we're better off living with the unknown. Not having all the answers makes life far more interesting.

Of course, the unknown is also what conjures fear. We humans tend not to like the things we don't know and don't understand. Things like unexplainable noises, strange people, and different ideas. So to most people, ghosts are scary. Yet witnessing such a thing should provide a sense of relief and awe instead. If you believe in what you've seen, a ghost is your ultimate answer about life after death. A ghost means there's something more. Maybe that something more includes various states of being, whether it's ignorance about being dead, a struggle to right a wrong, or existence on an entirely different plane. Maybe it means our best attempts to connect with the living come through electricity, mental imprints, blinking lights, tossed objects, or even a good old-fashioned knock on wood.

All we know is that no one knows. If any theories or paranormal experiences presented in this book have even an ounce of truth, it means we don't just die and turn to dust. We don't just live on in memories. We become something new in the afterlife. Whatever form that takes, it sounds a lot like heaven. Dead in a box is hell. Which do you want to believe in?

# BIBLIOGRAPHY

Ghosts may be elusive, but lore, legends, written accounts, scientific studies, and other reports about them are not. In addition to interviews with many knowledgeable sources, the following books, websites, podcasts, and articles—including many with colorful descriptions of events from Victorian-era newspapers—were valuable resources in my research.

## Ghosts of Humans Past

"Angels and Demons." https://swedenborg.com/emanuel-swedenborg/explore/angels-and-demons (accessed October 23, 2020).

Aridjis, Eva, and Joanna Ebenstein, eds. "Death in Ancient and Present-Day Mexico." *Death, a Graveside Companion*. London: Thames & Hudson, 2017.

Attar, Rob. "Guidebook to the Ancient Egyptian afterlife." History Extra, December 2010. https://www.historyextra.com/period/ancient-egypt/ancient-egyptian-guide-afterlife-death-book-dead-journey-facts (accessed October 5, 2020).

Ayton, William Alexander. *The Life of John Dee: Translated from the Latin of Dr. Thomas Smith*. London: Theosophical Publishing Society, 1908.

Bouyer, Louis. *Dictionary of Theology*. New York: Desclee Co., Inc., 1965.

Brennan, J. H. *Whisperers: The Secret History of the Spirit World*. New York: Overlook Duckworth, 2013.

Bruce, Scott G., ed. *The Penguin Book of the Undead*. New York, Penguin, 2016.

Casaubon, Meric. *A True & Faithful Relation of What Passed for many Years Between Dr. John Dee and Some Spirits*. London: D. Maxwell, 1659.

Crooke, William. *The Popular Religion and Folk-lore of Northern India*. London: A. Constable & Company, 1896.

"Dee, John." Occult World. https://occult-world.com/dee-john (accessed October 25, 2020).

Dee, John, and James Orchard Halliwell-Phillipps, eds. *The Private Diary of Dr. John Dee*. London: Camden Society, 1842.

Defoe, Daniel. *The Secrets of the Invisible World Disclosed*. New York: Svantovit Press, 1999.

Easting, Robert. "Peter of Bramham's account of a chaplain's vision of purgatory (c.1343?)" *Medium Aevum* 65, issue 2, 1996.

Heaphy, Linda. "Hungry Ghosts: Their History and Origin." Kashgar - Life for the Modern Nomad (website). https://kashgar.com.au/blogs/tribal-culture/hungry-ghosts-their-history-and-origin (accessed November 2, 2020).

Hearn, Lafcadio. *Kwaidan: Stories and Studies of Strange Things*. Boston: Houghton Mifflin Co., 1911.

"Inside Information." Lore podcast, episode 143, May 25, 2020.

James, M. R. "Twelve Medieval Ghost-Stories." *English Historical Review* XXXVII, issue CXLVII, July 1922.

Kowalewski, David, PhD. *Death Walkers: Shamanic Psychopomps, Earthbound Ghosts, and Helping Spirits in the Afterlife Realm*. Bloomington, IN: iUniverse, 2015.

Lavater, Ludwig. *Of ghostes and spirites, walking by night: and of straunge noyses, crackes, and sundrie forewarnings: which commonly happen before the death of men: great slaughters, and alterations of kingdoms*. London: Thomas Creede, 1596.

Lewis, Nell Battle. "Incidentally." *News and Observer*, August 28, 1938.

Lindley, Charles, Viscount Halifax. *Lord Halifax's Ghost Book*. New York: Didier Publishing Company, 1944.

Mark, Joshua J. "Ghosts in the Ancient World." World History Encyclopedia, October 30, 2014. http://www.ancient.eu/ghost (accessed November 7, 2020).

"Miscellany: A Propos de Bhoots." *Manchester Guardian*, December 24, 1926.

Onion, Amanda. "Scientists Explain Red Sea Parting and Other Miracles." ABC News, February 12, 2004. https://abcnews.go.com/Technology/story?id=99580&page=1 (accessed November 1, 2020).

Owens, Susan. *The Ghost: A Cultural History*. London: Tate Publishing, 2017.

Rivenburg, Roy. "Purgatory." *Los Angeles Times*, October 20, 1995.

Ruickbie, Dr. Leo. *A Brief Guide to Ghost Hunting: How to Identify and Investigate Spirits, Poltergeists, Hauntings and Other Paranormal Activity*. London: Robinson, 2013.

Swedenborg, Emanuel. *Heaven and Its Wonders, the World of Spirits, and Hell: From Things Heard and Seen*. New York: American Swedenborg Printing and Publishing Society, 1885.

Thorpe, T. E. "John Dee." *Nature*, December 2, 1909.

Whitby, Christopher Lionel. John Dee's Actions with Spirits. New York: Garland Publishing, 1988.

## Conversations with the Dead

Abbott, Karen. "The Fox Sisters and the Rap on Spiritualism." Smithsonianmag.com, October 30, 2012. https://www.smithsonianmag.com/history/the-fox-sisters-and-the-rap-on-spiritualism-99663697 (accessed August 23, 2020).

"Agnes Repplier Urges Ouija-Board Control." *Current Opinion*. October 1918.

Alford, Terry. "The Spiritualist Who Warned Lincoln Was Also Booth's Drinking Buddy." *Smithsonian* magazine, March 2015. https://www.smithsonianmag.com/history/the-spiritualist-who-warned-lincoln-was-also-booths-drinking-buddy-180954317 (accessed July 11, 2020).

"Among the New Books: Recent Fiction." *Detroit Free Press*, August 26, 1917.

"Anniversary of Spiritualism Observed at Hydesville." *Rochester Democrat and Chronicle*, April 1, 1962.

Aykroyd, Peter H., with Angela Narth. *A History of Ghosts: The True Story of Séances, Mediums, Ghosts, and Ghostbusters*. Emmaus, PA: Rodale, 2009.

Baker, Jean H. *Mary Todd Lincoln: A Biography*. New York: W. W. Norton & Company, 2008.

Barnum, Phineas Taylor. *The Humbugs of the World*. New York: Coachwhip Publications, 2008.

"Biting a Spook." *Auckland Star*. December 27, 1923.

"Books and Authors." *Living Age*, October 20, 1917.

Braude, Ann. *Radical Spirits: Spiritualism and Women's Rights in Nineteenth-Century America*. 2nd ed. Bloomington: Indiana University Press, 2001.

Carrington, Hereward. "A Last Word on Palladino." *New York Times*, May 31, 1918.

———. *Eusapia Palladino and Her Phenomena*. New York: B. W. Dodge & Company, 1909.

———. *The Coming Science*. New York: American Universities Publishing Company, 1920.

Christopher, Milbourne. *The Illustrated History of Magic*. New York: Thomas Y. Crowell Company, 1973.

———. *Mediums, Mystics & The Occult*. New York: Thomas Y. Crowell Company, 1975.

"Court Action to Stop 'Jap Herron': Harper & Bros. Ask Court to Stop Publication." *Hartford Courant*, August 23, 1918.

"The Davenport Brothers." *Spiritual* magazine V, no. 11, November 1864.

"Davis's Revelations." *New York Daily Tribune*, August 3, 1847.

Davis, Andrew Jackson. *Beyond the Valley*. Boston: Colby & Rich, 1885

———. *The Principles of Nature, Her Divine Revelations, and A Voice to Mankind*. New York: S. S. Lyon, and Wm. Fishbough, 1847.

De Heredia, Carlos María. *Spiritism and Common Sense*. New York: P. J. Kenedy & Sons, 1922.

"Dead Spiritualist Silent. Detroit Woman Awaits Message, But Denies Any." *New York Times*, February 8, 1921.

Diotrephes, Doctor [pseud.]. *"The Knockings" Exposed!* New York, 1850.

Doyle, Arthur Conan. *The New Revelation*. New York: George H. Doran Company, 1918.

———. *The History of Spiritualism, Vol. 1*. London: Cassell and Company, Ltd., 1926.

"Ectoplasm, An Established Marvel or a Flimsy Myth?" *Current Opinion*, October 1, 1922.

"Eusapia Palladino." *New York Times*, October 6, 1909.

"Eusapia Palladino, Puzzle of the Scientific World." *Sun*, November 21, 1909.

Evans, Henry Ridgely. *Hours with the Ghosts or Nineteenth Century Witchcraft*. Chicago: Laird & Lee, 1897.

———. *The Old and the New Magic*. Chicago: Open Court Publishing Co., 1906.

———. *The Spirit World Unmasked*. Chicago: Laird & Lee, 1897.

"The Foot of Palladino." *Washington Post*, Feb 7, 1910.

"Ghost Artists Make Fortunes for Mediums." *St. Louis Post-Dispatch*, March 5, 1905.

Greeley-Smith, Nixola. "Sir Oliver Lodge's Declaration That He Has Had Messages from the Dead Recalls Mrs. Piper's Powers, Even if Celestial Wiretappers Are at Work." *Evening World*, February 1, 1908.

Gresham, William Lindsay. *Houdini, the Man who Walked Through Walls*. New York: Henry Holt and Co., 1959.

Hardinge, Emma. *Modern American Spiritualism: A Twenty Years' Record of the Communion Between Earth and the World of Spirits*. New York: New York Printing Company, 1870.

Hartzman, Marc. "Rope Escapes, Musical Ghosts, and the Mysterious Magic of the Davenport Brothers." Weird Historian, March 24, 2020. https://www.weirdhistorian.com/rope-escapes-musical-ghosts-and-the-mysterious-magic-of-the-davenport-brothers (accessed July 9, 2020).

Higgie, Jennifer. "Longing for Light: The Art of Hilma af Klint." Hilma Af Klint: Painting the Unseen, March 3–May 15, 2016, press release, Serpentine Gallery.

"Hilma af Klint - Biography and Legacy." The Art Story. https://www.theartstory.org/artist/af-klint-hilma/life-and-legacy (accessed August 24, 2020).

"Hints of Séances at White House." *New York Times*, May 19, 1926.

Hintz, Charlie. "Thomas Bradford: Spiritualist Who Committed Suicide to Prove the Afterlife Was Real." Cult of Weird. https://www.cultofweird.com/paranormal/thomas-bradford-experiment (accessed July 7, 2020).

Home, Dunglas Mme. *D. D. Home: His Life and Mission*. London: Kegan Paul, Trench, Trubner & Co., 1921.

Horn, S. G. *The Next World Interviewed*. Chicago: Progressive Thinker Publishing House, 1896.

Houdini, Harry. *A Magician Among the Spirits*. New York: Harper & Brothers, 1924.

———. *Houdini Exposes the Tricks Used by the Boston Medium "Margery" to Win the $2500 Prize Offered by the Scientific American*. New York, Adams Press Publishers, 1924.

Hutching, Emily Grant. "A 'Spirit Novel' from Mark Twain?" *San Francisco Chronicle*, August 26, 1917.

Hyslop, James. "Patience Worth: A Psychic Mystery." *Journal of the American Society for Psychical Research*, April 1916.

Jaher, David. *The Witch of Lime Street*. New York: Crown, 2015.

*Jap Herron: A Novel Written from the Ouija Board*. New York: Mitchell Kennerley, 1917.

Kardec, Allan. *The Spirits' Book*. Boston: Colby and Rich, 1893.

"Kate Fox: Still in the Meshes of the Law, She Is a Woman of Impenetrable Mystery." *Cincinnati Enquirer*, May 6, 1888.

Kiddle, Henry. *Spiritual Communications*. New York: Authors' Publishing Company, 1879.

"Latest Works of Fiction." *New York Times*, September 9, 1917.

"Lincoln Spiritualist, He Says." *Rochester Democrat and Chronicle*, October 22, 1906.

Maskelyne, John Nevil. *Modern Spiritualism: A Short Account of its Rise and Progress, with Some Exposures of So-Called Spirit Media*. London: Frederick Warne & Co., 1876.

Mattison, Hiram. *Spirit-Rapping Unveiled!* New York: J. C. Derby, 1855.

"The medium who makes sceptics pant and tremble like nervous horses." Europaranormal. https://europaranormal.com/evidence-for-psi/the-medium-who-makes-sceptics-pant-and-tremble-like-nervous-horses (accessed August 22, 2020).

"Mediums Enliven Hearing in House." *Evening Star* (Washington, D.C.), May 20, 1926.

"Mere Tricks: Expose of Spiritualism by its Author." *Boston Daily Globe*, October 21, 1888.

"Mina 'Margery' Crandon (1888–1941)." First Spiritual Temple website. https://www.fst.org/margery.htm (accessed July 28, 2020).

"More Ouija Board Novels." *New York Tribune*, September 30, 1917.

Muchnic, Suzanne. "Portraying the Invisible." *Los Angeles Times*, November 16, 1986.

Munroe, A. F. "Do the Dead Talk to the Living?" *Cincinnati Enquirer*, February 27, 1921.

Murchison, Carl, ed. *The Case For and Against Psychical Belief*. Worchester: Clark University, 1927.

Myers, Arthur. "Fox Cottage Burns." Pamphlet, Lily Dale Historical Society.

Nabity, Katherine, ed. *David P. Abbott in The Open Court*. Entangled Continua Publishing, 2016.

Nagy, Ron. *Precipitated Spirit Paintings*. Lakeville, MN: Galde Press, Inc., 2006.

"Palladino Again Mystifies Science." *New York Times*, August 25, 1907.

Palladino, Eusapia. "My Own Story." *Cosmopolitan* 48, 1910.

Peebles, Dr. J. M. "Mediumship Vindicated: Dr. Peebles Saw Picture Produced—Calls Work of Bangs Sisters Genuine." *Self-Culture (A Monthly Journal & Review)*. February–March 1911.

"The Phenomena. Spirit Painting Baffles Police." *Sunflower*, April 8, 1905.

Phifer, Charles Lincoln. *Hamlet in Heaven*. Girard, Kansas: self-published, 1916.

Piper, Alta L. *The Life and Work of Mrs. Piper*. London: Kegan Paul, Trench, Trubner & Co., Ltd., 1929.

Podmore, Frank. *Modern Spiritualism, Vol. 2*. London: Methuen & Co., 1902.

"Powerful Manifestations of Spirits." *Richmond Indiana Palladium*. February 9, 1855.

"Professor Dies to Solve Spirit World Mystery." *San Francisco Chronicle*, February 13, 1921.

"Psychics Here Bow in 'Walter' Feud: American Society Concedes It Erred on the 'Ectoplasmic Prints' Evoked in Boston." *New York Times*, May 12, 1935.

"A Public Exhibition of Spirit Drawings." *Spiritual* magazine, June 1, 1871.

Richet, Charles. "Concerning the Phenomenon Called Materialisation." *Annals of Psychical Science*, II, July–December 1905.

*Rochester Knockings!: Discovery and Explanation of the Source of the Phenomena Generally Known as the Rochester Knockings*. New York: WM. H. Graham and Co., 1851.

Sandford, Christopher. *Houdini and Conan Doyle*. London: Duckworth Overlook, 2012.

"Savants Scrap Over Palladino." *Los Angeles Times*, January 20, 1910.

"Say Lawmakers Consult Mediums: Washington Spiritualists Fight Bill." *New York Times*, February 27, 1926.

Shatford, Sarah Taylor. *Shakespeare's Revelations by Shakespeare's Spirit.* New York: Torch Press, Inc., 1919.

Spence, Lewis. *An Encyclopædia of Occultism: A Compendium of Information on the Occult.* New York: Dodd, Mead & Company, 1920.

"Spirit Mediums Outdone: Lively Rappings in the Academy of Music." *New York Tribune*, October 22, 1888.

"Spirit Portraits." *Sunflower*, April 15, 1905.

"Spiritual Phenomena Again!" *Daily Morning Post* [Pittsburgh], July 27, 1855.

"Spiritualism, As Related to Religion and Science." *Fraser's* magazine LXXI, January 1865.

"Spiritualists Riot at Paris Congress: Mob Fights Police." *Washington Post*, September 12, 1925.

Steinmeyer, Jim. *Hiding the Elephant: How Magicians Invented the Impossible and Learned to Disappear.* New York: Carroll & Graf, 2003.

"Summer-Land: The Next World According to Seers and Spirits." *Chicago Daily Tribune*, October 18, 1874.

Tanner, Amy. *Studies in Spiritism.* New York: D. Appleton and Company, 1910.

Thornton, Gregory. *Sonnets of Shakespeare's Ghost.* Sydney: Angus & Robertson, 1920.

Truesdell, John W. *The Bottom Facts Concerning the Science of Spiritualism.* New York: G. W. Carleton & Co., 1883.

Tymn, Michael. "Leonora Piper." Psi Encyclopedia, Society for Psychical Research, February 14, 2015. https://psi-encyclopedia.spr.ac.uk/articles/leonora-piper#Hodgsons_First_Encounter (accessed August 22, 2020).

Von Schrenck-Notzing, Albert. *Phenomena of Materialisation.* London: Kegan, Paul, Trench, Truber & Co. Ltd., 1923.

Wallis, E. W. "Spiritualism in America." *Light*, April 15, 1899.

"Woman Denies She Entered Pact with Dead Spiritualist." *New York Tribune*, February 8, 1921.

## Ghost Sightings and Paranormal Phenomena

Adams III, Charles J. *Philadelphia Ghost Stories.* Reading, PA: Exeter House Books, 2001.

Allen, Tom. "A Haunted House Is Not a Home." *Daily News*, March 9, 1958.

Allsop, Kenneth. "Was Borley Rectory Haunted?" *Sydney Morning Herald*, February 19, 1955.

Associated Press. "'Amityville Horror' reported to be fiction." July 27, 1979.

Auerbach, Loyd. *Ghost Hunting: How to Investigate the Paranormal.* Berkeley: Ronin Publishing, 2004.

Bovsun, Mara. "Tale from the Crypt." *New York Daily News*, October 13, 2019.

Brennan, Zoe. "What IS the truth about the Enfield Poltergeist?" *Daily Mail*. October 29, 2011.

Brittle, Gerald. *The Demonologist: The Extraordinary Career of Ed and Lorraine Warren.* Authors Guild Backinprint.com Edition, 2002.

Burns, Charles. "Famed 'Ghost' Due Back in '35 After 107 Year Absence." *Des Moines Register*, September 29, 1935.

Carrington, Hereward, and Nandor Fodor. *Haunted People: Story of the Poltergeist Down the Centuries.* New York: E. P. Dutton & Co., 1951.

"Closs's Column." *Roanoke Rapids Herald*, May 15, 1941.

Combes, Alan. "The Chance of a Ghost." *Guardian*, October 27, 1988.

Counter, Rosemary. "Why do so many kids 'see ghosts'? We asked some psychologists." *Washington Post*, October 28, 2019. https://www.washingtonpost.com/lifestyle/2019/10/28/why-do-so-many-kids-see-ghosts-we-asked-some-psychologists (accessed September 12, 2020).

Curran, Bobby. "For Amityville Residents, Only 'Horror' Is Steady Parade of Gawking Tourists." Gannett News Service. *Courier News*, July 23, 1979.

"Eastern State Penitentiary Historic Structures Report." Eastern State Penitentiary Task Force of the Preservation Coalition of Greater Philadelphia, vol. II, July 21, 1994.

Edwards, Frank. *Strange People.* New York: Lyle Stuart, 1961.

Fort, Charles. *The Book of the Damned: The Collected Works of Charles Fort.* New York: Jeremy P. Tarcher/Penguin, 2008.

"Foul Play Suspected." *Staunton Spectator and Vindicator*, March 4, 1897.

"Ghostly Witness Settles Will Case Without Appeal to Court." *News and Observer* (Raleigh, NC), February 6, 1927.

"A Ghost Story." *Greenbrier Independent*, January 28, 1897.

Glennon, Patrick. "From the start, there was terror behind Eastern State's imposing walls." *Philadelphia Inquirer*, October 12, 2017. https://www.inquirer.com/philly/opinion/commentary/eastern-state-prison-terror-solitary-confinement-20171012.html (accessed September 14, 2020).

"Greenbrier Ghost." Occult World. https://occult-world.com/greenbrier-ghost (accessed August 13, 2020).

Hall, Warren. "The Last Spook Has Left England's Most Haunted House." *San Francisco Examiner*, January 20, 1957.

"House for Homeless Ghosts?" *Sun*, November 9, 1924.

"Individual Treatment: How It Is Administered in a Pennsylvania State Prison." *Chicago Tribune*, October 22, 1887.

Irwin, Virginia. "Did You Ever Meet a Poltergeist?" *St. Louis Post-Dispatch*, April 27, 1960.

Jerreat, Jessica. "'Women trouble', immorality and post traumatic stress from fighting in the civil war: The reasons patients were admitted to a lunatic asylum in the 1800s." *Daily Mail*, September 5, 2013. https://www.dailymail.co.uk/news/article-2413131/Immorality-post-traumatic-stress-Reasons-patients-admitted-lunatic-asylum-1800s.html (accessed September 19, 2020).

Lewis, Nell Battle. "This Tar Hell Ghost Talked." *News and Observer* (Raleigh, NC), November 25, 1956.

Lowe, Ed. "The Amityville Horribles." *Cincinnati Enquirer*, May 11, 1980.

"The Mad Chair: The Most Haunted Prison in America." Travel Dudes, February 6, 2015. https://www.traveldudes.org/images/mad-chair-most-haunted-prison-america/64391 (accessed September 14, 2020).

"'Manse of the Spooks' Is Opened to Public." *Los Angeles Times*, November 18, 1923.

Miller, Joy. "If You Must Have Them, Noisy Ghosts Are Best." Associated Press. *Chattanooga Daily Times*, February 7, 1960.

"A Modern Haunted House." *Age*, December 14, 1940.

"Mrs. Mary J. Heaster, the Mother of Mrs. Shue, Sees Her Daughter in Visions." *Greenbrier Independent*, July 1, 1897.

"Mrs. Winchester's Extraordinary Spook Palace." *American Weekly*, 1928.

"Mystery House." *99% Invisible* podcast, episode 162, April 28, 2015.

"Mystery of the Walled-Up 'Spook' of Borley Rectory." *Pittsburgh Sun Telegraph*, September 22, 1929.

Nickell, Joe. "Enfield Poltergeist." *Skeptical Inquirer*, July/August, 2012.

Pombeiro, Beth Gillin. "Amityville: The Real Horror Won't Go Away." *Miami Herald*, August 17, 1979.

Price, Harry. *Confessions of a Ghost-Hunter.* London: Putnam & Company, 1936.

———. *The Most Haunted House in England: Ten Years' Investigation of Borley Rectory.* London: Longmans, Green and Co., 1940.

"Scratches on Her Face Left by the Evil Spirit's Claws." *San Francisco Examiner*, December 19, 1926.

Sheppard, Fergus. "'We had everything *The Exorcist* had except green slime.'" *Scotsman*, July 6, 2006.

Sloan, Jenna. "I felt cold hands . . . a force pulled me out of bed and into the air." *Sun*, April 25, 2015.

Snopes staff. "Is the 'Poltergeist' Curse Real?" Snopes. https://www.snopes.com/fact-check/poltergeist-curse (accessed October 14,

2020).

"The Testimony of a Ghost." *Brooklyn Times Union*, July 3, 1897.

"Trial of Trout Shue." *Staunton Spectator and Vindicator*, July 8, 1897.

"Two Feet Short of Jailbreak." *Washington C. H. Record Herald*, February 17, 1940.

Warren, Jane. "'We shared our house with a poltergeist': The chilling tale of supernatural suburbia." *Express*, April 27, 2015. https://www.express.co.uk/news/weird/572761/Shared-house-poltergeist-chilling-tale-supernatural-suburbia (accessed September 20, 2020).

"Witchcraft in the Southland." *Times Picayune*, July 26, 1894

"Zügun, Eleonore." Encyclopedia.com. https://www.encyclopedia.com/science/encyclopedias-almanacs-transcripts-and-maps/zugun-eleonore-1914 (accessed September 4, 2020).

## Ghosts in the Machines

"And the Call Was Coming from the Basement." *This American Life*, episode 319, October 27, 2006. https://www.thisamericanlife.org/319/and-the-call-was-coming-from-the-basement (accessed September 26, 2020).

Asbury, Herbert. "Delicate Devices of Inventors to Weigh Spirit Powers." *Great Falls Tribune*, February 3, 1921.

Bander, Peter. *Voices from the Tapes: Recordings from the Other World*. New York: Drake Publishers Inc., 1973.

Berman, Connie, and Susan Katz. "Here's a Ghostly Guidebook to New York." *New York Daily News*, February 17, 1974.

Boshears, Bill. "'Paranormal' Voices Speak Beyond Grave." *Cincinnati Enquirer*, July 20, 1975.

Brown, Denny. "On the Air with Denny Brown." *Winnipeg Tribune*, March 14, 1936.

Buckner, John E, V and Rebecca Anders Buckner. "Talking to the Dead, Listening to Yourself." *Skeptic Magazine* 17, no. 2, 2012.

Bullock, Helen. "Voices from beyond the grave?" *Leader Post*, March 13, 1982.

"Can See the Soul." *Auckland Star*, February 12, 1898.

Carrington, Hereward. "Ghost-Hunting Machine Is Invented: 'Psychic-Howler' Will Catch Spooks." *Seattle Star*, March 22, 1922.

———. *Laboratory Investigations into Psychic Phenomena*. Philadelphia: David McKay Company, 1939.

———. *Modern Psychical Phenomena*, New York: Dodd, Mead and Company, 1919.

———. "Scientists Claim Spirit Communication." *St. Louis Post Dispatch*, March 29, 1914.

Cloutier, Crista. "Photographs of Spirits: Mumler's Ghosts." In *The Perfect Medium: Photography and the Occult* edited by Clément Chéroux. New Haven, CT: Yale University Press, 2005. Originally published as *Le troisième œil: la photographie et l'occult* (Paris: Editions Gallimard, 2004).

Donnay, Albert. "A True Tale of a Truly Haunted House." Ghostvillage.com, October 31, 2004. https://ghostvillage.com/a-true-tale-of-a-truly-haunted-house (accessed September 26, 2020).

Ede, Charisse. "Lecturer has lowdown on ghosts. IT man says sounds can help trigger visions." *Birmingham Post* (UK), July 21, 1998.

"Edison at Work on Machine to Talk with Dead." *Baltimore Sun*, October 1, 1920.

Edison, Thomas, and Dagobert D. Runes, eds. *The Diary and Sundry Observations of Thomas Alva Edison*. New York: Philosophical Library, 1948.

"Edison's Own Secret Spirit Experiments." Modern Mechanix. http://blog.modernmechanix.com/edisons-own-secret-spirit-experiments (accessed August 3, 2020).

"Extraordinary Delusion." *New Zealander*, May 2, 1863.

Hartzman, Marc. "Photographing Thoughts and Souls with Hippolyte Baraduc." Weird Historian, June 16, 2018. https://www.weirdhistorian.com/thought-photography-hippolyte-baraduc (accessed

August 8, 2020).

———. "Thomas Edison Talked to the Dead, Almost." Weird Historian, December 24, 2016. https://www.weirdhistorian.com/thomas-edison-talked-to-the-dead (accessed July 31, 2020).

———. "William Mumler and the Great Spirit Photograph Craze of the 1860s." Weird Historian, August 21, 2018. https://www.weirdhistorian.com/mumler (accessed August 29, 2020).

"Has Weighed a Departing Soul." *Burlington Free Press and Times*, July 27, 1911.

Hitt, Jack. "This Is Your Brain on God." *Wired*, November 1, 1999. https://www.wired.com/1999/11/persinger (accessed September 3, 2020).

Holzer, Hans. *Ghosts I've Met*. New York: Bobbs-Merrill Company, Inc., 1965.

———. *Ghosts of the Golden West*. New York: Ace Books, 1968.

Kaplan, Louis. *The Strange Case of William Mumler Spirit Photographer*. Minneapolis: University of Minnesota Press, 2008.

Moon, Chris, and Paulette Moon. *Ghost Box: Voices from Spirits, ETs, Shadow People & Other Astral Beings*. Woodbury, MN: Llewellyn Publications, 2017.

Podmore, Frank. *Modern Spiritualism, Vol. 2*. London: Methuen & Co., 1902.

Prince, Walter Franklin. "Supplementary Report on the Keeler-Lee Photographs." In *Proceedings of the American Society for Psychical Research* 13, 1919. New York.

O'Sullivan, J. L. "Spirit Photographs." *Gallery of Spirit Art*. Brooklyn: C. R. Miller & Co., November 1883.

"Plan to Weigh Souls." *Washington Post*, March 12, 1907.

"Press Conference remarks by George Meek, April 6, 1982." Transcript. http://www.worldditc.org/h_07_meek_pressconf1982.htm (accessed August 9, 2020).

Raudive, Konstantin. *Breakthrough: An Amazing Experiment in Electronic Communication with the Dead*. Buckinghamshire: Colin Smythe Limited, 1971.

"Researches in Spiritualism." *Human Nature*, May 1875.

Roach, Mary. *Spook: Science Tackles the Afterlife*. New York: W. W. Norton, 2005.

"Science finds sound theory for ghosts." *Calgary Herald*, June 29, 1998.

Simmonds-Moore, Christine, Donadrian Rice, and Chase O'Gwin. "My Brain Is Cool: A Thematic Analysis of Exceptional Experiences Among Sceptics." *Journal of the Society for Psychical Research* 83, no. 4 (2019): 193–211.

Simmonds-Moore, Christine, Donadrian L. Rice, Chase O'Gwin, and Ron Hopkins. "Exceptional Experiences Following Exposure to a Sham 'God Helmet': Evidence for Placebo, Individual Difference, and Time of Day Influences." *Imagination, Cognition and Personality* 39, no. 1 (2019): 44–87.

Speigel, Lee. "Dave Schrader and Alexandra Holzer." *Edge of Reality* podcast, season 1, October 24, 2019.

"Spirit Trap Constructed." *Evening Republican*, April 15, 1913.

Stollznow, Karen. "Turn On, Tune Out, Drop Off." *Skeptic* 16, issue 1, 2010.

Tandy, Vic. "Something in the Cellar." *Journal of the Society for Psychical Research* 64.3, no. 860, July 2000.

Tandy, Vic, and Tony R. Lawrence. "The Ghost in the Machine." *Journal of the Society for Psychical Research* 62, no. 851, April 1998.

Tang, Jean. "There are no bad deeds, just deeds." *Salon*, March 13, 2003. https://www.salon.com/2003/03/12/noe (accessed September 26, 2020).

"The Weighing of a Soul." *Washington Times*, April 7, 1907.

Williams, Grant. "'Spiricom' to let you phone the dead." *Sun*, April 7, 1982.

# INDEX

## A

Abbott, David P., 100–101
Adams, Paul, 158
af Klint, Hilma, 102–3
alchemy, 41–44
Alden, William, 96–97
Alexander ab Alexandro, 38
Alford, Terry, 82–83
Alvanez, Natalie, 141–42
Amityville Horror house, 160–61
ancient and medieval ghost tales: Aztec
 afterlife and Día de los Muertos, 30;
 biblical ghosts, 31; *Book of the Dead*,
 24–26; Dante's ghost, 37; Dee and
 Philosopher's Stone, 41–44; Greek
 underworld, 27–28; "hungry ghosts"
 of Asia, 28–30; Lady Beresford and
 ghost of Lord Tyrone, 18–21; making
 sense of, 32–33; nature of medieval
 ghosts, 38–40; Pliny the Younger's tale
 of Athenodorus, 21–22; purgatory, 33–36; Salem witch trials, 49;
 shamans as ghost messengers, 22–24,
 25; Swedenborg and astral projection,
 45–47
Andrews, Louisa, 93
angels, 34–35, 46, 48, 67
apophenia, 222, 238
Aquinas, Thomas, 33
astral projection, 45–47
astrology, 41
Athenodorus, 21–22
Auerbach, Loyd, 153–54, 162, 184,
 186–87, 189, 243–45
Austin, B. F., 85
automatic writing, 83–84
Aztec afterlife, 30

## B

Bagans, Zak, 12
Bander, Peter, 220–23
Bangs, Lizzie and May, 97–101
Baraduc, André, 208
Baraduc, Hippolyte, 207–12
Baraduc, Nadine, 208
Barnett, Thomas, 141
Barnum, P. T., 70, 199–200
Battle of Gettysburg ghosts, 143–46
Beck, Julian, 176
*Beetlejuice*, 24
Bell, Betsy, 165–66, 167–68
Bell, John, 165, 166–67, 168
Bell, Richard Williams, 167
Bell Witch of Robertson County, Ten-
 nessee, 165–68
Bender, Hans, 220
Béraud, Marthe (Eva Carrière), 116–19
Beresford, Lady, 18–21, 77

Beresford, Lord Tristram, 18–19
Beresford, Marcus, 19, 20, 21
*bhoots*, 29
biblical ghosts, 31
biblical miracles, 32
Bird, J. Malcolm, 123–24, 130
Bisson, Juliette, 117
Black, William, 198
*Book of the Dead*, 24–26
Booth, John Wilkes, 82–83
Borley Rectory, 155–59
Boucicault, Dion, 73
Bouyer, Louis, 33
Bradford, Thomas Lynn, 114–15
Braude, Ann, 126
Bremond, Paul, 200
Brown, Denny, 216–17
Brown, J. H., 204
Brown, John, 141–42
Buddhism, "hungry ghosts" in, 28–30
Buguet, Édouard, 202–5
Bull, Harry, 156
Bull, Henry Dawson Ellis, 155
Burton, Tim, 24

## C

Cage, Nicolas, 147
Cahill, Robert Ellis, 49
Caidin, Martin, 187
Campbell, Allen, 98
carbon monoxide hallucinations,
 234–35
Carlson, Anton J., 210
Carrière, Eva, 116–19
Carrington, Hereward, 109–12, 123,
 127, 129, 130, 164, 208–9, 210,
 212–16
celebrity ghosts, 87–91
Chaffin, James L., 180–81, 182
Chaffin, James P., 180–81, 182
Chaffin, John, 180
Chaffin, Marshall, 180, 181
Charon, 27
Christiansen, Jill, 49
clothes, worn by ghosts, 189
Coates, Jane B., 122
Cocke, J. R., 104
Colchester, Charles, 82–83
Collins, Jim, 129
Comstock, Daniel F., 123, 128
Cooke, George, 73–74
Corey, Giles, 49
Corey, Martha, 49
Coventry Cathedral cellar, 228–29
Crandon, Le Roi, 124–25, 129, 130
Crandon, Mina (Margery, the Witch of
 Lime Street), 123–30, 172
Crandon, Walter, 124

Cromarty, Barbara, 161
Cromarty, James, 161
Crookes, Sir William, 79–80
Curran, Pearl, 89, 90

## D

Dante, 37
Davenport, Ira, 70–74
Davenport, William, 70–74
Davenport cabinet, 70–72
Davis, Andrew Jackson, 66–69
Dee, John, 41–44
DeFeo, Ronald, 160
Defoe, Daniel, 17, 31
Día de los Muertos, 30
Dickens, Charles, 149
Dingwall, Eric, 118
disease, 150, 151
*Divine Comedy* (Dante), 37
Dodson, John M., 210
Donnay, Albert, 235
dopamine, 159
Doran, Ruth, 114–15
Doten, Lizzie, 87
Doyle, Jean, 122–23
Doyle, Sir Arthur Conan, 62–63,
 119–23, 125, 129, 205–7
Duhl, Harriet, 99
Dunne, Dominique, 176
Dunninger, Joseph, 121
dynamistograph, 213–16

## E

Eastern State Penitentiary, 148–50
Ebenstein, Joanna, 32, 33
ectoplasmic ghosts, 116–19
Edison, Thomas, 194–96, 237
Egyptians, 24–26
electromagnetism, 193, 231–34
electronics, and poltergeists, 162–64. *See
 also* machines, ghosts in
electronic voice phenomena (EVP),
 219–28, 241–42
Elizabeth I, 41, 210
Ellis, David, 222
Emancipation Proclamation, 82
emotions, photos of, 207–9
Endor, witch of, 31
Enfield poltergeist, 173–75
Engstrom, Fred, 223–24, 227
escape artists, 70–74
ESP, 172
Estes Method, 238–41
Evans, Henry Ridgley, 71, 96
eyes, and scientific reasons for seeing
 ghosts, 204

# PHOTO CREDITS

10 Photo by author.

11 Photo by author.

18 *The Star Press*, March 13, 1916.

21 Henry Justice Ford, 1913. Public domain, via Wikimedia Commons.

27 Johann Heinrich Füssli, circa 1800. Public domain, via Wikimedia Commons.

28 Unknown artist, late twelfth century. Public domain, via Wikimedia Commons.

31 Edward Henry Corbould, "Saul and the witch of Endor," 1860. Public domain, via Wikimedia Commons.

37 Illustration by Gustave Doré for Canto XXVIX of *Divine Comedy: Inferno* by Dante Alighieri (1857). Public domain.

39 British Library. Public domain.

42 **LEFT:** From *A True & Faithful Relation of What Passed for Many Yeers Between Dr. John Dee and Some Spirits* by Meric Casaubon (D. Maxwell, 1659). **TOP RIGHT:** Ebenezer Sibley, "John Dee and Edward Kelly evoking a spirit." Circa 1825. Public domain, via Wikimedia Commons. **BOTTOM RIGHT:** From *A True & Faithful Relation of What Passed for Many Yeers Between Dr. John Dee and Some Spirits* by Meric Casaubon (D. Maxwell, 1659).

45 Wellcome Collection.

49 From *Witchcraft Illustrated* by Henrietta D. Kimball (G.A. Kimball, 1892).

55 *San Francisco Examiner*, November 27, 1927.

58 Published by N. Currier, New York. Public domain, via Wikimedia Commons.

65 Photo by author.

68 From *The Principles of Nature, Her Divine Revelations and A Voice to Mankind* by and through Andrew Jackson Davis (S. S. Lyon, and Wm. Fishbough, 1847).

71 *The Spirit World Unmasked* by Henry Ridgely Evans (Laird & Lee, 1897). Author's collection.

72 From *The Davenport Brothers, the World-Renowned Spiritual Mediums: Their Biography, and Adventures in Europe and America* (William White and Company, 1869).

77 Armand DeGregoris Collection.

78 From *Les Mystères de la Science* by Louis Figuier (Librairie illustrée, 1880).

87 *St. Louis Post-Dispatch*, July 30, 1916.

93 *Medium and Daybreak*, October 6, 1876. International Association for the Preservation of Spiritualist and Occult Periodicals (iapsop.com).

97, 98 Photo by author.

108, 111 From *Mysterious Psychic Forces* by Camille Flammarion (Small, Maynard and Company, 1907).

114 *San Francisco Chronicle*, February 13, 1921.

116 From *Phenomena of Materialisation: A Contribution to the Investigation of Mediumistic Teleplastics* by Albert von Schrenck Notzing (E. P. Dutton & Co., 1923).

117 *San Francisco Examiner*, July 15, 1923.

**120** *Motion Picture News*, November 3, 1923.

**121** John Cox Collection.

**127** Libbet Crandon de Malamud Collection.

**136, 138, 140-141** Courtesy of the Winchester Mystery House.

**143** Photo by author.

**148** Courtesy of Eastern State Penitentiary Historic Site.

**149** Collection of Eastern State Penitentiary Historic Site, gift of the family of John D. Shearer.

**150** Photo by author.

**152** West Virginia and Regional History Center, WVU Libraries.

**155** *Pittsburgh Sun-Telegraph*, September 22, 1929.

**160** Everett Collection.

**165** *Democratic Herald*, August 5, 1897.

**166** *Des Moines Register*, September 29, 1935.

**169** *San Francisco Examiner*, December 19, 1926.

**176** Everett Collection.

**177** Image courtesy of the Greenbrier Historical Society.

**179** National Archives and Records Administration. Public domain.

**194** *Baltimore Sun*, October 1, 1920.

**197** The J. Paul Getty Museum, Los Angeles.

**199** From the collection of the College of Psychic Studies, London.

**201** Author's collection.

**202** Buguet (Paris). Public domain, via Wikimedia Commons.

**204** From *Spectropia or Surprising Spectral Illusions Showing Ghosts Everywhere* by J. H. Brown (James G. Gregory, 1864).

**205** Ada Deane. Public domain, via Wikimedia Commons.

**206** The National Media Museum, Bradford.

**211** *Washington Times Magazine*, April 7, 1907. Chronicling America, Library of Congress.

**213** *St. Louis Post-Dispatch*, March 29, 1914.

**217** *Times*.

**224–226** *Spiricom* by the Metascience Research Team (Metascience Foundation, 1982).

**238** Photo by Karl Pfeiffer.

**242** Photo by author.

# ACKNOWLEDGMENTS

Many of the Spiritualists I wrote about in this book had the help of ghosts guiding their hand to write from the Other Side. I had no such help from the dead, but I did receive a wealth of assistance from those still among the living.

Loyd Auerbach and John Kruth were generous with their time on the phone and through email, and if you're interested in classes at the Rhine Education Center, I recommend them both as teachers. Lily Dale Assembly's historian, Ron Nagy, met with me at Squirrel Alter Park and stood six feet away as he fielded questions through his COVID mask (as dozens of squirrels congregated behind us to noisily munch on nuts and seeds). Bonnie White, one of Lily Dale's many mediums, shared her personal experiences and beliefs after a spirit art session with my daughter Lela and me. And as I traveled from western New York through Pennsylvania, Niki Saunders and Vivian Vega took the time to chat with a stranger dropping in at the Farnsworth House Inn.

Many others within both the paranormal and cultural history fields kindly answered all my questions and offered opinions either by phone or email, sent photos, and truly helped make this book possible: Paul Adams, Natalie Alvanez, Mark Boccuzzi, Brandon Callihan, Jill Christiansen, John Cox, Joanna Ebenstein, John Fraser, Rebecca Jordan-Gleason, Alexandra Holzer, Brandon Hodge, Andrea Janes, Margee Kerr, Dr. David Kowalewski, Dr. Christine Simmonds-Moore, Julia Mossbridge, Alan Murdie, Valarie Myers, Greg Newkirk, Harley Newman, Karl Pfeiffer, Drs. Carl and Elena Procario-Foley, Connor Randall, Todd Robbins, Vivienne Roberts, Tom Ruffles, Dr. Leo Ruickbie, Sarah Shepherd, Lee Speigel, Dan Sturges, Shannon Taggart, Jackie Thomson, Anna Thurlow, Rabbi Eric Wasser, Robyn and Philip Wilson, Richard Wiseman, and Michael Yudin.

Thank you all for everything.

In addition, I'd like to thank a few friends and strangers who gave suggestions, provided imagery, connected me to others, or were willing to share their personal experiences: Pauletta Engrav, Todd Field, Jason Lambert, Rebecca Lazaroff, James Lynn, Anthony Monahan, Armand DeGregoris, Linda Briscoe Myers, Nancy Roberts, Gail Schoenberg, Steve Seril, Sarah Shepherd, Philip David Treece, and Lemley Mullett.

This ghost adventure began with my agent Katie Boyle, who suggested I write a book like this years ago. As always, thank you for your passion and guidance throughout my research and writing. I'm grateful for all that you do.

To my editor, Jhanteigh Kupihea, thank you for spending the last several years journeying from Mars to the beyond with me. Your enthusiasm and suggestions have undoubtedly made this a better book. To the rest of the Quirk team, including my copy editor Jane Morley; designer Ryan Hayes; illustrator Lauren O'Neill; Nicole De Jackmo, Jen Murphy, and Christina Tatulli in marketing and publicity; and John McGurk and Mandy Sampson in production: thank you for helping bring all the spirits within these pages to life.

Lastly, I want to thank my family. My aunt, Dr. Reva Wolf, discussed precipitated paintings and art history movements with me. During a summer weekend, Dr. Mark and Laura Tebbitt took me around western Pennsylvania in search of ghosts and gave me a quiet place to write. My parents, Bev and Paul Hartzman, bought me books about ghosts during my childhood and planted the supernatural seed. And my wife, Liz, and daughters, Lela and Scarlett, let me work and talk about ghosts perhaps more than they wanted. Thank you all for your love and support.